Leonard Benton Seeley

Mrs. Thrale, Afterwards Mrs. Piozzi

A Sketch of Her Life and Passages from Her Diaries, Letters and Other Writings

Leonard Benton Seeley

Mrs. Thrale, Afterwards Mrs. Piozzi
A Sketch of Her Life and Passages from Her Diaries, Letters and Other Writings

ISBN/EAN: 9783337813147

Printed in Europe, USA, Canada, Australia, Japan

Cover: Foto ©Thomas Meinert / pixelio.de

More available books at **www.hansebooks.com**

MRS. THRALE

AFTERWARDS Mrs. Piozzi

*A SKETCH OF HER LIFE
AND PASSAGES FROM HER DIARIES, LETTERS
& OTHER WRITINGS*

EDITED BY

L. B. SEELEY, M.A.
Late Fellow of Trinity College, Cambridge

WITH NINE ILLUSTRATIONS AFTER
Hogarth, Reynolds, Zoffany, & others

LONDON
SEELEY AND CO., LIMITED
Essex Street, Strand
1891

THE Editor of the following pages desires to express his acknowledgments to Messrs. Longman and Co. for kindly permitting him to make use of the 'Autobiography of Mrs. Piozzi,' edited by the late Mr. Abraham Hayward, and published by them about thirty years ago. Much of the matter contained in these two interesting volumes was, of course, common property; but the extracts from the 'Thraliana,' and other autobiographical notes which they contained, were then published for the first time, and Mr. Hayward's comments and criticisms could be overlooked by no one now undertaking to deal with the subject. The source of passages quoted from his work has been carefully indicated.

November, 1890.

CONTENTS.

CHAPTER I.

A Welsh Pedigree—Heroic Ancestors—Katharine of Berain—Richard Clough—Bâchygraig—The Cottons of Combermere—Parentage and Birth—Brought to London—James Quin—David Garrick—School in Queen Square—East Hyde—Sir Thomas Salusbury—Offley Place—Lady Salusbury—Dr. Collier—Hester a favourite—Hogarth—The Lady's Last Stake—Portents of Change—Mrs. King—Henry Thrale 1-11

CHAPTER II.

Origin of the Thrale Family—Edmund Halsey—The Anchor Brewhouse—Lord Cobham—Ralph Thrale—His Son's Education—The Cobham Cousins—Henry Thrale's Bachelorhood—Arthur Murphy—Hester's Courtship—A Family Dispute—Sudden Death of her Father—His Will—Sir Thomas Salusbury—Hester's Marriage—First Experiences of Matrimony—Dr. Fitzpatrick—Birth of a Daughter—Character of Thrale—Murphy introduces Johnson—Growth of the Acquaintance—Johnson's Hypochondria—Streatham—Deadman's Place—The Globe Theatre—House at Brighton—Johnson's Menagerie—Macbean—Miss Williams—Robert Levet—Domestication with the Thrales—Mrs. Salusbury—Johnson's Peculiarities—His Dress—Appetite—Taste in Food—Affects the Epicure—Love of Late Hours—Fondness for Tea—Want of Taste for Music and Painting—Mode of Entering a Room—Inarticulate Utterances—Twitchings—Ejaculations—A Favourite with Women—Characteristics of Mrs. Thrale—Her Personal Appearance—Her Dress—Influence over Johnson—He goes more into Society 12-43

CHAPTER III.

Thrale enters Parliament—Mrs. Thrale gains Influence—Her Acquirements—Outshines her Husband—Her Conversation—Miss Williams's Miscellanies—Floretta—The Three Warnings—Dissolution of Parliament—John Wilkes—Thrale re-elected—Boswell at Streatham—Literary Talk—Johnson's Political Pamphlets—Verses at the Theatre—Thrale in Difficulties—Humphrey Jackson—Mrs. Thrale shows herself a Woman of Business—Johnson's Advice—Thrale out of Health—Alteration in him—Mr. Perkins—Conversations at Streatham—Johnson's Estimate of Mrs. Thrale—Thrale created Doctor—Death of Mrs. Salusbury—Johnson's Visit—His Letters to Mrs. Thrale—His Ode written in Skye—He will not suffer Boswell to slight Mrs. Thrale—Death of Sir Thomas Salusbury—Disappointment and Misfortunes—'The

Journey to the Western Islands '—Excursion to Wales—Visits to Lleweny Hall and Bâchygraig—Johnson accuses his Mistress of Meanness—Bodvil—Visits to Lords Sandys and Lyttelton—General Election—Electioneering with Johnson—Project of bringing Johnson into Parliament . . . 44-75

CHAPTER IV.

Mrs. Abington's Benefit—Johnson created Doctor—Marriages with Inferiors in Rank—Thrale not a Wit—Baretti—Account of Him—Tried for Murder—Enters Thrale's Family—His Character drawn by Mrs. Piozzi—Dr. Thomas Campbell—His Diary of a Visit to England—His Impressions of Baretti and Johnson—Dinners at Thrale's—Tour to France—Baretti makes Himself Useful—Johnson's Letter and Diary—Johnson Intractable—Disagreements—Verses to Mrs. Thrale—She translates an Epigram Impromptu—Johnson removes to Bolt Court—Boswell again in London—He goes with Johnson to the Midlands—Sudden Death of Thrale's only son—Johnson and Boswell return to London—Johnson comforts the Parents—Proposed Tour to Italy given up—Garrick's Retirement—His Acting—The Thrales at Bath with Johnson—Visit from Boswell—Johnson Severe to Mrs. Thrale—He returns to London—Dines with Wilkes—Pressed to go again to Bath—Quarrel with Baretti—Mrs. Thrale describes the Rupture—Johnson's Account—Baretti's Version—Apparent Reconciliation—Thraliana—Thrale described by his wife 76-104

CHAPTER V.

Visit to Dr. Burney's—The Lives of the Poets—Progress of the Brewery—Advice about 'Thraliana'—Boswell at Ashbourne—Dr. Taylor's Cattle and Waterfall—Mrs. Thrale in Low Spirits—Letters from Johnson—Her alleged Inaccuracy—A Lecture—Precept and Practice—Johnson and Lord Marchmont—Cornelius Ford—A Ghost Story—Thrale over-brews himself—'Evelina' Published—Miss Burney Introduced at Streatham—Kindly Received—Second Visit—Johnson as an Inmate—His Opinions on Dress—Family Life at Streatham—Johnson's Domestic Economy—Lady Lade—Johnson's Portrait—The Brewery Prospers—The Black Dog—Discord in Bolt Court—Sopby Streatfield—Dr. Collier—Mrs. Thrale Jealous—Tears at Command—The Thrales at Brighton—Mr. Thrale has a Fit—Johnson's Sympathy—Thrale's Health Improves—Mrs. Thrale's Dislike of the Borough 105-139

CHAPTER VI.

Mr. Thrale has a Second Fit—Recruits at Bath—Anxiety about him—Society at Bath—Melmoth—An Election in Prospect—Mrs. Thrale visits Southwark—Her Activity—Johnson Flattered—The Life of Congreve—The Gordon Riots—Alarm at Bath—The Brewery Saved—Address of Perkins—The Thrales Flee from Bath—Quiet Restored in London—Zeal of John Wilkes—Anecdotes—Perkins Rewarded—Johnson and Queeney—Mrs. Cholmondely—Seventy-Two—Bolt Court—Thrale Loses his Seat—His Health Declines—The Streatham Portraits—Verses on them by Mrs. Thrale—The Library at Streatham Park—Grosvenor Square—Conversazione—Other Entertainments—A Foreign Tour Projected—Signs of Danger—Voracious Appetite—Sudden Death—Johnson's Grief—He Comforts the Widow—The Will—The Executors—Distress of Mrs. Thrale—The Trade to be Carried on—

Johnson's Mercantile Ardour — The Brewery Sold — The Barclays — The Summer at Streatham — Johnson and Pepys — Piozzi and Sacchini — Mrs. Thrale and Fanny Burney 140-170

CHAPTER VII.

Introduction to Piozzi — Account of him — He goes Abroad — Second Sight — Piozzi Returns — Beginning of Uneasiness — Good Resolutions — Harley Street — The Widow Watched — Fears for Johnson — Death of Levet — Verses on him — Johnson's Emotion — Social Comforts — Mrs. Thrale has an Assembly — Literary Women — Mrs. Thrale Described — Rumours of her marrying Again — Johnson Ill and Dispirited — A Lecture on Peevishness — Dr. Lee — Modern Refinement — Burton on Melancholy — Johnson and the Quakers — His Position at Streatham — A Disastrous Lawsuit — Reasons for Quitting Streatham — The Park Let to Lord Shelburne — The Last Summer there — Madame d'Arblay's Recollections — Johnson's Farewell to Streatham — He Accompanies Mrs. Thrale to Brighton — His Severity — Mrs. Thrale confesses her Attachment — Conduct of her Daughters and Miss Burney — Her Mental Struggles — Piozzi Dismissed — Embarrassments — Argyll Street — Resolution to leave London — Removal to Bath — The Parting with Piozzi — Mrs. Thrale loses her Youngest Daughter — Resentment 171-201

CHAPTER VIII.

Discontent — Johnson has a Stroke — Mrs. Thrale's Situation — Sir Philip Jennings Clerk — An Old Friend — Mrs. Thrale's Health — Miss Burney's Sympathy — Repinings — Irritation — Want of Society — Piozzi Recalled — The News told to Johnson — Correspondence — Rupture — Farewell — Return of Piozzi — The Marriage — Baretti's Attack 202-218

CHAPTER IX.

Departure for the Continent — Calais — Aspect of the Country — Chantilly — The Prince of Condé — Paris — The Palais Royal — The Parisians — Beaumarchais — The English Austin Nuns — An Air Balloon — Animal Magnetism — Mont Cenis — Italian Costume — Milan — Christmas Festivities — Free Manners — The Theatre of La Scala — The Lower Classes — Cremona — The Bells — Dr. Burney — Verona — Venice — Venetian Society — The Po — Ferrara — Talassi's Visit to Streatham — Bologna — The Painters of the Bolognese School — Journey to Florence 219-242

CHAPTER X.

Florence — An English Inn — Sir Horace Mann — Forests — An Eulogium on Captain Cook — A Cardinal — The *Lingua Toscana* — Hasty Burials — Lucca — Completion and Despatch of the 'Anecdotes' — The Bagni di Pisa — Illness of Mr. Piozzi — Insects — First View of Rome — The Coliseum — The King of Sweden — Queen Christina — Dislike of Perfumes — Insanitary Streets — Escape of Mr. Piozzi from Assassination — Arrival at Naples — Vesuvius — St. Januarius — The King of Naples — The Grotto del Cane — Reminiscence of the Southwark Brewery — The Hermit of Vesuvius — Return to Rome — The Carnival — Kissing the Slipper — Anecdote of the Emperor — Angelica Kauffman — Loretto — Correggio — Return to Milan — The Emperor Joseph's

Reforms—Lugano—Farewell to Italy—Innsbruck—Munich—Salzburg—Vienna—The Emperor—Metastasio—Prague—Dresden—Berlin—Antwerp—Return to England 243-273

CHAPTER XI.

Macaulay's Account of the Flight to Italy—Obloquy—Insults from Baretti—Continuing Regard for Johnson—His Death—Projected Work on Him—The Florence Miscellany—The 'Anecdotes'—Rupture with Boswell—Inaccuracies in the 'Anecdotes'—Shows Resentment against Johnson—Walpole's Censures—Sale of the Book—Peter Pindar—Bozzy and Piozzi—Extracts—Miss Thrale—The Piozzis Return to England—Their Reception—Miss Seward's Impressions of Mrs. Piozzi and her Husband . . 274-290

CHAPTER XII.

Life in England—Publication of the Letters—Opinions on them—Baretti's Libels—Mrs. Piozzi's Character of him after his Death—'The Sentimental Mother'—The Blues Ashamed—The Book of Travels—Walpole's Sentence—Miss Seward's Opinion—Samuel Rogers—Conduct of the Daughters—Mrs. Piozzi and Miss Burney—Return to Streatham Park—Gaieties there—Mr. Piozzi lays out Money—Society in London—Dr. Parr—Boswell's Life Published—Boswell's Attack on her—Walpole Sides with her—'British Synonymy'—Gifford's Opinion on it—Walpole's Criticism—Removal to Wales—Brynbella—Piozzi's Amiable Character—His Prudent Economy—Adoption of an Heir—Sir John Salusbury—'Retrospection'—Piozzi's Gout—Her Cares of him—Her Irrepressible Spirits—Miss Thrale marries Lord Keith—A Visit from Dr. Burney—Death of Piozzi—His Will . . 291-314

CHAPTER XIII.

Cession of Brynbella—Subsequent Life—Lavish Expenditure—Sir James Fellowes—Attempt to Dispose of Streatham—A Bath Cat—The Streatham Portraits Sold by Auction—Improvements in London—Bath Life—Mr. Mangin's Account of her—Her Handwriting—Rouge—Anecdotes of Johnson—Acquirements—Literary Conversation at Bath—Sir William Pepys—Miss Hawkins—Fickleness of Public Taste—Bennet Langton—Fazio—Miss O'Neill—The Conway Episode—Renewed Acquaintance with Madame d'Arblay—Moore's Impression of her—Celebration of her Eightieth Birthday—Her Death and Will—Madame d'Arblay's Parallel between her and Madame de Staël—Mr. Hayward's Criticism—His Estimate of Mrs. Piozzi—Sayings and Anecdotes 315-336

LIST OF ILLUSTRATIONS.

	PAGE
MRS. PIOZZI, *after* J. Jackson, R.A.	*Frontispiece.*
WILLIAM HOGARTH, after a Picture by Himself	10
ELIZABETH AND MARIA GUNNING, *after* F. Cotes, R.A.	18
JOSEPH BARETTI, *after* Sir J. Reynolds	78
MRS. ABINGTON, *after* Sir J. Reynolds	84
GARRICK, AS ABEL DRUGGER, *after* J. Zoffany	94
HENRY THRALE, *after* Sir J. Reynolds	122
SIR JOSHUA REYNOLDS, after a Picture by Himself	156
MISS O'NEILL, *after* A. W. Davis	328

MRS. THRALE

CHAPTER I.

A Welsh Pedigree—Heroic Ancestors—Katharine of Berain—Richard Clough—Bâchygraig—The Cottons of Combermere—Parentage and Birth—Brought to London—James Quin—David Garrick—School in Queen Square—East Hyde—Sir Thomas Salusbury—Offley Place—Lady Salusbury—Dr. Collier—Hester a favourite—Hogarth—The Lady's Last Stake—Portents of Change—Mrs. King—Henry Thrale.

'I ONCE heard it asserted that few men of ever so good a family could recollect, immediately on being challenged, the maiden names of their four great grandmothers.' So wrote the subject of the following pages, at the outset of a short account which, in her later days, she drew up of her own early life. Persons thus forgetful, she added, could not be Welshmen. The clever lady who figured for many years in English society, first as Mrs. Thrale, and afterwards as Mrs. Piozzi, was a true Welshwoman, and could do much more than this. She had at her fingers' ends the pedigree of her race, beginning with 'Adam of Salzburg, younger son to Alexander, Duke of Bavaria, who came to England with the Conqueror, and obtained for his valour a fair house in Lancashire.'

Her memory was stored with

> 'a hoard of tales that dealt with knights,
> Half legend, half historic, counts and kings
> Who laid about them at their wills and died.'

Among the early descendants of the first father Adam, she celebrated Henry Salusbury, surnamed 'the Black,' who was said to have taken three Emirs with his own hand in the first Crusade, and on his return to have built Lleweny* Hall, in Denbighshire, setting on its highest tower a brazen figure of the Bavarian lion which adorned his shield. The story ran that, besides knighting Black Sir Harry on the field of battle, Cœur de Lion rewarded his prowess by adding to his blazonry the three crescents which his successors subsequently displayed on their coat-of-arms. Coming further down, the genealogist told of another Henry Salusbury who gave quarter to a beaten foe in the great battle at Barnet, and whose name, carved on a stone by the roadside there, she remembered, or believed she remembered, to have been pointed out to her by her father when she was a child. In confirmation of the latter authentic incident, she could appeal to the fact that her family for generations had flaunted the motto, ' *Satis est prostrasse leoni.*'

The author of this magnanimous boast had fought on the side of the White Rose, but the inhabitants of North Wales were generally adherents of the opposite faction. We are on firmer ground when we read that, in the reign of Queen Elizabeth, John Salusbury, son and heir of Sir John Salusbury, of Lleweny, wedded her Grace's cousin, the fair Katharine of Berain, in the same county, who was also descended from the marriage between Owen Tudor and Katharine of France, the widow of Henry V.†

---

* It appears that *Llew* in Welsh signifies *a devourer, a lion.*

† Mrs. Piozzi traced the descent thus: 'Owen Tudor had three sons by Queen Katharine. The first of these, Edmund, Earl of Richmond, was father to Henry VII.; the second was Jasper, Earl of Pembroke; the third was Fychan Tudor, of Berain. Fychan's son married Jasper's daughter, and had an only child, who, wedding Constance d'Aubigné, favourite lady to Anne de Bretagne, was father to the famous heiress, Katharine Tudor of Berain.' — 'Piozziana,' p. 27.

Having survived her husband, this lady, after a brief courtship, gave her hand to another Welshman, Richard Clough, who had acquired wealth and distinction in commerce, both as a merchant on his own account, and as factor, or agent, for that prince of merchants, Sir Thomas Gresham. In his youth Clough had made a pilgrimage to Jerusalem, and had there been created a Knight of the Holy Sepulchre, in consequence of which Pennant and other popular writers, including Mrs. Piozzi, have styled him 'Sir' Richard Clough. He afterwards fixed his abode at Antwerp, where he was employed, under Gresham's direction, in negotiating loans, and in smuggling money, arms, and goods, on behalf of the English Government. In 1567 he returned to Wales, where his marriage presently took place, and in the same year he began building in a retired valley near Denbigh the house of Bâchygraig, and at a little distance another house, to which he gave the name of Plâs Clough. Both houses were built in the Dutch style, and probably by Dutch workmen.

Clough* died in 1570, at the age of about forty, leaving two daughters, of whom the elder, Anne, inherited Bâchygraig, and married Roger Salusbury, younger brother of her mother's first husband. Katharine of Berain, when left a widow for the second time, became the wife of Morris Wynn, of Gwydyr, in Caernarvonshire. There is a story that she was addressed by this Morris as she returned from following John Salusbury to the grave, and told him that she had engaged herself to Richard Clough, but that if she were unfortunate enough to survive *him* she consented to be lady of Gwydyr. Having

* For an account of Richard Clough, see Fuller's Worthies, Flintshire, ed. 1662, pp. 39, 40, and 'Dictionary of National Biography,' vol. xi. Clough appears to have suggested to Gresham the idea of the Royal Exchange (Pennant's 'Account of London,' ed. 1814, p. 299).

duly performed both contracts, she took for her fourth and last husband Edward Thelwall, of Plas y Ward, in Denbighshire; and with *his*, says Mrs. Piozzi, *her* bones repose.

Mrs. Piozzi relates that Roger Salusbury, the husband of Anne Clough, having quarrelled with the head of his family, tore down the lion from the tower of Lleweny, and fixed it on the roof of his own wife's house. From this pair, by a descent of which the historian was familiar with every step, her father, John Salusbury, was lineally sprung, and died the owner of Bâchygraig, while the elder branch soon terminated in a female heiress, Hester, who, marrying Sir Robert Cotton, of Combermere, gave him and her issue by him the name of Salusbury Cotton. This Lady Salusbury Cotton had a granddaughter, Hester Maria, who married John Salusbury, of Bâchygraig, and in their only child, whose life is now to be told, the blood of the two stocks was united.

The match between these two distant cousins was neither a very prudent, nor a very fortunate alliance. The lady, indeed, combined the charms of wealth with those of beauty and amiability. She is stated to have had £10,000—an excellent portion in those days—besides an annuity of £125 for the life of her mother, who had barely reached middle age. She was also warmly attached to her kinsman, and though living gaily with her brother, Sir Robert Salusbury Cotton, and his wife, Lady Betty Tollemache, refused all other suitors whom the attractions of her purse and person brought to her feet. The gentleman, however, appears to have had nothing to recommend him beyond a reputation for gaiety and spirit. He was not only a man of wayward temper, but unsteady in his conduct and spendthrift in his habits. Unchecked by the care of a father, who died during the infancy of his sons, John Salusbury had wrecked the family estate, as far as the settlement on his mother, Lucy Salusbury, permitted. So completely had he done this, that when his marriage took place in 1739, the bride's £10,000 scarcely sufficed to pay his debts, and furnish the couple a cottage at Bodvel in Caernarvonshire. There, after one or two disappointments, they had a daughter, who was their only child, and was baptized Hester, after her mother, and Lynch, from the maiden name of her maternal grandmother, Lady Cotton. Hester Lynch Salusbury, afterwards Mrs. Thrale, and later on Mrs. Piozzi, was born on January 16, 1740, old style, or January 27, 1741, new style.

The child from infancy showed quick parts and a lively disposition, which made her the plaything and almost the sole occupation of her parents, who were compelled by their circumstances to remain at Bodvel until either the death of the dowager Mrs. Salusbury, or some other accident should occur to improve their situation. The looked-for events were not long in coming: Mrs. Salusbury of Bâchygraig died; and Sir Robert Salusbury Cotton, having lost Lady Betty, who left her husband childless, manifested an inclination to attach himself to his sister and her little girl. Hester, with her parents, was invited to Lleweny, and came to the old Hall, which she remembered in after-years as hung round with armour, and where she won the heart of her uncle, who called her Fiddle, and was amused by the readiness and freedom of her talk. The baronet, who was displeased with an unequal match made by his only brother, and could not brook the indolent pride of his sister's impecunious husband, began to think of altering his will, and leaving his niece the portion of a daughter.

It seems to have been shortly after the conclusion of

this visit to Lleweny Hall that little Hester, now turned five years of age, was carried by her parents up to London. They went by invitation to her uncle Sir Robert's house in Albemarle Street, whither he had promised to follow them within two months. Before the end of the time mentioned, news came that he had died of apoplexy. His sudden end prevented the fulfilment of his intention to make provision for the child, his whole fortune going under the existing will to his brother, Sir Lynch Salusbury Cotton.

John Salusbury next fell into the hands of projectors, who pretended to find lead on his encumbered estate; but he left his wife and little Hester in town. The latter became a favourite with the Duke and Duchess of Leeds, who had some previous knowledge of the Salusburys. Under their roof she often met the great actor James Quin, who taught her to recite Satan's address to the sun in 'Paradise Lost.'* Afterwards, she says, she was taken to the play to see him act Cato, and when he appeared on the stage, to the great amusement of both Duchess and player, the child went to the front of the box, and made him a formal curtsey. The next incident that impressed itself on her memory was the display of fireworks for the Peace of Aix-la-Chapelle. She remembered sitting on a terrace to see them, and being fed with sweetmeats by David Garrick, who was charmed because, on his asking 'why those things that blew up were called Gerbes in the programme,' she answered at once: 'Because they are like wheat-sheaves, you see, and *gerbe* is French for a wheat-sheaf.' When Garrick was intimate at Streatham

* Frederick, Prince of Wales, appointed Quin to instruct his children in elocution, and under his direction there were amateur performances at Leicester House, in which the young Princes and Princesses took part. When told how well George III. delivered his first speech, the old actor exclaimed proudly: 'Ah, it was I who taught the boy to speak!' And the King placed his old master on the civil list.

Park more than twenty years afterwards, she adds, he did not like that story—it made him feel too old.

'Lord Halifax,' continues the writer, 'was now, or soon after, head of the Board of Trade, and wished to immortalize his name—he had no sons—by colonizing Nova Scotia. Cornwallis and my father, whom he patronized, were sent out, the *first persons* in every sense of the words; and poor dear mamma was left *sine pane* almost, I believe, certainly *sine nummo*, with her odd little charge, a girl without a guinea, whose mind, however, she ceased not to cultivate in every possible manner. For French, writing and arithmetic, I had no instructor but herself; and when she went from home where I could not be taken, my temporary abode was the great school in Queen Square, where Mrs. Dennis and her brother, the Admiral Sir Peter Dennis, said I was qualified, at eight years old, for teacher rather than learner; and he actually did instruct me in the rudiments of navigation, as the globes were already familiar to me.'

The small-pox and measles having interrupted her studies, her grandmother, Lady Cotton, invited her with her mother to spend a summer at East Hyde, a country seat belonging to her ladyship near Luton, on the borders of Bedfordshire and Hertfordshire. 'At East Hyde I learned to love horses; and when my mother hoped I was gaining health by the fresh air, I was kicking my heels on a corn-bin, and learning to drive of the old coachman, who, like everybody else, small and great, delighted in taking me for a pupil. Grandmamma kept four great ramping war-horses for her carriage, with immense long manes and tails, which we buckled and combed; and when, after long practice, I showed her and my mother how two of them (poor Colonel and Peacock) would lick my hand for a lump of sugar or fine white bread, much were they amazed; much more when my skill in guiding them round the courtyard on the break could no longer be doubted or denied, though forbidden to be exercised for the future.'

Not far from East Hyde is Offley, in Hertfordshire, where lived Sir Henry Penrice, the Judge of the Admiralty Court, who, by an heiress of the Spencer family, was the father of an only daughter, the destined successor to the fortunes of both her parents. Now John Salusbury had a younger brother Thomas, who, after passing through Cambridge, had studied the Civil Law, and was now in full practice in Doctors' Commons. This rising advocate was a constant visitor at Offley Place, and became a candidate for the hand of the accomplished Anna Maria Penrice. The young lady was by no means averse from his suit, and sought the friendship of his sister-in-law, while she bestowed her favour freely on Hester. Mrs. John Salusbury was by no means disposed to forward the match, considering that her absent husband's interest had been neglected by his brother, who had undertaken to act for him while abroad. Love, however, was Dr. Thomas's apology; Mrs. John Salusbury's complaints were hushed, and the lovers married. Satisfied with the great wealth he had acquired, Sir Henry resigned his office in 1751, after a tenure of thirty-six years, and died in the following year. He was succeeded both in his post and his estate by his son-in-law, who had now became Sir Thomas Salusbury.*

'My father,' continues Hester, 'meanwhile behaved

---

* At the end of Burrell's Admiralty Reports, edited by Marsdon, will be found printed, 'Letters Patent under the Great Seal of Great Britain, dated the 19th December, 1752, granted to the Right Worshipful Sir Thomas Salusbury, Knight and Doctor of Laws, for the office of Judge of the High Court of Admiralty of England, so long as he shall behave himself, with a salary of £400 *per annum*.' He had previously held the post of Advocate-General for the office of Lord High Admiral.

perversely, quarrelling and fighting duels, and fretting his friends at home. My mother and uncle, taking advantage of a gloomy letter, begged him to return and share the gaieties of Offley Place. . . . Here I reigned long a fondled favourite.' Lady Salusbury, though her health soon began to decline, took care that her young charge should be instructed in Latin and modern languages. For this purpose she employed the aid of a certain Dr. Collier, who is frequently mentioned by his pupil. This gentleman appears to have been the eldest son of Arthur Collier, a writer on metaphysics, who, in the early part of the eighteenth century, worked out for himself a system similar to that of Bishop Berkeley. The younger Collier bore his father's Christian name, and engaged in the profession of a lawyer, in which, however, he did not achieve any extraordinary distinction.* He is described by the author of the 'Lives of the Civilians'† as an ingenious, but unsteady and eccentric man, the confidential law-adviser of the notorious Duchess of Kingston, whose marriage with the Duke he had a large share in promoting. He undertook the tuition of Hester Salusbury in 1757, but in March, 1759, her kind aunt died.

'Study,' wrote the pupil, in after years, ' was my delight, and such a patroness would have made stones students. . . . Felicity in this world, however, lasts not long. Poor Lady Salusbury died, at forty-one years old, of dropsy in the breast, and uncle said he had no kindness but for me. I think I did share his fondness with his stud; our stable was the first for hunters of enormous value—for racers, too; and our house, after my aunt's death, was even haunted by young men who made court to the niece, and expressed

---

* He frequently appears as a counsel conducting cases in the volume of Law Reports mentioned in our last note.

† 'Sketches of the Lives and Characters of Eminent English Civilians,' by one of the members of the College (Charles Coote, LL.D.), London, 1804.

admiration of the horses. Every suitor was made to understand my extraordinary value. Those who could read were shown my verses; those who could not were judges of my prowess in the field. It was my sport to mimic some, and drive others back, in order to make Dr. Collier laugh, who did not perhaps wish to see me give a heart away which he held completely in his hands, since he kindly became my preceptor in Latin, logic, rhetoric, etc. . . . A friendship more tender, or more unpolluted by interest or by vanity, never existed; love had no place at all in the connection, nor had he any rival but my mother. Their influence was of the same kind, and hers was the stronger.'

Hester and her mother spent a large part of each year in Hertfordshire, but removed for the winter to London, where John Salusbury had a house of his own. It was during one of these winters that she sat to Hogarth for the principal figure in his painting of 'The Lady's Last Stake.' She tells us that the painter was very intimate with her father during her girlhood, and that she was no more than fourteen when this picture was executed. There may be some mistake about the date,* but a likeness is clearly discernible between her avowed portraits and the features of the lady in Hogarth's picture, which was engraved, at Lord Macaulay's suggestion, for the edition of her 'Remains' published by Mr. Hayward.

During the later years in which Hester and her mother spent their summer at Offley Place, they had the greatest difficulty in managing her father's hot temper. It constantly threatened them with the loss of Sir Thomas Salusbury's favour, and during the last season of their

---

* We have somewhere seen it stated that this picture was painted in 1761. If so, Hester would be twenty at the time. The figure represented is a woman about twenty-four.

W. Howarth

residence there further portents of change appeared from more than one quarter. A new neighbour took up her abode close to the park gate. This was the Honourable Mrs. King, a widow, who rapidly effected a conquest of Sir Thomas. His frequent visits to her made the mother and daughter not sorry when the time came for their removal to their London house. Meanwhile, Lord Halifax had become Lord-Lieutenant of Ireland, and when, in the early part of 1752, he went to take possession of the Viceroyalty, Hester's father had gone with him as one of his suite, flattered to attend his patron through his own country, and show him the wonders of Wales. Mrs. John Salusbury remained at Offley doing the honours. Sir Thomas went to town for a day or two, and returned with the tidings that he had met with an excellent young man, whose merits he proceeded to extol, ending with the eulogy that he was a real sportsman. Seeing his niece disposed to laugh, 'he looked,' she says, ' very grave, and observed, " He expected us to like him, and that seriously."' Next day the young man, whose name was Henry Thrale, appeared in person, and applied himself diligently to win the favour of the mother, while in a certain formal way he commenced paying his addresses to the daughter.

CHAPTER II.

Origin of the Thrale Family—Edmund Halsey—The Anchor Brewhouse—Lord Cobham—Ralph Thrale—His Son's Education—The Cobham Cousins—Henry Thrale's Bachelorhood—Arthur Murphy—Hester's Courtship—A Family Dispute—Sudden Death of her Father—His Will—Sir Thomas Salusbury—Hester's Marriage—First Experiences of Matrimony—Dr. Fitzpatrick—Birth of a Daughter—Character of Thrale—Murphy introduces Johnson—Growth of the Acquaintance—Johnson's Hypochondria—Streatham—Deadman's Place—The Globe Theatre—House at Brighton—Johnson's Menagerie—Macbean—Miss Williams—Robert Levet—Domestication with the Thrales—Mrs. Salusbury—Johnson's Peculiarities—His Dress—Appetite—Taste in Food—Affects the Epicure—Love of Late Hours—Fondness for Tea—Want of Taste for Music and Painting—Mode of Entering a Room—Inarticulate Utterances — Twitchings — Ejaculations — A Favourite with Women—Characteristics of Mrs. Thrale—Her Personal Appearance—Her Dress—Influence over Johnson—He goes more into Society.

TOWARDS the close of the seventeenth century, Edmund Halsey, son of a miller at St. Albans, quarrelled with his father, and ran away to London with a very few shillings in his pocket. 'He was eminently handsome,' writes Mrs. Piozzi, 'and old Child, of the Anchor Brewhouse, Southwark,* took him in as what we call a broomstick clerk, to sweep the yard,' etc. The young man behaved so well that he was soon preferred to be a house-clerk, and then, having free access to his master's table, married his only daughter, and succeeded to the business upon Child's decease. Halsey was returned to Parliament in 1711, as member for the Borough, but the House of Commons displaced him in favour of a rival candidate. He was again returned in 1722, and retained the seat

* The Borough was famed for its breweries from an early period. Chaucer speaks of 'The ale of Southwark' in his time.

from that time until his death. Having, like his father-in-law, no child but a daughter, he matched her with the wealthy and aspiring founder of the great house of Temple.

Sir Richard Temple, who had served in Flanders under the Duke of Marlborough, was ennobled on the accession of George I., and, four years later, obtained a patent, raising him to the rank of Viscount Cobham, with remainder to his sister, Hester Grenville and her issue male. Having later on taken an active part against Sir Robert Walpole, he was gratified, upon the fall of that statesman, with the truncheon of a Field-Marshal, and for a short time held the post of Commander-in-Chief. Though now best remembered as the friend of Pope, and creator of the gardens at Stowe, Cobham was chiefly known to his contemporaries as the most restless of political intriguers. Not even his nephew and successor, the first Earl Temple, was better versed, or more diligent, in all the tactics of party. A peer so dignified, so busy, and of such large possessions, could have no leisure for the affairs of a brewhouse, even had the prejudices of that age permitted the wearer of a coronet to be connected with any trading concern. But nothing was further from the noble son-in-law's thoughts than to throw away the important position which Halsey had made his own on the south side of London Bridge.

Mrs. Piozzi relates that when Halsey became rich, he turned his eyes homewards, where he learned that his sister had married a hard-working man at Offley, named Thrale, and had many children. What was the precise station in life of this family we are not informed. It appears, however, that the name of Thrale was of some consideration in the neighbouring town of St. Albans ; in the Abbey Church there is, or was, a handsome monument to the memory of Mr. John Thrale, late of London, merchant, who died in 1704.* 'Halsey,' proceeds Mrs. Piozzi, 'sent for one of his sister's children, my Mr. Thrale's father, to London; said he would make a man of him, and did so; but made him work very hard, and treated him very roughly.' According to an account with which Boswell was furnished by Johnson, Ralph Thrale—so the new-comer was called—was employed in the brewery for twenty years at six shillings a week. This does not sound very probable. According to Mrs. Piozzi, the nephew, though he remained a servant, ' made himself, in course of time, so useful to Halsey that the weight of the business fell entirely on him; and while the uncle was canvassing the borough and visiting the Viscountess, Ralph Thrale accumulated money both for himself and his principal.' Both accounts agree that any hopes which Ralph had cherished of receiving the brewery as a bequest from its owner were disappointed, and it seems that he did not take a guinea under Halsey's will. The brewer's entire fortune and the goodwill of his trade were left to the sole disposition of Lord Cobham. Halsey's churlishness to his nephew is said to have been caused in part by jealousy. Ralph Thrale was remarkable—as the senior had been—for personal beauty; and the latter, who affected the character of an old beau, was piqued at finding a younger rival preferred to himself.

Halsey died about 1730,† and after some delay Lord Cobham sold the brewery to my lady's cousin for £30,000. Mrs. Piozzi says that Ralph paid the money out of his savings; Boswell, that he gave security on the property, and discharged the debt in eleven years.

---
* Boswell's Johnson (Dr. Birkbeck Hill's edition), vol. i., p. 491, n. 1.
† The return of the election for Southwark, on the vacancy occasioned by his death, is dated January 23, 1729-30.

Whatever was the fact, the purchaser was rich enough by 1741 to stand for Southwark in the decisive General Election of that year. He came into Parliament on the crest of the great wave which overwhelmed Walpole. Boswell, in a tone of superiority well becoming so great a man, observes that 'the esteem which Thrale's good conduct procured him from the nobleman who had married his master's daughter made him be treated with much attention.' We cannot be wrong in inferring from this statement that the member for the Borough voted steadily on the side of his aristocratic connections.

Ralph Thrale lived until 1758, and amassed a large fortune. Beyond sitting a few sessions in the House of Commons, and serving the office of High Sheriff of Surrey, he made no figure in the world, but was remembered for the liberality with which he used his riches. He gave his son and three daughters the best education in his power. His son Henry, both at school and at the University of Oxford, was encouraged and aided to associate with young men of the first rank. To the Cobhams were allied a whole clan of junior kinsmen, Grenvilles, Lytteltons and Pitts. These were the Boy Patriots who had joined in the league against Sir Robert Walpole. The late Minister had been used to call them 'the Cobham cousins.' Old Thrale was careful to connect his heir with a coterie of such distinction. 'He lent them money,' observes Mrs. Piozzi, 'and they furnished assistance of every other kind.' Thus Henry Thrale, before he attained manhood, was familiar with Stowe and some other great houses, and had been abroad with Mr. Lyttelton, afterwards Lord Westcote, who accompanied him, at the expense of his father, as a kind of dignified tutor, 'His allowance after he left college,' adds Boswell, 'was splendid—not less than a thousand a year.' Recollecting that a thousand a year in the middle of last century was equivalent to an income of at least double that amount in the present day, we may echo the biographer's remark, that, in a man who had risen as Ralph Thrale did, this was a very extraordinary instance of generosity. He used to say, 'If this young dog does not find so much, after I am gone as he expects, let him remember that he has had a great deal in my own time.'

One of his three daughters married a Mr. Rice; another, Sir John Lade, a baronet of large fortune, and member for Camelford; the third, a few months after the old man's death, wedded Mr. Arnold Nesbit, member for Winchelsea.

Henry Thrale succeeded his father at the age of thirty,* inheriting, besides the brewery, a house in the Borough, and a villa standing in a large paddock, near the village of Streatham. Though he applied himself diligently to business, his hours of leisure, until he married, appear to have been given chiefly to the pleasures of Ranelagh and the green-room. Boswell, who did not make his acquaintance till he was the father of several children, describes his manners as presenting the character of a plain, independent English squire. On this Mrs. Piozzi has the note: 'No, no! Mr. Thrale's manners presented the character of a gay man of the town; like Millamant, in Congreve's comedy, he abhorred the country and everything in it.' Evidently the lady's thoughts went back to what her first husband had been in the time of his bachelorhood and early marriage. And her 'Remains' contain several passages showing that, in his younger days, Henry Thrale saw a good deal of the sort of life which is depicted in 'The Way of the World.' Arthur Murphy, nearly of the same age as himself, was his

* He was born in 1728.

chosen friend. Even Horace Walpole allowed that the 'writing actor was good company.' Murphy's talents, literary acquirements, and gentle manners made him a general favourite; but his morals were undeniably lax. He and Thrale were partners in many a careless adventure. The worthy pair, we are told, sought out the beautiful Gunnings on their arrival in England, presented to them a hanger-on of their own in the character of a young nobleman, and were ignominiously turned into the street for their pains, the impostor having betrayed himself by the use of a low Irish exclamation. The Duchess of Hamilton never forgave this impudent frolic; Lady Coventry, more prudently, pretended to forget it. Yet, according to the standard of that age, these were no mere common rakes. Murphy was not only a wit, but a scholar, as his translation of Tacitus bears witness. Thrale, though no wit, was, if we may believe Johnson, something of a scholar. Whatever other excesses they indulged in, the friends do not seem to have found their merriment in wine. Thus in May 1760, Murphy wrote to Garrick: 'You stand engaged to Mr. Thrale for Wednesday se'ennight. You need not apprehend drinking; it is a very easy house.'

When Henry Thrale, with all his advantages of education and social experience, went down to Offley to visit his father's birthplace, he appeared to his future wife a very handsome and well-accomplished gentleman. 'The people,' she says, 'all looked with admiration at his giving five shillings to a poor boy who lay on the bank, because he was sure his father had been such a boy. In a week's time the country caught up the notion that Miss Salusbury's husband had been suddenly found by meeting Sir Thomas at the house of Mr. Levinz, a well-known *bon vivant* of those days, who kept a gay house at Brompton, where he entertained the gay fashionists of 1760.* The chaplain of Offley Place, a distant relation of ours, having undisclosed hopes of his own to get the heiress, not only took alarm, but cunningly conveyed that alarm to my father, who, when he came home, said he saw his girl already half disposed of without his consent, and swore I should not be exchanged for a barrel of porter.

'Vain,' she continues, 'were all my assurances that nothing resembled love less than Mr. Thrale's behaviour; vain my promises that no step on my part should be taken without his concurrence; although I clearly understood, and wrote Dr. Collier word, that my uncle made this marriage the condition of his favour quite apparently, and that certain ruin would follow my rejection. The letter, perhaps, still exists, in which I declared my resolution to adhere to the maxims of filial duty. . . . By this time the brothers quarrelled, and met no more. My father took us to London. My uncle solaced himself with visiting the widow; and after a miserable winter, which visits from Mr. Thrale to my mother rendered terrifying to *me* every day from papa's violence of temper, a note came, sent in a sly manner, from Dr. Collier, to tell me—it was written in Latin—that Sir Thomas would certainly marry Mrs. King the Sunday following, and begged I would not say a syllable till the next day, when *he* would come and break the dreadful tidings to my father.

'My countenance, however, showed, or his acuteness discovered, something he did not like; an accusation followed that I received clandestine letters from Mr. Thrale, a circumstance I had certainly every just reason to deny.' A family quarrel ensued, which was prolonged till four o'clock in the morning, when Mr. John Salusbury

---

* The writer is using round numbers here; Sir Thomas and Henry Thrale do not appear to have met before the summer of 1762.

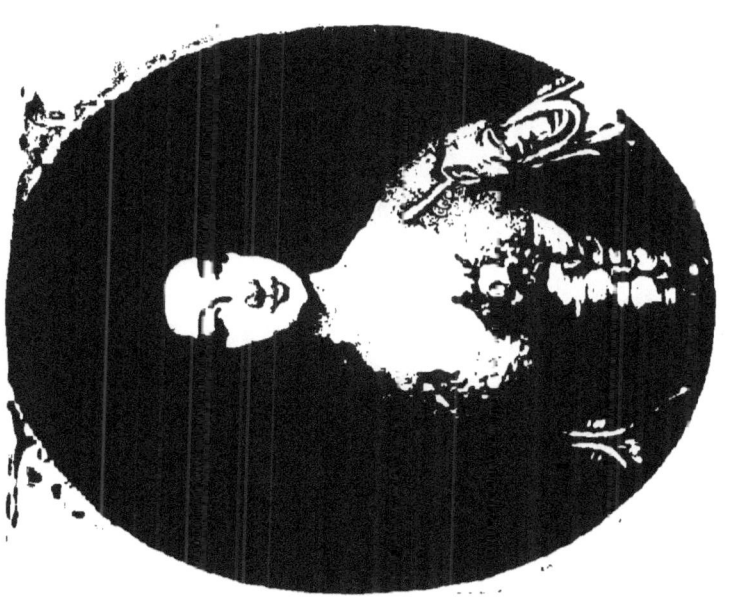

gained possession of the fatal billet, and had to ask pardon of his daughter for having disbelieved her denial. At nine o'clock the father went out to consult his brother-in-law, Sir Lynch Salusbury Cotton. As the whole party had been made ill by their dispute, a medical friend was invited to dinner, but by the time he arrived John Salusbury had died, and was brought home a corpse before the dining hour. This was in December,* 1762.

'His will,' proceeds the narrative, ' gave to my mother his Bâchygraig house and estate for life, charged with £5,000 for me, to which my uncle added £5,000 more; with which, and expectations, of course, Mr. Thrale deigned to accept my undesired hand, and in ten months from my poor father's death were both the marriages he feared accomplished. My uncle went himself with me to church, gave me away, dined with us at Streatham Park, returned to Hertfordshire, wedded the widow, and then scarce ever saw or wrote to either of us; leaving me to conciliate as I could a husband who was indeed much kinder than I counted on to a *plain girl*, who had not one attraction in his eyes, and on whom he never had thrown five minutes of his time away, in any interview unwitnessed by company, even till after our wedding-day was done.'

Mrs. Piozzi's statements respecting the disposition of her father's estate are not very clear. She elsewhere says that, by her parents' marriage settlement, the property, in the event of their having no son, was entailed on Sir Thomas Salusbury and his issue male, in priority to female issue of their own. It is possible, however, that power was reserved to John Salusbury to limit a life-estate to his widow, and to charge portions in favour of daughters. Mrs. John Salusbury, as we shall see, died in

* On the 18th. See *Gents. Mag.*, 1762, p. 601.

the summer of 1773; Sir Thomas died without issue in the following October; and shortly after the latter date we hear that Thrale, in right of his wife, had come into possession of the house and lands of Bâchygraig. Sir Thomas Salusbury left no mark on the history of English jurisprudence. In the 'Lives of the Civilians' he is spoken of as a respectable judge, but not equal in ability to Sir William Scott.* The same thing may be said of nineteen out of twenty of the judges who have presided in the Court of Admiralty. Some years after his death a monument by Joseph Nollekens was erected in the parish church of Offley to the memory of Sir Thomas, at the expense of his second wife, who long survived him. It represents the pair standing in front of an oak-tree. There is a tradition in the family that, during their engagement, a misunderstanding arose between them, by which the match was broken off. A short time afterwards they both, unconscious of each other's presence, sought shelter from a shower under the same tree. They quickly discovered the awkwardness of their situation, but the drops continued to fall so heavily that retreat was impossible. The result was that they made up their difference, and before the rain ceased were once more betrothed.† So much for the power of sentiment over middle-aged lovers! We return to the more prosaic history of the lively Hester and her unimpassioned bridegroom.

Their wedding-day was October 11, 1763. The young wife's mother remained with her, as did also her cousin Hester Salusbury Cotton. Of other society she saw hardly any, save a few of her husband's bachelor friends. 'Mr. Murphy,' she says, 'was introduced, and the

---

* Afterwards Lord Stowell.
† Cussans' 'History of Hertfordshire,' ii. 104.

facetious Georgey Bodens,* as the men called him.' Another visitor was the notorious Simon Luttrell.† Besides these, she was thrown with a very sickly old physician, 'who seemed as if living with us,' Dr. Fitzpatrick, a Roman Catholic. Her reign had not begun. There was no sign as yet of the noble hospitality that was to render Streatham famous.

'When winter came,' the story goes on, 'I was carried to my town residence, Deadman's Place, Southwark, which house, no more than that in Surrey, had been seen by me till called upon to inhabit it. Here, too, my mother quitted us, and lived at our old mansion, in Dean Street, Soho, then no unfashionable part of the world; and thither I went—oh, how willingly!—to visit her every day.' Thrale's sisters now called, took a survey of their reserved brother's bride, and asked how she liked Dr. Fitzpatrick, his Jesuit friend. The question led her to cultivate a man who was supposed to have so much influence. She found that the aged physician possessed no more influence than herself, but, from his long acquaintance with the Thrales, he was able to satisfy her curiosity on some points. 'From him in due time I learned what had determined my husband's choice to me, till then a standing wonder. He had, the old man said, asked several women, naming them, but all, except *me*, refused to live in the Borough; to which, and to his business, he observed that Mr. Thrale was as unaccount-

---

* He is mentioned by Miss Burney. At the commencement of the Gordon riots she writes to her father: 'Dr. Johnson has written to Mrs. Thrale, without even mentioning the existence of this mob; perhaps, at this very moment, he thinks it "a humbug upon the nation," as George Bodens called the Parliament.'—Mme. d'Arblay's Diary, i. 293.

† It was told of him that he challenged his son, the Colonel Luttrell (afterwards Earl of Carhampton) of Middlesex election celebrity, who refused to fight him, 'not because he was his father, but because he was not a gentleman.' —Hayward's 'Piozzi,' ii. 23.

ably attached now as he had been in his father's time averse from both.

'So summer came again, and Streatham Park was improving, and autumn came, and a daughter* came, and I became of a *little* more importance. Confidence was no word in our vocabulary; and I tormented myself to guess who possessed that of Mr. Thrale; not his clerks, certainly, who scarce dared approach him—much less come near me; whose place, he said, was either in the drawing-room or the bed-chamber. We kept, meantime, a famous pack of foxhounds at a hunting-box near Croydon; but it was masculine for ladies to ride. We kept the finest table possible at Streatham Park, but *his* wife was not to *think of the kitchen.* So I never knew what was for dinner till I saw it. Driven thus on literature as my sole resource, no wonder if I loved my books and children. From a *gay* life my mother held me fast. Those pleasures Mr. Thrale enjoyed alone; with *me*, indeed, they never would have suited, I was too often and too long confined.' Elsewhere she records that she never was in a theatre from her first wedding-day till her daughter, born in 1764, went with her.

So far Henry Thrale has not appeared in a very favourable light. There could be little sympathy between a husband phlegmatic, uncommunicative, impenetrable, intent on the cares of business and the pursuit of private indulgences, and a wife thirteen years his junior, full of spirits, quick in feeling, hungry for companionship, unable to be content without society. Yet the self-contained brewer's character had a better side to it, and this was now to reveal itself. 'It is but justice to Mr. Thrale,' observes the smooth Murphy, in the tone of a man com-

---

* Born September 17, 1764; baptized by the name of Hester, but usually called Queeney; married in 1808 to Admiral Viscount Keith.

bating a general prejudice, 'to say that a more ingenuous frame of mind no man possessed. His education at Oxford gave him the habits of a gentleman; his amiable temper recommended his conversation, and the goodness of his heart made him a sincere friend.' There was a kindness of long standing between Murphy and Dr. Johnson, as well as between Murphy and Thrale. The good-natured Irishman determined to bring his two friends together, thinking, no doubt, that an acquaintance between them would promote Thrale's credit as much as Johnson's comfort. Mrs. Thrale does not appear to have had any voice or part in the matter,* though she was more than ready to second Murphy's proposal. 'Mr. Hogarth,' she writes, 'was used to be very earnest that I should obtain the acquaintance, and if possible the friendship, of Dr. Johnson, whose conversation was to the talk of other men like Titian's painting compared with Hudson's, he said. . . . . Of Dr. Johnson, when my father and he were talking together about him one day, "That man," says Hogarth, "is not contented with believing the Bible, but he fairly resolves, I think, to believe nothing *but* the Bible. Johnson," added he, " though so wise a fellow, is more like King David than King Solomon; for he says in his haste that *all men are liars.*" † This character did not at all deter the Thrales from seeking his society. The brewer, a strong man, though a silent one, felt quite able to protect himself, while his wife was justly confident in her powers of pleasing, as well as eager to forward her husband's interest.

* 'That Johnson's introduction into Mr. Thrale's family was owing to her desire for his conversation,' says Boswell, 'is very probable, and the general supposition; but it is not the truth.' The biographer might have added that so far from giving any countenance to the general supposition, Mrs. Thrale herself supplied the correction of it which he printed.
† 'Anecdotes of Samuel Johnson.'

The introduction took place in January, 1765.* Murphy had wrought upon Thrale to desire it, extolling the lexicographer as one of the most eminent and worthiest characters of the age. The wish to know him having been awakened, the question next arose how his company was to be obtained. Evidently some excuse was considered necessary for inviting a distinguished man of letters to dine at the brewery. At last it was resolved that one Woodhouse, a shoemaker, who had gained some passing notoriety by writing verses, should be asked and made a temptation to Johnson to meet him. Accordingly, at the time appointed, Murphy brought the great man, having previously warned their hostess not to be surprised at his figure, dress, or behaviour. 'Mr. Johnson,' writes the lady, 'liked his new acquaintance so much that from that time he dined with us every Thursday through the winter and in the autumn. . . . . he followed us to Brighthelmstone, whence we were gone before his arrival: so he was disappointed and enraged, and wrote us a letter expressive of anger, which we were very desirous to pacify and to obtain his company again. Mr. Murphy brought him back to us again very kindly, and from that time his visits grew more frequent, till in the year 1766 his health, which he had always complained of, grew so exceedingly bad, that he could not stir out of his room in the court† he inhabited for many weeks together—I think, months.

'Mr. Thrale's attentions and my own now became so acceptable to him, that he often lamented to us the horrible condition of his mind, which he said was nearly

---

* 'Thraliana.' Johnson also places the date in 1765. Boswell, Hill's ed., iv. 85, n. 1. In the 'Anecdotes' Mrs. Piozzi states that the acquaintance began in 1764; but the 'Anecdotes' were written in Italy, without reference to documents.

† In 1766 Johnson was living in Johnson's Court, Fleet Street.

distracted; and though he charged *us* to make him odd solemn promises of secrecy on so strange a subject, yet, when we waited on him one morning, and heard him in the most pathetic terms, beg the prayers of Dr. Delap,* who had left him as we came in, I felt excessively affected with grief, and well remember my husband involuntarily lifted up one hand to shut his mouth, from provocation at hearing a man so wildly proclaim what he could at last persuade no one to believe, and what, if true, would have been so very unfit to reveal. Mr. Thrale went away soon after, leaving me with him, and bidding me prevail on him to quit his close habitation in the court, and come with us to Streatham, where I undertook the care of his health, and had the honour and happiness of contributing to its restoration.'†

Johnson at all ages suffered from hypochondria. He was liable to terrible fits of depression: at such times he was racked with dread of disease or madness, tortured by remorse for imaginary sins, in an agony of despair about the world to come. It may be truly said of this great but unhappy man, that 'through fear of death he was all his lifetime subject to bondage.' It is difficult to fix the precise date of this particular attack, the duration of which the narrator, writing from memory, has probably exaggerated; but it must have occurred some time in the former half of 1766. We know from Boswell that in that year he was with the Thrales from before Midsummer till after Michaelmas. From the time of this visit he became domesticated with the family, and began to influence the course of their life in many ways. He used to call their house his home, and to speak playfully of its owners as his 'master' and 'mistress.' This connection with Streatham lasted for sixteen years, and did not

* Rector of Lewes, and a friend of the Thrales.   † 'Anecdotes.'

cease till Thrale was dead, and his widow let the property to Lord Lansdowne.

Streatham Place, also known as Thrale Place, and later as Streatham Park, was on the south side of Tooting Beck Common, between Streatham and Tooting. The house was a large white building of three floors, having a slightly projecting centre, and wings with, on the right, a semicircular termination. It stood in well-timbered, park-like grounds of about a hundred acres in extent. The inclosure was girdled by a gravel walk of nearly two miles in circumference. The wealth and luxury of the owner appeared in the kitchen gardens belonging to the villa, which were of surprising extent, and surrounded by brick walls fourteen feet in height, built for the reception of forcing-frames, and producing a great abundance of fine fruit. Miss Burney, on her first visit, naïvely expressed her astonishment at the quantity of grapes, melons, peaches, nectarines that she saw daily at table, adding, 'We have not once missed a pineapple since I came.' No hospitality could be better suited to Johnson's taste than this, and no pains were spared to make him comfortable. He had his own room, his established seat at the table and the fireside; the library was his sanctum, and the books added to it were of his own selection. In course of time his favourite walk in the grounds became known as Dr. Johnson's Walk, and his resting-place there as Dr. Johnson's Summer-house.

The house was pulled down, and the materials sold by auction, in May, 1863. It had previously undergone considerable alteration at the hands of Mrs. Thrale and her second husband. No trace now remains of the Streatham Place of Thrale and Johnson.

Streatham, of course, in their time, was a quiet rural village, and the short journey between it and London was not without its risks in those days of highwaymen. In 1763 a man had been hanged on Kennington Common for robbing Mr. Thrale there. In the winter, when days were dark, roads mire, and travelling specially dangerous, the household were settled in the Borough. Thrale's house there was situated in Deadman's Place, a name said to be a corruption of Desmond's Place, and to indicate the site where the Earl of Desmond had had a mansion in the time of Elizabeth. If we may trust an account written by Mrs. Piozzi at the age of eighty, the residence belonging to the brewery had another historical association of greater interest. 'For a long time,' she says, ' my fate was bound up with the old Globe Theatre, upon the Bankside, Southwark, the alley it had occupied having been purchased and thrown down by Mr. Thrale to make an opening before the windows of our dwelling-house.' She adds that there were really curious remains of the old Globe Playhouse, meaning, we must suppose, of the foundations, for the structure itself was removed in 1644 to make room for tenements in the alley above mentioned.* In Deadman's Place, as well as at Streatham Place, Johnson had his own peculiar apartment.

Thrale had also his house at Brighton—a neat, small house in West Street, 'which,' says Miss Burney, writing from it, 'is the Court end of the town here as well as in London.' The family usually resorted to the Sussex coast for some weeks in the autumn; and here, too, they were frequently joined by Johnson.

During all this time, however, Johnson retained a home of his own in one or other of the courts off Fleet Street. ' He turned his house,' says Macaulay, 'into a place of

* According to another account, Deadman's Place derived its name from the number of bodies buried there during the great plague; and Thrale's brewery itself occupied the site of the Globe Theatre. It is certain, at any rate, that both brewhouse and dwelling-house stood close to the spot where Shakespeare once trod the boards on the Bankside.

refuge for a crowd of wretched old creatures who could find no other asylum ; nor could all their peevishness and ingratitude weary out his benevolence.'* In his sketch of Johnson's life he writes: 'At the head of the establishment he had placed an old lady named Williams, whose chief recommendations were her blindness and her poverty. But in spite of her murmurs and reproaches, he gave an asylum to another lady who was as poor as herself — Mrs. Desmoulins, whose family he had known many years before in Staffordshire. Room was found for the daughter of Mrs. Desmoulins, and for another destitute damsel, who was generally addressed as Mrs. Carmichael, but whom her generous host called Polly. An old quack doctor called Levet, who bled and dosed coalheavers and hackney coachmen, and received for fees crusts of bread, bits of bacon, glasses of gin, and sometimes a little copper, completed this menagerie.'†

The menagerie certainly resembled such a collection of discordant animals as the showmen of London used to train to live together in one cage, and exhibit under the name of 'a happy family.' But Macaulay has omitted one of the inmates, the Scotchman Macbean,‡ and describes two of the others in a strain of caricature. The presence of Macbean in the group shows how purely humorous was Johnson's professed dislike of the Scotch. He spoke of Macbean with respect, as a man of great learning, who knew many languages, and knew them well, but knew nothing of life. Miss Williams was the daughter

---

* Essay on Johnson's life.
† 'Miscellaneous Writings,' i. 293.
‡ Alexander Macbean had been one of Johnson's amanuenses in the compilation of the Dictionary. 'He had afterwards,' says Boswell, 'the honour of being librarian to Archibald, Duke of Argyle, for many years, but was left without a shilling. Johnson wrote for him a preface to "A System of Ancient Geography," and, by the favour of Lord Thurlow, got him admitted a poor brother of the Charterhouse.' This was about the end of 1780.

of a physician, and belonged to a good Welsh family. She was a woman of uncommon talents, great accomplishments, and agreeable conversation. She had a small income of her own, and in her latter days Johnson persuaded Garrick to give her a benefit, and Mrs. Montagu to give her a pension. Robert Levet was no quack doctor. Though he began life as a waiter at a coffee-house in Paris, he afterwards studied medicine under the ablest French professors, and while living with Johnson attended John Hunter's lectures. He was indebted to Johnson for little more than house room, maintaining himself for the most part by a practice among the lower class of tradesmen, from whom he took all that was offered him by way of fee, including meat and drink, although he demanded nothing from the poor. He acted for many years as surgeon and apothecary to Johnson under the direction of Dr. Lawrence. The writer who collected these particulars adds that 'Johnson never wished him to be regarded as an inferior, nor treated him like a dependent.' Though Johnson, in his letters to Mrs. Thrale, often laments the discord among the inmates of his house, it is clear that in the society of Miss Williams and Levet he found real pleasure. It became his regular custom to spend the middle of each week with the Thrales, joining his own family on Saturday afternoon to give them three good dinners, and his company before he went back to his master and mistress on the Monday evening. His other associates presently began to complain that this new connection estranged him from his old friendships. Thus Goldsmith, in the 'Haunch of Venison':*

> 'My friend bade me welcome, but struck me quite dumb
> With tidings that Johnson and Burke would not come;
> For I knew it (he cried), both eternally fail,
> The one with his speeches, and t'other with Thrale.'

---

* Written in 1771, though not published till two years after the author's death.

A difficulty which the Thrales at first had with their new guest was to preserve peace between him and the mother-in-law, Mrs. Salusbury, who was by this time domiciled under their roof. That excellent woman, like many other elderly ladies, had a passion for studying the newspapers and discussing politics, especially foreign politics. Now, nothing more exasperated the philosopher of Fleet Street than to be pestered with topics of the day. References to ancient history offended him; he would be rude to anyone who mentioned the Punic wars or Catiline's conspiracy; but talk of 'what the Swede intends and what the French,' goaded him almost to madness. 'This unmeaning stuff spoils all my comfort,' he would say. If we may credit the story, he repaid Mrs. Salusbury's tattle by composing, in his well-known style, sundry marvellous accounts of events that never happened, and publishing them in her favourite journals, greatly to the good lady's indignation. Thus, in the words of Baretti, Johnson could not much bear Mrs. Salusbury, nor Mrs. Salusbury him, when they first knew each other. But apart from her vicious propensity to political gossip, the widow was a woman of bright parts, and of the 'sound principles' which, in the sage's estimation, often covered a multitude of faults much more serious than hers. As years went on, his hearty interest in her daughter's family, and his sympathy for herself, when sinking under a lingering and mortal disease, reconciled them to each other, and at the close of her life they were on cordial, and even affectionate, terms.

At the commencement of his acquaintance with the Thrales, Johnson was fifty-six years of age. No more extraordinary inmate was ever admitted into a gentleman's household. His habits had been formed in penury and solitude. His ordinary dress has been made familiar to us by numerous descriptions: a rusty suit of brown clothes; a little, shrivelled, unpowdered wig, too small for his head; black worsted stockings ill drawn up. When indoors, the neck and sleeves of his shirt, and the knees of his breeches were left unfastened, and he wore a pair of unbuckled shoes by way of slippers. By his own confession, he had no passion for clean linen. He remembered the time, he said, when people in England changed a shirt only once a week; those who sat near him were sometimes tempted to think that he kept up the old custom. The foretops of all his wigs were burned away by too near approach to the candle, which he held, being short-sighted, between his eyes and a book. For this reason, Mr. Thrale's valet had always a becoming wig ready, with which he met Johnson at the parlour door, when he came down to dinner, and as he went upstairs to sleep, the same man followed him with another. In some other respects the great man's external appearance altered for the better after he joined the Streatham circle. Boswell tells us that he got better clothes, and the dark colour from which he never deviated was enlivened by metal buttons. The biographer, having on one occasion accompanied him to purchase a pair of silver buckles, attributes that expense to the influence of Mrs. Thrale. The lady, in a note on this passage, disowns the soft impeachment, and transfers the responsibility to her husband. While attentive to the comfort of their friend, she deemed it no part of her duty to advise him respecting the adornment of his person.

On one subject the brewer was by no means well qualified to correct the aberrations of his guest. Both of them were men of inordinate appetite. Both may be said to have shortened their days by excessive indulgence in the pleasures of the table. That Thrale did so is certain, and though Johnson lived to be seventy-five, his powerful frame would probably have lasted still longer had it not been called upon to perform impossible feats of digestion. 'When at table, he was totally absorbed in the business of the moment; his looks seemed riveted to his plate, nor would he, unless when in very high company, say one word, or even pay the least attention to what was said by others, till he had satisfied his appetite, which was so fierce, and indulged with such intenseness, that while in the act of eating, the veins of his forehead swelled, and generally a strong perspiration was visible.'* A leg of pork boiled till it dropped from the bone, a veal pie with plums and sugar, or the outside cut of a salt buttock of beef, were his favourite dainties.† His attack on a pie was not at all slackened by the circumstance that the crust had been made with rancid butter. He would eat lobster sauce with plum pudding, pour capillaire into his port wine, and melted butter into his chocolate. Nor was his mode of feeding more delicate than his choice of food: he astonished a fellow-traveller at an inn dinner by devouring a plateful of stewed carp with the assistance of his fingers only. Fermented drinks he judged not at all by their flavour, but solely by their intoxicating effect. Claret for boys, port for men, brandy for heroes, was his well-known maxim. Rather than become a boy, he preferred to give up the use of wine altogether, and did so before the end of 1765. But though he spared the cellar at Streatham, in the fruit-garden he ran riot. According to the 'Anecdotes,' 'he usually ate seven or eight large peaches of a morning before beakfast began, and treated them with proportionate attention after dinner again; yet I have heard him protest that he never had quite as much as he wished of wall-fruit, except once in his life.'

* Boswell. † 'Anecdotes.'

Johnson, though not temperate in eating or drinking, could be abstemious for what seemed to him sufficient reason. His host and hostess found that he kept fast in Lent, particularly during Holy Week, with a rigour which they thought very dangerous to his general health; they believed, though he would not own it, that he had left off wine from religious motives. He told Boswell that he had fasted two days without inconvenience, and that he had never been hungry but once. What his condition could have been on that exceptional occasion was a mystery to those who witnessed the destruction done by his ordinary appetite. Yet this very valiant trencherman affected the character of a fastidious epicure. When he had dined out anywhere, he would recollect minutely, and criticise the dishes which had been served at table. During his Scotch tour* he observed of one entertainment: 'As for Maclaurin's imitation of a made dish, it was a wretched attempt;' and with the performances of Lord Elibank's French cook he was so much enraged that he expressed a wish to 'throw such a rascal into the river.' Even when invited by an intimate friend, he resented being put off with a plain dinner. 'It was a good dinner enough,' he would say, 'but not a dinner to *ask* a man to.'* He had certainly no reason to grumble at the hospitality of Streatham or the Borough; nor do we find that he ever did so. When Thrale was gone, and his own death was approaching, he wrote to Mrs. Thrale: 'I have now an inclination to luxury which even your table did not excite. . . . I remember you commended me for seeming pleased with my dinners when you had reduced your table; I am able to tell you with great veracity that I never knew when the reduction began, nor should have known that it was made had not you told me.'†

* Boswell.   † 'Piozzi Letters,' ii. 362.

'Johnson loved late hours extremely, or, more properly,' says Mrs. Piozzi, 'hated early ones. Nothing was more terrifying to him than the idea of retiring to bed, which he never would call going to rest, or suffer another to call so. "I lie down," said he, "that my acquaintance may sleep; but I lie down to endure oppressive misery, and soon rise again to pass the night in anxiety and pain." By this pathetic manner, which no one ever possessed in so eminent a degree, he used to shock me from quitting his company, till I hurt my own health not a little by sitting up with him when I was myself far from well; nor was it an easy matter to oblige him even by compliance, for he always maintained that no one forbore his own gratification for the sake of pleasing another, and if one did sit up it was probably to amuse himself. Some right, however, he certainly had to say so, as he made his company exceedingly entertaining when he had once forced one not to quit the room, but to sit quietly and make tea for him, as I often did in London, till four o'clock in the morning. At Streatham, indeed, I managed better, having always some friend who was kind enough to engage him in talk and favour my retreat.'* One of these self-sacrificing persons was Dr. Burney. He told Boswell that about 1776† he had many long conversations with Johnson at Streatham, often sitting up as long as the fire and candles lasted, and much longer than the patience of the servants subsisted.

The Great Cham of literature avowed himself 'a hardened and shameless tea-drinker, who with tea amuses the evening, with tea solaces the midnight, and with tea welcomes the morning.' He protested that 'the infusion of this

---

* 'Anecdotes.'
† Boswell says in 1775, but Dr. Burney has mentioned 1776 as the year in which his acquaintance with the Thrales began.

fascinating plant' had never caused him the least inconvenience. But it may be doubted whether his indulgence in tea had not something to do with the bad nights of which he constantly complained. Among other stories told of his excesses, it is related that Lady Macleod, having poured out for him sixteen cups of tea, asked him if a small basin would not save him trouble, and be more agreeable. 'I wonder, madam,' answered he roughly, 'why all the ladies ask me such questions. It is to save yourselves trouble, madam, and not me.' The lady was silent, and resumed her task.* If the number of cups which he is reported to have consumed on several occasions sounds incredible, we must remember the space of time over which the imbibition was extended. Four o'clock was the usual dinner-hour at Thrale's. If the urn was brought soon after the other guests had finished their wine, and Johnson his lemonade, there remained many hours to be filled with talk and tea before the reluctant talker could be prevailed on to take his chamber candlestick.†

Johnson's love of tea was closely connected with that social temper which was the marked feature of his character. When not engaged in writing or reading, conversation was almost his only employment. He had, indeed, scarcely any other resource outside the literature of which his mind was full. For painting and music he cared nothing. 'His utter scorn of painting,' says Mrs. Thrale, 'was such that I have heard him say that he would sit very quietly in a room hung round with the works of the greatest masters, and never feel the slightest

---

* Northcote's 'Reynolds,' i. 81.

† Supper, in those days a usual and even fashionable meal, was not served in Mr. Thrale's house. Thus Miss Burney writes : ' Just as we got our biscuits and toast-and-water, which make the Streatham supper, and which, indeed, is all there is any chance of eating after our late and great dinners,' etc. Madame d'Arblay's Diary, i. 50. (We refer always to the Revised Edition of this book.)

disposition to turn them if their backs were outermost, unless it might be for the sake of telling Sir Joshua that he had turned them.'* Of music he said: 'It excites in my mind no ideas, and hinders me from contemplating my own.'† When he could find no one to talk to, he would amuse himself by watering and pruning a vine which grew in his garden at Bolt Court, or try small chemical experiments. His new friends humoured this scientific fancy. 'We made up a sort of laboratory at Streatham, and diverted ourselves with drawing essences and colouring liquors. But the danger which Mr. Thrale found his friend in one day, when he had got the children and servants round him to see some experiments performed, put an end to all our entertainment.'‡

He was a man who, as he once said, loved to fold his legs and have his talk out. When his heavy tread was heard approaching a room, the company within prepared themselves, but several minutes frequently elapsed before he made his appearance. He was bound by some mysterious spell to cross the passage in a certain number of steps, and enter at the door with one particular foot foremost. If he failed to pace the charm aright at the first trial, there was nothing for it but to turn back, and repeat the attempt until it proved successful.§ When seated, he constantly moved his body backwards and forwards on the chair,‖ rubbing his left knee in the same direction with the palm of his hand. His voice was loud, and his utterance slow and deliberate. When not speaking, he would give vent to various inarticulate sounds. Boswell, who observed him with the minute attention of a naturalist studying some new species of animal, has distinguished

---

* 'Anecdotes.'   † Hawkins.   ‡ 'Anecdotes.'
§ Boswell. The same eccentric habit is mentioned in 'Piozziana,' p. 20.
‖ Boswell. Miss Burney frequently describes him as 'see-sawing on his chair.'

several varieties of these. Sometimes the philosopher clucked like a hen; when pleased, he emitted a half-whistle; when annoyed or embarrassed, as on the memorable occasion of his being cajoled into dining with Jack Wilkes at the Messieurs Dilly's in the Poultry, he would mutter '*too, too, too*' under his breath. At the close of a violent dispute, 'he used to blow out his breath like a whale,' as though to signify that he had made the arguments of his opponent 'fly like chaff before the wind.' His countenance was disfigured by scars of the scrofulous evil, for which in childhood he had been touched by Queen Anne, and which had destroyed the sight of one eye, as well as impaired his hearing; when he mused, strange nervous twitchings convulsed his mouth and fingers; while the effect of all he uttered was made peculiar by uncouth movements of his arms and legs. His gestures, his enunciation, the air, the starts, the pauses which set off his most familiar talk, no less than his emphatic discourse, were the constant subject of Garrick and Boswell's conversation and mimicry.

If the topic in hand failed to interest him, he would rise from his seat, quit the circle, and talk in an undertone to himself. It used to be imagined at Mr. Thrale's, when Johnson retired to a window or corner of the room, by his lips being perceived to move, and a low murmur becoming audible, that he was at prayers. This was not mere conjecture. Sometimes his voice grew stronger, and fragments of the Lord's Prayer were overheard. His friend Tom Davies (of whom Churchill said, 'That Davies hath a very pretty wife'), when Johnson muttered, 'Lead us not into temptation,' used to whisper his better half, 'You, my dear, are the cause of this.' But further observation showed that the solemn smothered utterances which passed for pious ejaculations had occasionally a more mundane character. Dr. Burney, being once engaged in writing near the place of his retreat, found that he was repeating over and over to himself some lines from an ode of Horace. The truth is that his fits of abstraction, as well as his fits of melancholy, his transports of rage, his disregard of social usages, his superstitious fancies, and most of his other eccentricities, were in great measure morbid products of a mind that for many years had been driven to feed upon itself.

At Thrale's he was, for the first time, introduced to the comforts of a well-appointed household, and the softening influences of refined domestic life. 'In that society he began to wear off the rugged points of his character.'* He would not, indeed, have acknowledged that he stood in any want of the file. Though conscious that he was irritable, and apt to be vehement in discussion, he considered himself a very polite man. He one day astonished Mrs. Thrale by bidding her observe that he was 'well-bred to a degree of needless scrupulosity.' But he was ready to make the most of the new situation in which he found himself. He had a fondness for young children, and prided himself, not without warrant, on being acceptable to ladies. Negligent, coarse, ungainly as he was, the old man's bodily infirmities, the masculine vigour of his spirit, his commanding authority, the tenderness of his heart, and that abounding sympathy of his which no superficial faults of prejudice or temper could long disguise, and, even more than all these, his strong pleasure in the company of women, rendered him an object of great interest to most of his female acquaintance.

And by no more agreeable family than the Thrales could he have been entertained. A lively group of little

* Murphy.

ones sprang up around him. Their mother, 'short, plump, and brisk,'* was always in a good humour, always eager to please, and often brilliant in conversation, though not always perfectly discreet in what she said. Someone has affirmed that there was a vein of romance at the bottom of Johnson's nature. Certainly he had idealized the elderly wife, in whom no one but himself could discover the least attraction. Perhaps he in some degree idealized the kindly and sprightly dame† who indulged his weaknesses, heaped his plate with dainties, forbore to count his cups of tea, and was able, besides, to follow his Latin quotations, and to join him in the critical remarks on English poets, which he relished more than any other talk.

Though not beautiful, she may fairly be said to have been very pretty. Twelve years after her introduction to Johnson, she was thus described by Fanny Burney: 'Mrs. Thrale is a pretty woman still, though she has some defect in the mouth that looks like a cut or scar; her nose is very handsome, her complexion very fair, and her eyes are blue and lustrous.'‡ This was written after a first meeting, and before anything had occurred which could raise the least suspicion of flattery. In her old age she would not allow that she had ever possessed any comeliness of feature. Sometimes, when visiting her friend Mr. Mangin,§ she used to look at her little self, as she called it, and speak drolly of what she once was, as if speaking of someone else; and one day, turning to him,

---

* Boswell.

† 'Mrs. Thrale's enchantment over him seldom failed,' says Boswell in his 'Journal of a Tour to the Hebrides.'

‡ In a letter to Mr. Crisp, written in 1777 : 'Memoirs of Dr. Burney,' by Mme. d'Arblay, ii. 87.

§ Author of 'Piozziana ; or, Recollections of the late Mrs. Piozzi, with Remarks by a Friend.'—Moxon, London, 1833. We shall have more to say of these 'Recollections' later on.

she exclaimed: 'No, I never was handsome; I had always too many strong points in my face for beauty.' On his expressing a doubt of this, and hinting that Dr. Johnson was certainly an admirer of her personal charms, she replied that his devotion was at least as warm towards the table and the tablecloth at Streatham.

In speaking thus, however, she certainly did justice neither to the Doctor nor to herself. According to the writer just cited, who became acquainted with her after she had passed her seventieth year, she was short and, though well-proportioned, broad and deep-chested. Her hands, he says, were muscular and almost coarse; but he speaks of her very erect carriage and most expressive face. He mentions the defect in the mouth noticed by Miss Burney, describing it as a trivial deformity of the lower jaw, caused by her horse trampling on her after having thrown her in Hyde Park. In short, allowing for the lapse of more than thirty years, we discover nothing in Mr. Mangin's account to make us doubt the truth of the picture drawn by Miss Burney. That Johnson found the person of his hostess attractive, as well as her conversation, appears in many passages. Take, for instance, the following:

'One day when he was ill and exceedingly low-spirited, and persuaded that death was not far distant, I appeared before him in a dark-coloured gown, which his bad sight and worse apprehensions made him mistake for an iron-gray, "Why do you delight," said he, "thus to thicken the gloom of misery that surrounds me? Is not here sufficient accumulation of horror without anticipated mourning?" "This is not mourning, sir," said I, drawing the curtain, that the light might fall upon the silk, and show it was a purple mixed with green. "Well, well!" replied he, changing his voice, "you little creatures should never wear these sort of clothes, however; they are unsuitable in every way. What! have not all insects gay colours?"'*

'During the years when he was domesticated at Streatham,' says Macaulay, 'his chief pleasures were derived from what the astronomer of his Abyssinian tale called the "endearing elegance of female friendship." Mrs. Thrale rallied him, soothed him, coaxed him, and, if she sometimes provoked him by her flippancy, made ample amends by listening to his reproofs with angelic sweetness of temper. When he was diseased in body and in mind, she was the most tender of nurses. No comfort that wealth could purchase, no contrivance that womanly ingenuity, set to work by womanly compassion, could devise, was wanting to his sick-room. He requited her kindness by an affection pure as the affection of a father, yet delicately tinged with gallantry, which, though awkward, must have been more flattering than the attention of a crowd of fools who gloried in the names, now obsolete, of Buck and Macaroni.'†

As for Thrale, the brewer's figure, 'tall, well-proportioned, and stately,'‡ was an index of his disposition—proud, reserved, strong-willed, but liberal, hospitable, and sluggishly beneficent. He very soon gained an ascendancy over his visitor which no one else could rival. To the control of this tradesman the literary dictator submitted himself with surprising docility. A word, even a look, from his host generally sufficed to bring him to order. 'Mr. Thrale,' wrote his wife, 'had a very powerful influence over the Doctor, and could make him suppress many rough answers. He could likewise prevail on him to change his shirt, his coat, or his plate, almost before it became

---

* 'Anecdotes.'
† Lord Macaulay's 'Miscellaneous Writings,' i. ‡ Boswell.

indispensably necessary to the comfort of his friends.' He could also, which was more difficult, by some cold, curt speech, arrest the excessive flow of the great talker's eloquence. 'There, there,' he would say, 'now we have had enough for one lecture, Dr. Johnson. We will not be upon education any more till after dinner, if you please.'

Nothing, Boswell was constrained to admit, could have been more fortunate for Johnson than this connection with the Thrales. He had no bad attacks of hypochondria under their roof. His bursts of passion became less frequent and more controllable. He even went hunting with the brewer. 'He certainly,' says the lady, 'rode on Mr. Thrale's old hunter with a good firmness, and though he would follow the hounds fifty miles on end sometimes, would never own himself either tired or amused. I think no praise ever went so close to his heart as when Mr. Hamilton called out one day upon Brighthelmstone Downs, "Why, Johnson rides as well, for aught I see, as the most illiterate fellow in England."'* He learned in Mrs. Thrale's drawing-room to lay aside much of what Goldsmith called his bow-wow manner. 'A lady may be vain,' observed another member of the Literary Club, 'when she can turn a wolf-dog into a lap-dog.' The compliment was well deserved, though the credit of the change was due, in part, to the lady's husband. 'The vivacity of Mrs. Thrale's literary talk,' says Boswell, ' roused him to cheerfulness and exertion even when they were alone. She did more than this. She called forth a playfulness which the Scottish biographer was seldom able to elicit, and to which he has done no justice, while she accustomed her guest to chat with simple people on simple topics. A clergyman once complained to Mrs.

* 'Anecdotes,' p. 206.

Salusbury of the want of society where he lived: his parishioners, he said, talked of *runts*—that is, young cows. 'Sir,' replied the now reconciled old lady, 'Mr. Johnson would learn to talk of runts.' In course of time, as other men eminent for talents, learning, or wit were added to the Streatham circle, the old lion was entertained there with social enjoyments of the sort which he loved best; and when it became known that the Thrales had disciplined their strange inmate, the lion-hunters of London began to seek him for their parties, nor was he anything loath to accept their invitations. In the last years of his life he was more often to be found at fashionable houses, or the resorts of the blue-stockings, than at the tavern or the club which had been his earlier haunts. The leaders of the female world now paid him something of the homage which he had long received from men of letters. 'I have seen,' says Wraxall, 'the Duchess of Devonshire, then in the first bloom of youth, hanging on the sentences that fell from Johnson's lips, and contending for the nearest place to his chair.' Miss Burney describes a brilliant assembly which he attended at the house of Miss Monckton, afterwards Countess of Cork, where the display of dress was superb, and where he was 'environed with listeners.' Langton furnished Boswell with an account of another evening at Mrs. Vesey's, when the visitors consisted chiefly of ladies, among whom were the Duchess Dowager of Portland, the Duchess of Beaufort, Lady Lucan, Lady Clermont, and Mrs. Boscawen. 'As soon as Dr. Johnson was come in and had taken a chair, the company began to collect about him till they became not less than four, if not five deep, those behind standing, and listening over the heads of those that were sitting near him.'

CHAPTER III.

Thrale enters Parliament—Mrs. Thrale gains Influence—Her Acquirements—Outshines her Husband—Her Conversation—Miss Williams's Miscellanies—Floretta—The Three Warnings—Dissolution of Parliament—John Wilkes—Thrale re-elected—Boswell at Streatham—Literary Talk—Johnson's Political Pamphlets—Verses at the Theatre—Thrale in Difficulties—Humphrey Jackson—Mrs. Thrale shows herself a Woman of Business—Johnson's Advice—Thrale out of Health—Alteration in him—Mr. Perkins—Conversations at Streatham—Johnson's Estimate of Mrs. Thrale—Thrale created Doctor—Death of Mrs. Salusbury—Johnson's Visit—His Letters to Mrs. Thrale—His Ode written in Skye—He will not suffer Boswell to slight Mrs. Thrale—Death of Sir Thomas Salusbury—Disappointment and Misfortunes—'The Journey to the Western Islands'—Excursion to Wales—Visits to Lleweny Hall and Bâchygraig—Johnson accuses his Mistress of Meanness—Bodvel—Visits to Lords Sandys and Lyttelton—General Election—Electioneering with Johnson—Project of bringing Johnson into Parliament.

BUT, in the connection between them and Johnson, the benefits which the Thrales conferred were not greater than those which accrued to themselves. Under the influence of their new associate, the brewer improved his standing before the world, and the wife was allowed her just position in her husband's family. The remains of the bachelorhood disappeared. The foxhounds were sold. Thrale aspired to a seat in Parliament. This he presently obtained, being returned for Southwark at a by-election before the end of 1765. 'I grew useful now,' says the lady; 'almost necessary—wrote the advertisements, looked to the treats, and people to whom I was till then unknown, admired how happy Mr. Thrale must be in such a wonder of a wife.'* There can be no doubt,

* Hayward's 'Piozzi,' ii. 23.

too, that Johnson's good opinion of Mrs. Thrale's powers contributed greatly to raise her in the esteem of her husband. Though she sometimes provoked his censure, the sage treated her with deference, suffered her to argue with him on equal terms, and on occasion would even appeal to her as a literary authority. A few disparaging expressions which Boswell has put into Johnson's mouth must be read with due remembrance of the quarrel between the Doctor's biographers. It is perfectly true, doubtless, that no man was ever more master of his wife and family than Thrale, and that if he but held up a finger he was obeyed. But if Johnson ever said, as his Life alleges, that Thrale had ten times the learning of his wife, and that her learning was that of a school-boy in one of the lower forms, the remark must have been intended to apply to verbal scholarship alone. Mrs. Thrale's knowledge of Latin grammar may have been inaccurate, yet that her reading in Latin, as well as in modern languages, was considerable, her writings clearly show. Henry Thrale had passed through the University, but there is no record of his having preserved any permanent interest in books, beyond the statement in his epitaph, that '*Inter mille mercaturæ negotia, literarum elegantiam minimè neglexit*,'* which, after all, proves nothing, for the author was Johnson, who used to say that in lapidary inscriptions a man is not upon oath.

In social gifts Thrale bore no comparison with his wife. The utmost that Johnson could say for his friend's conversation was that, although it did not mark the minutes, it generally struck the hour pretty correctly. The brewer is described by Madame d'Arblay as a man who 'found a singular amusement in hearing, instigating,

* 'Though engaged in a very extensive business, he found some time to apply to polite literature.'

and provoking a war of words, alternating triumph and overthrow between clever and ambitious colloquial disputants.'* Hence he was mostly a listener at table, whether in his own house or another's. His wife attributed his taciturnity to the cares of business and the pressure of anxiety. But doubtless he had little or nothing to say on the topics which his company discussed. His silence sometimes provoked Johnson, who on one occasion blamed him for sitting at General Oglethorpe's without speaking, and observed that a man was to be censured for degrading himself to a nonentity. Mrs. Thrale was in no danger of incurring this reproach. She had a natural talent for conversation, which she improved by constant and assiduous practice, till she became one of the most famous female talkers of her time. Many testimonies to her brilliancy are on record, some of them showing the discipline exercised over her by Johnson. According to Madame d'Arblay, her celebrity exceeded that of either of the blue-stocking queens, Mrs. Vesey and Mrs. Montagu. 'Mrs. Vesey, indeed, gentle and diffident, dreamed not of any competition; but Mrs. Montagu and Mrs. Thrale were set up as rival candidates for colloquial eminence, and each of them thought the other alone worthy to be her peer. Whenever they met, therefore, a contest for superiority ensued.' Sir Nathaniel Wraxall says: 'Mrs. Thrale always appeared to me to possess at least as much information, a mind as cultivated, and more brilliancy of intellect than Mrs. Montagu; but she did not descend among men from such an eminence, and she talked much more, as well as more unguardedly, on every subject. She was the provider and conductress of Dr. Johnson, who lived almost constantly under her roof, or, more properly, under that of

* 'Memoirs of Dr. Burney,' ii. 104.

Mr. Thrale, both in town and at Streatham. He did not, however, spare her more than other women in his attacks, if she courted and provoked his animadversions.' Nevertheless, he valued himself extremely on his pupil. Miss Reynolds, in her 'Recollections,' mentions that he used to dwell on her praises with a peculiar delight, and paternal fondness that expressed his pride in being so intimately acquainted with her.

In 1766 Miss Williams, with Johnson's assistance, published a volume of 'Miscellanies.' Her protector furnished the preface, and contributed several pieces. Boswell ends his account of the collection by saying: '"The Fountains," a beautiful little fairy tale in prose, written with exquisite simplicity, is one of Johnson's productions; and I cannot withhold from Mrs. Thrale the praise of being the author of that admirable poem, "The Three Warnings."' The jealous biographer does not mention, perhaps he did not know, that the character of Floretta in 'The Fountains' was intended for Mrs. Thrale. Sixteen years later, when Thrale was dead, and the newspapers had begun to couple his widow's name with Piozzi's, she reminded her old friend of the compliment he had paid her. 'The newspapers,' she wrote in February, 1782, 'would spoil my few comforts that are left if they could; but you tell me that's only because I have the reputation, whether true or false, of being a *wit*, forsooth; and you rememember poor *Floretta*, who was teased into wishing away her spirit, her beauty, her fortune, and at last even her life, never could bear the bitter water which was to have washed away her wit, which she resolved to keep with all its consequences.'*

Mrs. Thrale was throughout her life a fluent writer of

---

* 'Letters to and from the late Samuel Johnson, published by Hester Lynch Piozzi,' ii. 233. We shall cite this book hereafter under the name of the Piozzi Letters.

verses. We give here the contribution to Miss Williams's 'Miscellany' as the earliest and best known among the extant specimens of her talent:

THE THREE WARNINGS.

A TALE.

The tree of deepest root is found
Least willing still to quit the ground;
'Twas therefore said by ancient sages,
That love of life increased with years.
So much, that in our latter stages,
When pains grow sharp and sickness rages,
The greatest love of life appears.
This great affection to believe,
Which all confess but few perceive,
If old affections can't prevail,
Be pleased to hear a modern tale.
When sports went round, and all were gay,
On neighbour Dobson's wedding-day,
Death called aside the jocund groom
With him into another room,
And looking grave, 'You must,' says he,
'Quit your sweet bride, and come with me.'
'With you! and quit my Susan's side?
With you!' the hapless husband cried.
'Young as I am! 'tis monstrous hard;
Besides, in truth, I'm not prepared.
My thoughts on other matters go,
This is my wedding-night, you know.'
What more he urged I have not heard,
His reasons could not well be stronger,
So Death the poor delinquent spared,
And left to live a little longer.
Yet calling up a serious look,
His hour-glass tumbled while he spoke,
'Neighbour,' he said, 'farewell. No more
Shall Death disturb your mirthful hour;
And further, to avoid all blame
Of cruelty upon my name,
To give you time for preparation,
And fit you for your future station,
Three several warnings you shall have
Before you're summoned to the grave:
Willing, for once, I'll quit my prey,
And grant a kind reprieve;
In hopes you'll have no more to say,
But when I call again this way,
Well pleased the world will leave.'
To these conditions both consented,
And parted perfectly contented.

The Three Warnings.

What next the hero of our tale befell,
How long he lived, how wise, how well;
How roundly he pursued his course,
And smoked his pipe, and strok'd his horse,
The willing muse shall tell.
He chaffer'd then, he bought, he sold,
Nor once perceived his growing old,
Nor thought of Death as near;
His friends not false, his wife no shrew,
Many his gains, his children few,
He passed his hours in peace;
But while he view'd his wealth increase,
While thus along life's dusty road
The beaten track content he trod,
Old Times, whose haste no mortal spares,
Uncalled, unheeded, unawares,
Brought him on his eightieth year.
And now one night in musing mood,
As all alone he sate,
Th' unwelcome messenger of fate
Once more before him stood.
Half stilled with anger and surprise,
'So soon returned!' old Dobson cries.
'So soon, d'ye call it!' Death replies.
'Surely, my friend, you're but in jest;
Since I was here before
'Tis six-and-thirty years at least,
And you are now fourscore.'
'So much the worse,' the clown rejoin'd,
'To spare the aged would be kind;
However, see your search be legal,
And your authority—is't regal?
Else you are come on a fool's errand,
With but a secretary's warrant.
Besides, you promised me three warnings,
Which I have looked for nights and mornings;
But for that loss of time and ease
I can recover damages.'
'I know,' cries Death, 'that at the best
I seldom am a welcome guest;
But don't be captious, friend, at least;
I little thought you'd still be able
To stump about your farm and stable;
Your years have run to a great length,
I wish you joy, tho', of your strength.'
'Hold,' says the farmer, 'not so fast,
I have been lame these four years past.'
'And no great wonder,' Death replies.
'However, you still keep your eyes;
And, sure, to see one's loves and friends,
For legs and arms would make amends.'
'Perhaps,' says Dobson, 'so it might,
But latterly I've lost my sight.'
'This is a shocking story, faith,

> Yet there's some comfort still,' says Death.
> 'Each strives your sadness to amuse,
> I warrant you have all the news.'
> 'There's none,' cries he : 'and if there were,
> I'm grown so deaf, I could not hear.'
> 'Nay, then,' the spectre stern rejoin'd,
> 'These are unjustifiable yearnings;
> If you are lame, and deaf, and blind,
> You've had your three sufficient warnings.
> So come along, no more we'll part,'
> He said, and touched him with his dart.
> And now old Dobson, turning pale,
> Yields to his fate—so ends my tale.

By the middle of 1767 Johnson's position in the Thrale household had become so settled that, in July of that year, he wrote to the lady from Lichfield : 'Though I have been away so much longer than I purposed or expected, I have found nothing that withdraws my affections from the friends whom I left behind, or which makes me less desirous of reposing at that place which your kindness and Mr. Thrale's allows me to call my *home*.'*

In the spring of 1768, Parliament was dissolved, and the elections took place in the midst of general excitement, aroused by the proceedings against Wilkes and the *North Briton*. The cause of the trouble, though rejected by the City of London, contrived to get himself returned as member for Middlesex, chiefly through the intimidation of the mob. The rioters stopped all carriages, and compelled the occupants to shout for Wilkes and liberty. The ferment extended to the Borough of Southwark, for which Thrale was again a candidate. The brewer being, as his epitaph assures us, *vulgi obstrepentis contemptor animosus*, took the matter with his accustomed coolness. But the contest was severe enough to occasion his wife and friends considerable anxiety. Several letters on the subject passed between Mrs. Thrale and Johnson, who was for the time at Oxford. The latter was very ill

---

* 'Piozzi Letters,' i. 4. He was away from London 'near six months.'

during this visit to his University, and the lady was expecting her confinement. On March 14 Johnson writes to her: 'If I can be of any use, I will come directly to London; but if Mr. Thrale thinks himself certain, I have no doubt. That they all express the same certainty, has very little effect upon those who know how many men are confident without certainty, and positive without confidence. We have not any reason to suspect Mr. Thrale of deceiving us or himself. . . . . This little dog does nothing, but I hope he will mend: he is now reading Jack the Giant-Killer. Perhaps so noble a narrative may rouse in him the soul of enterprise.'* The zeal and interest displayed by both the correspondents seem to show that they were each now in their master's confidence. In the end, Thrale was elected second on the poll.

Johnson does not appear to have been in any haste to make his faithful Boswell acquainted with the household at Streatham. Perhaps he found the comfort of having a retreat into which he could not be pursued by his admirer. But the introduction could not be evaded. Under the date of September 30, 1769, the biographer writes: 'I had last year the pleasure of seeing Mrs. Thrale at Dr. Johnson's one morning, and had conversation enough with her to admire her talents, and to show her that I was as Johnsonian as herself. Dr. Johnson had probably been kind enough to speak well of me, for this evening he delivered me a very polite card from Mr. Thrale and her, inviting me to Streatham.

'On the 6th of October I complied with this obliging invitation, and found at an elegant villa, six miles from town, every circumstance that can make society pleasing. Johnson, though quite at home, was yet looked up to

* 'Piozzi Letters,' i. 8.

with an awe, tempered by affection, and seemed to be equally the care of his host and hostess. I rejoiced at seeing him so happy.

'During the evening Mrs. Thrale disputed with him on the merit of Prior. He attacked him powerfully; said he wrote of love like a man who had never felt it: his love verses were college verses; and he repeated the song, "Alexis shunn'd his fellow swains," etc., in so ludicrous a manner as to make us all wonder how any-one could have been pleased with such fantastical stuff. Mrs. Thrale stood to her gun with great courage, in defence of amorous ditties, which Johnson despised, till he at last silenced her by saying, "My dear lady, talk no more of this. Nonsense can be defended but by nonsense!"

'Mrs. Thrale then praised Garrick's talent for light gay poetry, and, as a specimen, repeated his song in "Florizel and Perdita," and dwelt with peculiar pleasure on this line:

"I'd smile with the simple, and feed with the poor."*

'JOHNSON: "Nay, my dear lady, this will never do. Poor David! Smile with the simple—what folly is that? And who would feed with the poor that can help it? No, no; let me smile with the wise, and feed with the rich!"' Boswell adds that he repeated this sally to Garrick, and wondered to find his sensibility as a writer not a little irritated by it. In a note on the passage, Mrs. Thrale remarks, 'How odd to go and tell the man!'

Boswell went again to Streatham on November 10,

---

* '"Florizel and Perdita,"' says Boswell's latest editor, 'is Garrick's version of "The Winter's Tale."' He cut down the five acts to three. The line, which is misquoted, is in one of Perdita's songs:

'That giant ambition we never can dread;
Our roofs are too low for so lofty a head;
Content and sweet cheerfulness open our door,
They smile with the simple, and feed with the poor.'
Act ii., Sc. 1.

to take leave of Johnson before he himself returned to Scotland to be married. He did not again visit London for more than two years. The interval was a season of fierce political excitement. The Ministry were menaced by the popularity of Wilkes, and by the attacks of 'Junius.' Johnson took the field as a pamphleteer on their side.

On Wilkes being returned member for Middlesex at the election of 1768, he was declared by the House of Commons incapable of being elected, and a new writ was ordered. Twice he was re-elected without opposition, and twice was his election again declared void. On a fourth writ being issued, the Ministers provided another candidate, Colonel Luttrell; and the House pronounced that the poll taken for Wilkes was null and void, and that his opponent, though in a great minority of votes, had been duly elected. In defence of this high-handed proceeding, Johnson, in 1770, published a tract, entitled 'The False Alarm,' intended to prove that no breach of the constitution had been committed. '"The False Alarm,"' says Mrs. Thrale, 'his first and favourite pamphlet, was written at our house between eight o'clock on Wednesday night and twelve o'clock on Thursday night. We read it to Mr. Thrale when he came very late home from the House of Commons.'*

In 1771† appeared a second pamphlet from Johnson's pen, containing his character of the mysterious JUNIUS, 'executed,' as Boswell says, 'with all the force of his genius, and finished with the highest care. He seems to have exulted in sallying forth to single combat against the boasted and formidable hero who bade defiance to "principalities and powers, and the rulers of this world."'

* Anec., p. 41.
† It was entitled 'Thoughts on the Late Transactions respecting Falkland's Islands,' and was published without the author's name.

'I forget,' says Mrs. Thrale, 'which of his tracts contains the stroke at "Junius," but shall for ever remember the pleasure it gave him to have written it.'

We have few other records of this year relating either to Johnson or the Thrales. Mrs. Thrale, however, writes: 'One evening, in the oratorio season of the year 1771, Mr. Johnson went with me to Covent Garden Theatre; and though he was for the most part an exceedingly bad playhouse companion, as his person drew people's eyes upon the box, and the loudness of his voice made it difficult for me to hear anybody but himself, he sat surprisingly quiet; and I flattered myself that he was listening to the music. When we were got home, however, he repeated these verses, which he said he had made at the oratorio, and he bade me translate them.' [She then gives a copy of Latin sapphics, which are printed in the later editions of Boswell.]

She continues: 'I gave him the following lines in imitation, which he liked well enough, I think:

> 'When threescore years have chilled thee quite,
> Still can theatric scenes delight?
> Ill suits this place with learned wight,
>   May Bates or Coulson cry.
>
> 'The scholar's pride can Brent disarm?
> His heart can soft Guadagni warm?
> Or scenes with sweet delusion charm
>   The climacteric eye?
>
> 'The social club, the lonely tower,
> Far better suit thy midnight hour;
> Let each according to his power
>   In worth or wisdom shine!
>
> 'And while play pleases idle boys,
> And wanton mirth fond youth employs,
> To fix the soul, and free from toys,
>   That useful task be thine!'*

In was in the summer of 1771 that a laboratory was fitted up at Streatham for Johnson's amusement. In

* Anec., p. 72.

July he writes from Derbyshire to his mistress :—' When we come together to practise chemistry, I believe we shall find our furnaces sufficient for most operations. We have a gentleman here reading philosophical lectures, who performs the chemical part with furnaces of the same kind with ours, but much less; yet he says that he can in his little furnace raise a fire that will melt iron. I saw him smelt lead, and shall bring up some ore for our operations. The carriage will cost more than the lead perhaps will be worth, but a chemist is very like a lover—" And sees those dangers which he cannot shun." I will try to get other ore, both of iron and copper, which are all which this country affords, though *feracissima metallorum regio.*'*

In 1772 Thrale's affairs became seriously embarrassed through his own imprudence, and his wife was able to afford him material assistance. In fact, the brewer's fortunes appear to have been retrieved mainly through her tact and energy. After long wondering who had her husband's confidence, she found to her dismay that he had given it to an unworthy speculator. Here is her account of the discovery: 'A vulgar fellow, by name Humphrey Jackson, had, as the clerks informed me, all in a breath, complete possession of it. He had long practised on poor Thrale's credulity, till by mixing two cold liquors which produced heat, perhaps, or two colourless liquors which produced brilliancy, he had at length prevailed on him to think he could produce beer too, without the beggarly elements of malt and hops. He had persuaded him to build a copper somewhere in East Smithfield, the very metal of which cost £2,000, wherein this Jackson was to make experiments, and conjure some curious stuff which should preserve ships'

---

* ' Piozzi Letters,' i. 45.

bottoms from the worm; gaining from Government money to defray these mad expenses. Twenty enormous vats, holding 1,000 hogsheads each—costly contents!—ten more, holding 1,000 barrels each, were constructed to stew in this pernicious mess; and afterwards erected on, I forget how much ground, bought for the ruinous purpose.

'That all were spoiled, was but a secondary sorrow. We had, in the commercial phrase, no beer to start for customers. We had no money to purchase with. Our clerks, insulted long, rebelled and *ratted*, but I held them in. A sudden run menaced the house, and death hovered over the head of the principal.'*

During the crisis Johnson was at a distance from London. In October, 1772, he writes to Mrs. Thrale from Lichfield:—'Do not suffer little things to disturb you. The brewhouse must be the scene of action, and the subject of speculation. The first consequence of our late trouble ought to be an endeavour to brew at a cheaper rate; an endeavour, not violent and transient, but steady and continual, prosecuted with total contempt of censure or wonder, and animated by resolution not to stop while more can be done. Unless this can be done nothing can help us, and if this be done we shall not want help. Surely there is something to be saved; there is to be saved whatever is the difference between vigilance and neglect, between parsimony and profusion. The price of malt has risen again. It is now two pounds eight shillings the quarter. Ale is sold in the publichouses at sixpence a quart, a price which I never heard of before.'†

Johnson was so much pleased with the ability and

---

* Autobiographical Memoir, Hayward's 'Piozzi,' ii. 25.
† 'Piozzi Letters,' i. 37.

firmness displayed by his correspondent and her mother at this time of distress that he said, 'No man with two such women to console him could ever dream of committing suicide. Of all the bankrupts made that dreadful year,' he continued, 'none had destroyed themselves but married men; who would not have risen from the weeds undrowned had not the women clung about and sunk them, stifling the voice of reason with their cries?' Mrs. Salusbury lent her son-in-law the whole of her little savings, amounting to about £3,000; and her daughter, though expecting her confinement, drove down to Brighton to beg further help from an old friend of the Thrale family, a Mr. Scrase, who cheerfully found £6,000 more. 'Dear Mr. Scrase,' writes the grateful petitioner, 'was an old gouty solicitor retired from business, a contemporary of my husband's father. Other friends also gave their assistance. Mr. Rush lent us £6,000, Lady Lade £5,000. Our debts, including those of Humphrey Jackson, were £130,000, besides borrowed money. Yet in nine years was every shilling paid; one, if not two, elections well contested. . . . The baby that I carried lived an *hour*—my mother a year; but she left our minds easy. I lay awake twelve nights and days, I remember, 'spite of all art could do.'

In November of the same year Johnson writes from Ashbourne to his mistress:—

'So many days and never a letter! *Fugere fides, pietasque pudorque.* This is Turkish usage. And I have been hoping and hoping. But you are so glad to have me out of your mind.

'I think you were quite right in your advice about the thousand pounds, for the payment could not have been delayed long; and a short delay would have lessened credit, without advancing interest. But in great matters you are hardly ever mistaken. . . . I wish I could know how you brew, and how you go on; but you tell me nothing.'*

Again, two days later:—

'DEAR MADAM,

'After I had sent away my last letter I received yours, which was an answer to it; but, being not fully directed, had lain, I think, two days at the office.

'I am glad that you are at last come home, and that you exert your new resolution with so much vigour. But the fury of housewifery will soon subside, and little effect will be produced but by methodical attention and even frugality; nor can these powers be immediately attained. You have your own habits, as well as those of others, to combat: you have yet the skill of management to learn, as well as the practice to establish. Do not be discouraged either by your own failures, or the perverseness of others; you will, by resolution frequently renewed, and perseverance properly excited, overcome in time both them and yourself. . . . Mr. Thrale's money, to pay for all, must come from the sale of good beer. I am far from despairing of solid and durable prosperity. Nor will your success exceed my hopes, or my opinion of your state, if, after this tremendous year, you should annually add to your fortune three thousand pounds. This will soon dismiss all incumbrances; and when no interest is paid, you will begin annually to lay up almost five thousand. This is very splendid; but this, I think, is in your power.'†

For several months the state of Mr. Thrale and the

* 'Piozzi Letters,' i. 63. † *Ibid.*, i. 63.

perplexities of his business continued to be the source of great anxieties. 'Mr. Thrale,' wrote his wife,* 'was a very merry talking man in 1760, but the distress of 1772, which affected his health, his hopes, and his whole soul, affected his temper, too. Perkins called it being planet-struck, and I am not sure that he was ever completely the same man again.' Gradually, however, his condition improved. In March 1773, Johnson writes again to the lady: 'Notwithstanding my master has mended his share for one year, you must think of cutting in pieces and boiling him. We will at least keep him out of Jackson's copper. You will be at leisure now to think of brewing and negotiating, and a little of yours,' etc.†

Mr. Perkins was then the manager of the brewery, of which, after Thrale's death, he became one of the proprietors. Dr. Johnson esteemed him much. Boswell tells us that 'he hung up in the counting-house a fine proof of the admirable mezzotinto of Dr. Johnson by Doughty; and when Mrs. Thrale asked him somewhat flippantly, 'Why do you put him in the counting-house?' he answered, 'Because, madam, I wish to have one wise man there!' 'Sir,' said Johnson, 'I thank you. It is a very handsome compliment, and I believe you speak sincerely.'

From a collection of letters which passed between Perkins and Mrs. Thrale, and which Mr. Hayward was permitted to read, it appears that she paid the most minute attention to her husband's business during the period of his distress and illness, besides undertaking the superintendence of her family estate, when it fell to her shortly afterwards.

We have some notes by Boswell of conversations at

---

* In a marginal note written on a copy of the printed letters.
† 'Piozzi Letters,' i. 78.

Thrale's during the spring of 1773, in which the master of the house, as usual, sat mute, while Mrs. Thrale talked with knowledge and effect. One evening Johnson brought forward a favourite paradox of his against action in public speaking: 'Action can have no effect upon reasonable minds. It may augment noise, but it never can enforce argument. If you speak to a dog, you use action; you hold up your hand thus, because he is a brute; and in proportion as men are removed from brutes, action will have the less influence upon them.' The lady at once struck in: 'What, then, sir, becomes of Demosthenes's saying, "Action, action, action!"?' JOHNSON: 'Demosthenes, madam, spoke to an assembly of brutes, to a barbarous people.' 'The polished Athenians!' is Mrs. Thrale's natural exclamation in a marginal note on her copy of 'Boswell.'

On another occasion, when the flattery heaped on Garrick by Lord Mansfield and Lord Chatham was mentioned, Johnson remarked: 'When he whom everybody else flatters, flatters me, I then am truly happy.' MRS. THRALE: 'The sentiment is in Congreve, I think.' JOHNSON: 'Yes, madam, in "The Way of the World."'

'"If there's delight in love, 'tis when I see
The heart that others bleed for, bleed for me."'

Johnson sometimes complained that his mistress flattered him, but he was far from being displeased with her attentions, and repaid them in kind. In May, 1773, he wrote:—

'Never imagine that your letters are long; they are always too short for my curiosity. I do not know that I was ever content with a single perusal.

'Why should Mr. Thrale suppose that what I took the liberty of suggesting was concerted with you? He does not know how much I revolve his affairs, and how honestly I desire his prosperity. I hope he has let the hint take some hold of his mind. . . .

'My nights are grown again very uneasy and troublesome. I know not that the country will mend them; but I hope your company will mend my days. Though I cannot now expect much attention, and would not wish for more than can be spared from the poor dear lady [her mother], yet I shall see you and hear you every now and then; and to see and hear you is always to hear wit and to see virtue.'*

He did not, however, use language like this to the lady herself only. Miss Reynolds heard him pronounce an eloquent eulogium on Mrs. Thrale to Harris, the author of 'Hermes,' ascribing to her, not merely brilliant wit and a strong understanding, but solid virtue also:

> 'A genuine virtue of a vigorous kind,
> Pure in the last recesses of the mind.'†

In the summer of 1773, Thrale made an excursion to the country, leaving his business in charge of his wife. Among other places, he visited Oxford, where, on July 8, he received from the University the honorary degree of D.C.L.‡

On September 28 Mrs. Thrale wrote to Perkins, who was on a commercial journey:—

'Mr. Thrale is still upon his little tour; I opened a letter from you at the counting-house this morning, and am sorry to find you so much troubled with Grant and his affairs. How glad I shall be to hear that matter is settled to your satisfaction! His letter and remittance came while I was there to-day. . . . Careless, of the

---

* 'Piozzi Letters,' i. 82.
† Dryden's translation of Persius. In the original:—
  'Compositum jus fasque animo, sanctosque recessus
   Mentis, et incoctum generoso pectus honesto.'—Pers. Sat., ii. 73.
‡ 'Catalogue of Oxford Graduates,' 1851, p. 660.

"Blue Posts," has turned refractory, and applied to Hoare's people, who have sent him in their beer. I called on him to-day, however, and by dint of an unwearied solicitation (for I kept him at the coach-side a full half-hour), I got his order for six butts more as the final trial.'*

This was the year of the death of Mrs. Salusbury, on whom Johnson wrote an epitaph, and of Johnson's visit to Scotland. Her daughter describes Mrs. Salusbury and Johnson as 'excellent, far beyond the excellence of any other man and woman I ever yet saw. As her conduct extorted his truest esteem, her cruel illness excited all his tenderness. He acknowledged himself improved by her piety, and astonished at her fortitude,† and hung over her bed with the affection of a parent, and the reverence of a son.'‡ During his absence in the North, Johnson addressed frequent letters to Mrs. Thrale. From Aberdeen he wrote:—' The maids at the inns run over the house barefoot, and children, not dressed in rags, go without shoes or stockings. Shoes are, indeed, not yet in universal use; they came late into this country. One of the professors told us, as we were mentioning a fort built by Cromwell, that the country owed much of its present industry to Cromwell's soldiers. They taught us, said he, to raise cabbage and make shoes. How they lived without shoes may yet be seen; but in the passage through the villages it seems to him that surveys their gardens that when they had not cabbage they had nothing.'§ On reaching Skye: ' Little did I once think of seeing this region of obscurity, and little did you once expect a salutation from this verge of European life. I have now the pleasure of going where nobody goes, and seeing what nobody sees.'‖

But generally these letters, if they do not display much

---

* Hayward's 'Piozzi,' i. 70. † Anec., p. 131. ‡ Ibid., p. 129.
§ 'Piozzi Letters,' i. 116. ‖ Ibid., i. 120.

enthusiasm for the beauties of the scenes visited, show no disposition to disparage either the country or the inhabitants. 'They abound,' says Boswell, 'in such benignant sentiments towards the people who showed him civilities, that no man whose temper is not very harsh and sour can retain a doubt of the goodness of his heart.' From Skye he wrote: 'The hospitality of this remote region is like that of the golden age. We have found ourselves treated at every house as if we came to confer a benefit.'* In another letter, addressed from Inverary to Mr. Thrale, was inclosed the once famous Latin ode written in Skye.† 'About fourteen years ago,' wrote Sir Walter Scott in 1829, 'I landed in Skye, with a party of friends, and had the curiosity to ask what was the first idea on every one's mind at landing. All answered separately that it was this ode.' The poem has been thus translated by Lord Houghton:

> 'Where constant mist enshrouds the rocks,
> Sheltered in Earth's primæval shocks,
> And niggard Nature ever mocks
>   The labourer's toil,
>
> 'I roam through clans of savage men,
> Untamed by arts, untaught by pen;
> Or cower within some squalid den
>   O'er reeking soil.
>
> 'Through paths that halt from stone to stone,
> Amid the din of tongues unknown,
> One image haunts my soul alone,
>   Thine, gentle Thrale!
>
> 'Soothes she, I ask, her spouse's care?
> Does mother-love its charge prepare?
> Stores she her mind with knowledge rare,
>   Or lively tale?
>
> 'Forget me not! thy faith I claim,
> Holding a faith that cannot die,
> That fills with thy benignant name
>   These shores of Skye.'

The family at Streatham, and particularly his mistress,

* 'Piozzi Letters,' i. 155.   † *Ibid.*, i. 177.

occupied a large share of Johnson's thoughts during his northern expedition. He would not suffer Boswell to speak slightingly of Mrs. Thrale, nor allow him to jest about the relation between her and himself. 'I yesterday told him,' writes Boswell in the journal he kept of their tour, 'I was thinking of writing a poetical letter to him, *on his return from Scotland*, in the style of Swift's humorous epistle in the character of Mary Gulliver to her husband, Captain Lemuel Gulliver, on his return to England from the country of the Houyhnhnms:—

> '"At early morn I to the market haste,
> Studious in everything to please thy taste.
> A curious *fowl* and *sparagrass* I chose;
> (For I remember you were fond of those);
> Three shillings cost the first, the last seven groats;
> Sullen you turn from both, and call for OATS."

'He laughed, and asked in whose name I would write it. I said in Mrs. Thrale's. He was angry. "Sir, if you have any sense of decency or delicacy, you won't do that!" BOSWELL: "Then let it be in Cole's, the landlord of the Mitre Tavern, where we have so often sat together." JOHNSON: "Ay, that may do."'*

At Inverary Boswell writes: 'The prospect of good accommodation cheered us much. We supped well; and after supper Dr. Johnson, whom I had not seen taste any fermented liquor during all our travels, called for a gill of whisky. "Come," said he, "let me know what it is that makes a Scotchman happy." He drank it all but a drop, which I begged leave to pour into my glass, that I might say we had drunk whisky together. I proposed Mrs. Thrale should be our toast. He would not have her drunk in whisky, but rather "some insular lady"; so we drank one of the ladies whom we had lately left.'†

During Johnson's absence in Scotland his mistress

---

* 'Boswell,' Dr. Hill's Edition, v. 139. † *Ibid.*, v. 346.

suffered a series of misfortunes. She lost her uncle, Sir Thomas Salusbury, who died at Bath on October 23, leaving her nothing that he could will away to anyone else; she gave birth to her second son, a sickly infant, who did not long survive;* and she was distressed by the illness of one of her daughters, which soon ended fatally. On November 20 she wrote to the traveller, who was now in Edinburgh:—

'When things are so *very* bad as they are now with me, the best comforters are those who acknowledge them to be very bad. Your last letter says, very properly, that among all the possibilities of evil which your imagination could suggest, losing my uncle's estate was the most unlikely. Had you known his excessive tenderness for me when a girl, the surprise would not have been lessened. You *do* know that I married, to please him, a man of his own choice, and deserving of everybody's esteem—indeed, possessing it. You know that I have scarce seen him since; and certainly never disobliged him; and you know he had no other relation, except at a very great distance. You now know he has willed away his estate. I should think on this sorrow more, however, had I not other sorrows, perhaps providentially sent to hold my heart fixed on my husband and his concerns. Lucy's unaccountable illness, my own present situation, having brought a second son, who appears to have suffered something, though I know not what, from my late accumulation of misery; and Mr. Thrale's health —which has been shook by these confusions as well as my own—occupy all the thoughts I have in the world; and you can scarce believe how full my mind is, without a word of my uncle. Our generous master is not angry at *that* disappointment, though he has a right to be sorry;

* This boy, who was named Ralph, died in July, 1775.

for he doubtless married me with hopes and promises of the Hertfordshire estate.'*

Johnson replied :—

' This is the last letter that I shall write ; while you are reading it, I shall be coming home.

' I congratulate you upon your boy ; but you must not think that I will love him all at once as well as I love Harry, for Harry, you know, is so rational. I shall love him by degrees. . . . ' Do not suffer yourself to be dejected. Resolution and diligence will supply all that is wanting, and all that is lost. But if your health should be impaired, I know not where to find a substitute. I shall have no mistress, Mr. Thrale will have no wife, and the little flock will have no mother.'†

Johnson spent a hundred days in Scotland, and left Edinburgh for London on November 22, feeling, as he said, that Mrs. Boswell wished him well to go. ' In this,' says Boswell, ' he showed a very acute penetration. My wife paid him the most assiduous and respectful attention while he was our guest ; so that I wonder how he discovered her wishing for his departure.' The truth is, that his irregular hours and uncouth habits, such as turning the candles with their heads downwards, when they did not burn bright enough, and letting the wax drop upon the carpet, could not but be disagreeable to a lady. Besides, she had not that high admiration for him which was felt by most of those who knew him ; and, what was very natural to a female mind, she thought he had too much influence over her husband. She once in a little warmth, made, with more point than justice, this remark upon that subject : " I have seen many a bear led by a man ; but I never before saw a man led by a bear !" '

The first half of 1774 was marked in the Streatham

* ' Piozzi Letters,' i. 203. † *Ibid.*, i. 206.

circle by three principal matters of interest: the production of Johnson's 'Journey to the Western Islands,'* the illness and death of Oliver Goldsmith, and preparations for an excursion to North Wales, undertaken chiefly for the purpose of visiting Mrs. Thrale's birthplace and property. Respecting the last, Johnson, who was of the party, at the moment of departure wrote to his old friend, Bennet Langton: 'I have just begun to print my *Journey to the Hebrides*, and am leaving the press to take another journey into Wales, whither Mr. Thrale is going to take possession of at least five hundred a year, fallen to his lady.'

Of this tour to Wales Boswell says: 'I do not find that he kept any journal or notes of what he saw there. All that I heard him say of it was, that instead of bleak and barren mountains, there were green and fertile ones; and that one of the castles in Wales would contain all the castles that he had seen in Scotland.'

He had, however, kept a journal, which was preserved by his black servant, Frank Barber, and was edited and published by Mr. Duppa in 1816. Mrs. Thrale-Piozzi lent her assistance to this publication, and some notes by her, which came too late for insertion, were added by Croker. The diary begins on Tuesday, July 5, with the entry: 'We left Streatham 11 a.m. Price of four horses two shillings a mile. Barnet 1.40 p.m. On the road I read Tully's Epistles. At night at Dunstable.' It proceeds from day to day with similar notes, the contents being generally *bien maigres*, as Mrs. Piozzi confessed.

On July 26 we read: 'In the afternoon we came to West-Chester (my father went to the fair when I

---

* The Tour, however, was not published till late in the autumn.

had the small-pox). We walked round the walls, which are complete, and contain one mile, three quarters, and one hundred and one yards. Within them are many gardens. They are very high, and two may walk very commodiously side by side.' On this entry Mrs. Thrale made a manuscript note some time after it was written: 'Of those ill-fated walls Dr. Johnson might have learned the extent from anyone. He has since put me fairly out of countenance by saying, "I have known my mistress fifteen years, and never saw her fairly out of humour but on Chester wall." It was because he would keep Miss Thrale beyond her hour of going to bed to walk on the wall, where, from the want of light, I apprehended some accident to her, perhaps to him.'

On July 28, the party reached Lleweny Hall, then the residence of Mr. Robert Cotton, Mrs. Thrale's cousin-german,* and stayed there three weeks. 'In the lawn,' wrote the journalist, 'is a spring of fine water, which rises above the surface into a stone basin, from which it runs to waste in a continual stream through a pipe. There are very large trees.' After giving the dimensions of the hall, gallery, library, and dining parlours of the old house, he adds: 'It is partly sashed and partly has casements.'† Their first visit thence was paid to Mrs. Thrale's property, which the diary thus describes: 'Saturday, July 30. We went to Bâch y Graig, where we found an old house, built 1567, in an uncommon and incommodious form. My mistress chattered about tiring, but I prevailed on her to go to the top. The floors

---

* He was the eldest son of her uncle, Sir Lynch Salusbury Cotton, and the father of Lord Combermere.

† Mrs. Piozzi wrote in 1817: 'Poor old Lleweny Hall! pulled down after standing a thousand years in possession of the Salusburys.'—Hayward's 'Piozzi,' ii. 206.

have been stolen, the windows are stopped. The house was less than I seemed to expect. The river Clwyd is a brook with a bridge of one arch, about one-third of a mile. The woods have many trees, generally young; but some which seem to decay. They have been lopped. The house never had a garden. The addition of another story would make an useful house, but it cannot be great. Some buildings which Clough, the founder, intended for warehouses, would make store-chambers and servants' rooms. The ground seems to be good. I wish it well.' Mr. Duppa notes :

'Pennant gives a description of this house in a tour he made into North Wales in 1780: "Not far from Dymerchion lies, half buried in woods, the singular house of Bâch y Graig. It consists of a mansion of three sides, enclosing a square court. The first consists of a vast hall and parlour: the rest of it rises into six wonderful stories, including the cupola; and forms from the second floor the figure of a pyramid; the rooms are small and inconvenient. The bricks are admirable, and appear to have been made in Holland, and the model of the house was probably brought from Flanders, where this kind of building is not unfrequent. . . . The initials of Richard Clough's name are in iron on the front, with the date 1567, and on the gateway 1569."' To return to Johnson's diary:

'*August* 2.—We went to Dymerchion Church, where the old clerk acknowledged his mistress. It is the parish church of Bâch y Graig. A mean fabric; Mr. Salusbury' (Mrs. Thrale's father) 'was buried in it. Bâch y Graig has fourteen seats in it. As we rode by I looked at the house again. We saw Llannerch, a house not mean, with a small park very well watered. There was an avenue of oaks, which, in a foolish compliance with the present mode, has been cut down.* A few are yet standing. The way lay through pleasant lanes and overlooked a region beautifully diversified with trees and grass. At Dymerchion Church there is English service only once a month. This is about twenty miles from the English border. The old clerk had great appearance of joy at the sight of his mistress, and foolishly said that he was now willing to die. He had only a crown given him by my Mistress.'

'If Mr. Duppa,' wrote Mrs. Piozzi, when this was published, 'does not send me a copy of Johnson's Diary, he is as shabby as it seems our doctor thought me, when I gave but a crown to the old clerk. The poor clerk had probably never seen a crown in his possession before. Things were very distant A.D. 1774 from what they are 1816.' 'Mrs. Piozzi,' says Dr. Birkbeck Hill, 'writes as if Johnson's censure had been passed in 1816, and not in 1774.' Not so; she means, of course, that a reflection which might appear reasonable in 1816 was not just in 1774.

Johnson, as will be seen in our next extract, seems, like many other persons of limited income, to consider it incumbent on the rich to be careless of small sums. On August 4 the travellers visited Rhuddlan Castle and Bodryddan, the residence of the Stapylton family, of which the diary says:

'Stapylton's house is pretty; there are pleasing shades about it, with a constant spring that supplies a cold bath. We then went to see a cascade. I trudged unwillingly,

* Dr. Birkbeck Hill aptly quotes from the first book of Cowper's 'Task':—
'Not distant far a length of colonnade
Invites us. Monument of ancient taste,
Now scorned, but worthy of a better fate,
  * * *
Thanks to Benevolus, he spares me yet
These chestnuts ranged in corresponding lines,
And though himself so polished still reprieves
The obsolete prolixity of shade.'

and was not sorry to find it dry. The water was however, turned on, and produced a very striking cataract.* . . .'

'Mrs. Thrale lost her purse. She expressed so much uneasiness that I concluded the sum to be very great; but when I heard of only seven guineas, I was glad to find that she had so much sensibility of money.'

Mrs. Piozzi remarks on this passage: ' He teased Mrs. Cotton about her dry cascade till she was ready to cry.'

This Mrs. Cotton, afterwards Lady Salusbury Cotton, was one of five Stapylton co-heiresses. She married the eldest son of Sir Lynch Cotton, and was the mother of Field-Marshal Viscount Combermere. She said that Johnson, despite his rudeness, was at times delightful, having a manner peculiar to himself in relating anecdotes that could not fail to attract both old and young. Her impression was that Mrs. Thrale was very vexatious in wishing to engross all his attention, which annoyed him much. ' This I fancy,' says Mr. Hayward, ' is no uncommon impression when we ourselves are anxious to attract notice.'

The range of hills bordering the valley or delta of the Clwyd is very fine. On their being pointed out to him by his host, he exclaimed: ' Hills do you call them ? Mere mole-hills to the Alps or to those in Scotland!' On being told that Sir Richard Clough had formed a plan for making the river navigable to Rhuddlan, he broke out into a loud fit of laughter, and shouted: ' Why, sir, I could clear any part of it by a leap.'

On the way to Holywell he records : ' Talk with mistress about flattery,' on which she has the note: ' He said I flattered the people to whose houses we went. I was

---

* Bowles, the poet, on the unexpected arrival of a party to view his grounds, was overheard giving a hurried order to set the fountain playing, and curry the hermit his beard.—HAYWARD.

saucy, and said I was obliged to be civil for two, meaning himself and me.'* He replied nobody would thank me for compliments they did not understand. At Gwaynynog (the house of Mr. Middleton), however, he was flattered, and was happy, of course.'†

The Thrales are mentioned again in several subsequent passages:

'*August* 22.—We went to Bodvil, the place where Mrs. Thrale was born, and the churches called Tydweilliog and Llangwinodyl, which she holds by impropriation.'

'*August* 24.—We went to see Bodvil. Mrs. Thrale remembered the rooms, and wandered over them, with recollection of her childhood. This species of pleasure is always melancholy. The walk was cut down, and the pond was dry. Nothing was better.

'We surveyed the Churches, which are mean, and neglected to a degree scarcely imaginable. They have no pavement, and the earth is full of holes. The seats are rude benches; the Altars have no rails. One of them has a breach in the roof. On the desk, I think, of each lay a folio Welsh Bible of the black letter, which the curate cannot easily read. Mr. Thrale purposes to beautify the Churches, and if he prospers, will probably restore the tithes. . . .‡

'*August* 26.—Note. Queeney's goats, 149, I think.'

Of this last entry Mr. Duppa gives an explanation with

---

* Miss Burney reports Mrs. Thrale saying to Johnson at Streatham in September, 1778: 'I remember, sir, when we were travelling in Wales, how you called me to account for my civility to the people. "Madam," you said, "let me have no more of this idle commendation of nothing. Why is it that whatever you see, and whomever you see, you are to be so indiscriminately lavish of praise?" "Why, I'll tell you, sir," said I. "When I am with you, Mr. Thrale, and Queeney, I am obliged to be civil for four."'

† Hayward's 'Piozzi,' i. 75.

‡ In 1809 the whole income from Llangwinodyl, including surplice fees, amounted to £46 2s. 2d., and for Tydweilliog £43 19s. 10d., so that it does not appear that Mr. Thrale carried into effect his good intention.—DUPPA.

which, no doubt, he was furnished by Mrs. Piozzi: 'Mr. Thrale was near-sighted, and could not see the goats browsing on Snowdon, and he promised his daughter, who was a child of ten years old, a penny for every goat she would show him, and Dr. Johnson kept the account; so that it appeared her father was in debt to her one hundred and forty-nine pence. Queeney was an epithet, which had its origin in the nursery, by which (in allusion to Queen Esther) Miss Thrale was always distinguished by Johnson.' She was named, after her mother, Hester, not Esther.

Under date September 13 Johnson notes: 'We came to Lord Sandys's, at Ombersley, where we were treated with great civility.' It was at Ombersley Court, as he told Mrs. Thrale, that, for the only time in his life, he had as much wall-fruit as he liked. She wrote to him in 1778:* 'Mr. Scrase gives us fine fruit; I wished you my pear yesterday: but, then, what would *one* pear have done for you?'

Johnson was less pleased with a visit to Hagley, where the party spent three days with Thrale's early friend, Mr. Lyttelton, uncle of the then Lord Lyttelton, and afterwards himself, by successive creations, Lord Westcote and Lord Lyttelton; at whose house Johnson imagined that they did not meet with the respect and kindness to which they were entitled. Mrs. Thrale's explanation is: 'Mrs. Lyttelton forced me to play at whist against my liking, and her husband took away Johnson's candle that he wanted to read by at the other end of the room. Those, I trust, were the offences.'

The journey ended with a visit to Burke, at Beaconsfield, where they heard that Parliament was dissolved, and at once returned home. The dissolution was on

* 'Piozzi Letters,' ii. 36.

September 30; and Thrale, who was a strong supporter of Lord North, having again to encounter a contested election, Johnson came forward with his third political pamphlet, entitled 'The Patriot,' in defence of the Government. This tract, like its two predecessors, was written in a remarkably short space of time. 'It was called for,' said the author, 'by my political friends on Friday, and was written on Saturday.'

On October 16 Horace Walpole wrote that there had been outrageous rioting in Southwark, but that he knew nothing of the candidates, their connections, or their success.* In the end Thrale was again returned, though, as before, he was only second on the poll. He had not the popular manners necessary for a good candidate, and owed great part of his success to his wife, who threw herself heart and soul into the business of electioneering, for which she was as well qualified as the Duchess of Devonshire, or Mrs. Crewe. In later life Mrs. Thrale, having occasion to pass through Southwark, expressed her astonishment at no longer recognising a place every hole and corner of which she had three times visited as a canvasser.

On one of these expeditions Johnson accompanied her, and a rough fellow, a hatter by trade, seeing his beaver in a state of decay, seized it suddenly with one hand, and clapping him on the back with the other, cried out, 'Ah, Master Johnson, this is no time to be thinking about hats.' 'No, no, sir,' replied the Doctor in a cheerful tone; 'hats are of no use now, as you say, except to throw up in the air and huzza with,' accompanying his words with the true election halloo.†

On October 27 Johnson was able to write to Boswell that Thrale had happily surmounted a very

* 'Letters,' vi. 134.   † Anec., p. 214.

violent and acrimonious opposition; but, added he: 'All joys have their abatement: Mrs. Thrale has fallen from her horse, and hurt herself very much.'

Thrale's gratitude to Johnson, or his admiration of him, made him at one time anxious that his friend should be brought into Parliament. Sir John Hawkins says that Thrale had two meetings with the Minister, who at first seemed inclined to find Johnson a seat, but eventually discouraged the proposal. Lord Stowell told Mr. Croker that Lord North was afraid that Johnson's help might sometimes prove embarrassing. 'He perhaps thought, and not unreasonably,' added Lord Stowell, 'that, like the elephant in the battle, he was quite as likely to trample down his friends as his foes.' Boswell expresses a wish that the moralist had tried his hand in the House, and wonders that the Ministry did not make the experiment. On this Mrs. Thrale remarks very sensibly: 'Boswell had leisure for curiosity; Ministers had not. Boswell would have been equally amused by his failure as by his success, but to Lord North there would have been no joke at all in the experiment ending untowardly.'

CHAPTER IV.

Mrs. Abington's Benefit—Johnson created Doctor—Marriages with Inferiors in Rank—Thrale not a Wit—Baretti—Account of Him—Tried for Murder—Enters Thrale's Family—His Character drawn by Mrs. Piozzi—Dr. Thomas Campbell—His Diary of a Visit to England—His Impressions of Baretti and Johnson—Dinners at Thrale's—Tour to France—Baretti makes Himself Useful—Johnson's Letters and Diary—Johnson Intractable—Disagreements—Verses to Mrs. Thrale—She translates an Epigram Impromptu—Johnson removes to Bolt Court—Boswell again in London—He goes with Johnson to the Midlands—Sudden Death of Thrale's only Son—Johnson and Boswell return to London—Johnson comforts the Parents—Proposed Tour to Italy given up—Garrick's Retirement—His Acting—The Thrales at Bath with Johnson—Visit from Boswell—Johnson Severe to Mrs. Thrale—He returns to London—Dines with Wilkes—Pressed to go again to Bath—Quarrel with Baretti—Mrs. Thrale describes the Rupture—Johnson's Account—Baretti's Version—Apparent Reconciliation—Thraliana—Thrale described by his Wife.

In the spring of 1775 Boswell was again in London, and on Monday, March 27, breakfasted at Mr. Strahan's* with Johnson, where he learned that the latter was engaged to go that night to Mrs. Abington's† benefit. The two met again at Drury Lane Theatre in the evening. 'Sir Joshua Reynolds,' writes the biographer, 'at Mrs. Abington's request, had promised to bring a body of wits, and having secured forty places in the front boxes, had done me the honour to put me in the group. Johnson sat in the seat directly behind me; and as he could

* William Strahan, the King's printer. He was great-grandfather of Dr. Spottiswoode, the late President of the Royal Society.
† This celebrated actress was then at the zenith of her fame. Her range was large, extending from Ophelia and Beatrice to Miss Prue and Polly Peachum. Murphy dedicated to her his comedy of 'How to Keep Him,' and she was the original representative of Lady Teazle in 1777.

neither see nor hear at such a distance from the stage, he was wrapped up in grave abstraction, and seemed quite in a cloud, amidst all the sunshine of glitter and gaiety. He said very little. He was more disposed for talk next day at a dinner given by Mr. Thrale. He was then awaiting his diploma of Doctor of Laws from Oxford, and was understood to be highly pleased with the prospect of his new dignity.

Boswell, who was also a guest, records a little sparring between Johnson and their hostess respecting the poet Gray, whom the lady, to her credit, was disposed to admire, while Johnson reviled him as a dull fellow and a mechanical poet. The conversation next turned on the subject of unequal matches, a question arising how a woman who married a man much her inferior in rank should be treated by her relations. ' While I recapitulate the debate,' says its reporter, ' and recollect what has since happened, I cannot but be struck in a manner that delicacy forbids me to express. While I contended that she ought to be treated with an inflexible steadiness of displeasure, Mrs. Thrale was all for mildness and forgiveness, and, according to the vulgar phrase, making the best of a bad bargain.' Johnson, he adds, thought that when there was a gross and shameful deviation from rank it should be punished, so as to deter others from the same perversion. The allusion in this passage to Mrs. Thrale's second marriage is so pointed, as well as so unnecessary, that Scotch James's affectation of delicacy has the air of a studied impertinence.

On May 10 in this year, Boswell wrote to his friend Temple : ' I am at present in a *tourbillon* of conversations ; but how come you to throw in the Thrales, among the Reynoldses and the Beauclerks ? Mr. Thrale is a worthy, sensible man, and has the wits much about his house, but

he is not one himself. Perhaps you mean Mrs. Thrale.'*
This is not exactly the tone in which he distinguishes the
couple in his book.

The Thrale household now included another inmate,
who for some time was as much a constant member
of the family as Johnson himself. This was Joseph
Baretti, a native of Piedmont, who had been brought
to England by Lord Charlemont in 1750. According
to his own story, Baretti was the son of an architect
n the service of the King of Sardinia, and had inherited
a small property, which he had lost at play. He had
received the usual classical education, and had taught
himself, besides, English, French, Spanish, and Portuguese.
In this country his talents, knowledge, and force of mind
attracted the regard of many eminent friends, while the
roughness of his manners, and an unbridled arrogance
of temper also made him numerous enemies. The latter
accused him of falsehood and malevolence. The former
asserted that, throughout a life of poverty, his integrity was
unimpeached, and his distress never made known but in the
last extremity. Huggins, the translator of Ariosto, told a
story of his having lent Baretti a gold watch, which he
had afterwards to recover from a pawnbroker, to whom
the borrower had sold it. But it is fair to add that Huggins had quarrelled with both Baretti and Baretti's chief
friend, Johnson. The two last had suffered want together,
and Johnson always mentioned his old companion with kindness. In 1768 Johnson remarked: 'I know no man who
carries his head higher in conversation than Baretti.
There are strong powers in his mind. He has not,
indeed, many hooks, but with what hooks he has, he
grapples very forcibly.' On the other hand, Madame
d'Arblay, who knew him from a girl, was more impressed

* 'Letters of Boswell,' p. 192.

by his rudeness and violence than by his intellectual power.

In October, 1769, Baretti was tried at the Old Bailey, on a charge of murder, for killing with a pocket-knife one of three men who, with a woman of the town, had set upon him in the Haymarket. He was acquitted, and the incident is chiefly remarkable for the appearance of Burke, Johnson, and Beauclerk as witnesses to character. An Italian came one day to Baretti whilst he lay in Newgate to desire a letter of recommendation for the teaching of his scholars when the prisoner should have been hanged. 'You rascal!' replied Baretti in a rage, 'if I were not in *my own apartment* I would kick you downstairs directly!'

The exile earned a precarious subsistence by giving lessons in modern languages, and writing for the booksellers. The year after his trial he published 'Travels through Spain, Portugal, and France,' and made £500 by this book. The money was soon spent, and the author was again in difficulties, to relieve which he was persuaded by Johnson to accept Thrale's hospitality, and undertake the instruction of his host's daughters in Italian. As the teacher reserved the right of coming and going at his pleasure, he received no salary, but merely occasional presents in money. The arrangement was not a hopeful one; yet it lasted longer than might have been expected. The turbulent Italian lived for nearly three years in the Thrale family.

'Baretti,' wrote Mrs. Piozzi, while the subject of her remarks was still living, 'could not endure to be called, or scarcely thought, a foreigner, and, indeed, it did not often occur to his company that he was one; for his accent was wonderfully proper,* and his language always

* Malone says of Baretti that 'he was certainly a man of extraordinary talents, and perhaps no one ever made himself so completely master of a foreign language as he did of English.'—Prior's 'Malone,' p. 392.

copious, always nervous, always full of various allusions, flowing, too, with a rapidity worthy of admiration, and far beyond the power of nineteen in twenty natives. . . . He has, besides, some skill in music, with a bass voice, very agreeable, besides a falsetto, which he can manage so as to mimic any singer he hears. I would also trust his knowledge of painting a long way. These accomplishments, with his extensive power over every modern language, make him a most pleasing companion while he is in a good humour; and his lofty consciousness of his own superiority, which made him tenacious of every position, and drew him into a thousand distresses, did not, I must own, ever disgust me, till he began to exercise it against myself, and resolve to reign in our house by fairly defying the mistress of it. Pride, however, though shocking enough, is never despicable; but vanity, which he possessed too, in an eminent degree, will sometimes make a man near sixty ridiculous.'

Mrs. Piozzi gives the following instance of his skill in our low street language. Walking in a field near Chelsea he met a fellow, who, suspecting him from dress and manner to be a foreigner, said sneeringly: 'Come, sir, will you show me the way to France?' 'No, sir,' says Baretti instantly; 'but I will show you the way to Tyburn.' 'Such, however,' she adds, 'was his ignorance in a certain line, that he once asked Johnson for information who it was composed the "Pater Noster," and I heard him tell Evans the story of Dives and Lazarus as the subject of a poem he once had composed in the Milanese dialect, expecting great credit for his powers of invention.'*

A newer acquaintance than either Baretti or Boswell

---

* Hayward's 'Piozzi,' i. 93, 94. Evans was a clergyman, and Rector of St. George's, Southwark. The story of Baretti's ignorance about the 'Pater Noster' was also told by Johnson and Sir Joshua Reynolds. See Boswell's Johnson' (Hill's Edition), v. 121, and n. 4.

was sometimes to be seen at Thrale's house in the spring of 1775. This was an Irish clergyman, Dr. Thomas Campbell, who had come to this country chiefly with a view to see Dr. Johnson, for whom he entertained the highest veneration. ' He has since,' writes Boswell, ' published " A Philosophical Survey of the South of Ireland," a very entertaining book, which has, however, one fault, that it assumes the fictitious character of an Englishman.' A book purporting to be the ' Diary of a Visit to England in 1775,' by this gentleman, was published at Sydney in 1854. The manuscript was stated by the editor to have been discovered behind an old press in one of the offices of the Supreme Court of New South Wales. Some doubts have been entertained as to the genuineness of this work. Lord Macaulay, however, was convinced of its being authentic, and Dr. Birkbeck Hill shares this opinion. Several passages of the diary afford illustrations of the Thrale hospitalities:

' *March* 14*th*.—This day I called at Mr. Thrale's, where I was received with all respect by Mr. and Mrs. Thrale. She is a very learned lady, and joins to the charms of her own sex the manly understanding of ours. The immensity of the brewery astonished me.'

With Johnson he was disappointed:

' 16*th*.— Dined with Mr. Thrale, along with Dr. Johnson and Baretti. Baretti is a plain, sensible man, who seems to know the world well. He talked to me of the invitation given him by the College of Dublin, but said it (£100 a year and rooms) was not worth his acceptance; and if it had been, he said, in point of profit, still he would not have accepted it, for that now he could not live out of London. He had returned a few years ago to his country, but he could not enjoy it, and he was obliged to return to London, to those connections he had been making for near thirty years past. He told me he had several families with whom, both in town and country, he could go at any time and spend a month; he is at this time on these terms at Mr. Thrale's, and he knows how to keep his ground. Talking as we were at tea of the magnitude of the beer vessels, he said there was one thing in Mr. Thrale's house still more extraordinary, meaning his wife. She gulped the pill very prettily—so much for Baretti!

'Johnson, you are the very man Lord Chesterfield describes: a Hottentot, indeed, and though your abilities are respectable, you never can be respected yourself. He has the aspect of an idiot, without the faintest ray of sense gleaming from any one feature—with the most awkward garb, and unpowdered gray wig on one side only of his head; he is for ever dancing the devil's jig, and sometimes he makes the most drivelling effort to whistle some thought in his absent paroxysms.'

The Diarist mentions that Johnson this day, referring to his fourth political pamphlet then recently published, said that 'Taxation no Tyranny'* did not sell. On a subsequent day he remarked of the same tract, 'I think I have not been attacked enough for it. Attack is the reaction; I never think I have hit hard unless it rebounds.' We return to Dr. Campbell:

'*March* 25*th.*—Dined at Mr. Thrale's, where there were ten or more gentlemen, and but one lady besides Mrs. Thrale. The dinner was excellent; first course, soups at head and foot, removed by fish and a saddle of mutton; second course, a fowl they call galena at head, and a capon larger than some of our Irish turkeys at foot; third course, four different sorts of ices, pineapple, grape, rasp-

---

* 'An Answer to the Resolutions and Address of the American Congress.' This, like the pamphlet on 'Falkland's Islands,' was published anonymously.

berry, and a fourth; in each remove, I think, there were fourteen dishes. The two first courses were served in massy plate. I sat beside Baretti, which was to me the richest part of the entertainment. He and Mr. and Mrs. Thrale joined in expressing to me Dr. Johnson's concern that he could not give me the meeting that day, but desired that I should go and see him.'

'*April* 1.—Dined at Mr. Thrale's, whom, in proof of the magnitude of London, I cannot help remarking, no coachman, and this is the third I have called, could find without inquiry. But of this, by the way. There was Murphy, Boswell, and Baretti; the two last, as I learned just before I entered, are mortal foes, so much so that Murphy and Mrs. Thrale agreed that Boswell expressed a desire that Baretti should be hanged upon that unfortunate affair of his killing, etc. Upon this hint I went, and without any sagacity it was easily discernible; for upon Baretti's entering, Boswell did not rise, and upon Baretti's descry of Boswell he grinned a perturbed glance. Politeness, however, smooths the most hostile brows, and theirs were smoothed. Johnson was the subject both before and after dinner, for it was the boast of all but myself, that under that roof were the Doctor's fast friends. His *bon-mots* were retailed in such plenty that they, like a surfeit, could not lie upon my memory.'

'*April* 8. Dined with Thrale, where Dr. Johnson was, and Boswell (and Baretti as usual). The Doctor was not in as good spirits as he was at Dilly's.* He had supped the night before with Lady ——, Miss Jeffries, one of the Maids of Honour, Sir Joshua Reynolds, etc., at Mrs. Abington's. He said Sir C. Thompson, and some others who were there, spoke like people who had seen good

* Referring to a dinner to which the Diarist had been taken three days before by Boswell.

company, and so did Mrs. Abington herself, who could not have seen good company. He seems fond of Boswell, and yet he is always abusing the Scots before him, by way of joke.'

Boswell's account of the same evening runs:

'On Saturday, April 8, I dined with him at Mr. Thrale's, where we met the Irish Dr. Campbell. Johnson had supped the night before at Mrs. Abington's, with some fashionable people whom he named; and he seemed much pleased with having made one of so elegant a circle. Nor did he omit to pique his mistress a little with jealousy of her housewifery; for he said with a smile, "Mrs. Abington's jelly, my dear lady, was better than yours." Mrs. Thrale, who frequently practised a coarse mode of flattery by repeating his *bon-mots* in his hearing,* told us that he had said a certain celebrated actor was just fit to stand at the door of an auction-room with a long pole, and cry: "Pray, gentlemen, walk in;" and that a certain author, upon hearing this, had said that another still more celebrated actor was fit for nothing better than that, and would pick your pocket after you came out. JOHNSON: "Nay, my dear lady, there is no wit in what our friend added; there is only abuse. You may as well say of any man that he will pick a pocket; besides, the man who is stationed at the door does not pick people's pockets; that is done within by the auctioneer."'

In the summer of this year Johnson made his annual ramble into the midland counties. He was absent from the end of May till some time in August. He wrote to Mrs. Thrale from Oxford on June 1: 'Don't suppose

---

* Baretti, in a manuscript note in his copy of the 'Piozzi Letters,' i. 174, says: 'Johnson was often fond of saying silly things in strong terms, and the silly madam [Mrs. Thrale] never failed to echo that beastly kind of wit.' Here Boswell and Baretti appear on the same level.

that I live here as we live at Streatham. I went this morning to chapel at six.' On September 15 he set out on a short tour to France, with Mr. and Mrs. Thrale. The party, which on this occasion included Baretti as well as Queeney, were abroad about eight weeks.

'France,' says Mrs. Thrale, 'displayed all Mr. Baretti's useful powers. He bustled for us, he catered for us, he took care of the child, he secured an apartment for the maid, he provided for our safety, our amusement, our repose; without him, the pleasure of that journey would never have balanced the pain. And great was his disgust, to be sure, when he caught us, as he often did, ridiculing French manners, French sentiments, etc. I think he half cried to Mrs. Payne, the landlady at Dover, on our return, because we laughed at French cookery and French accommodations. Oh, how he would court the maids at the inns abroad, abuse the men perhaps! and that with a facility not to be exceeded, as they all confessed, by any of the natives. But so he could in Spain, I find, and so 'tis plain he could here.'*

In a letter to Levet, dated Paris, October 22, 1775, Johnson writes:

'We came yesterday from Fontainebleau, where the Court is now. We went to see the King and Queen at dinner, and the Queen was so impressed by Miss,† that she sent one of the gentlemen to inquire who she was. I find all true that you have ever told me of Paris. Mr. Thrale is very liberal, and keeps us two coaches and a very fine table; but I think our cookery very bad. Mrs. Thrale got into a convent of English nuns, and I talked with her through the grate, and I am very kindly used by the English Benedictine friars. But upon the

* Hayward's 'Piozzi,' i. 94.   † Miss Thrale.

whole I cannot make much acquaintance here; and though the churches, palaces, and some private houses are very magnificent, there is no very great pleasure, after having seen many, in seeing more; at least, the pleasure, whatever it be, must sometime have an end. . . . I ran a race in the rain this day, and beat Baretti. Baretti is a fine fellow, and speaks French, I think, quite as well as English.'

During part of this excursion, Johnson kept a journal similar to that which he had kept in Wales the year before, but even more brief and disappointing in its contents. We can find only one quotable allusion to his friends:

'*October* 23.—We went to Sans-terre, a brewer.* He brews with about as much malt as Mr. Thrale, and sells his beer at the same price, though he pays no duty for malt, and little more than half as much for beer. Beer is sold retail at sixpence a bottle. He brews 4,000 barrels a year.'

Johnson seems to have been ill at ease in France, and on the whole to have shown himself less tractable and accommodating than he had been either in Scotland or Wales. He would either talk Latin or not talk at all. Baretti said that he saw next to nothing of Paris, adding: 'He noticed the country so little that he scarcely ever spoke of it after.' As, however, he declared that Johnson never touched a pen in France, it is clear that the hot-tempered Italian's account is not altogether to be trusted.

'When we were at Rouen together,' says Mrs. Thrale, 'he took a great fancy to the Abbé Roffette, with whom he conversed about the destruction of the order of Jesuits, and condemned it loudly, as a blow to the general power of the Church, and likely to be followed with many and dangerous innovations, which might at length become fatal

* He commanded the troops at the execution of Louis XVI.

to religion itself, and shake even the foundation of Christianity. The gentleman seemed to wonder and delight in his conversation; the talk was all in Latin, which both spoke fluently, and Mr. Johnson pronounced a long eulogium upon Milton with so much ardour, eloquence, and ingenuity, that the Abbé rose from his seat and embraced him. My husband, seeing them apparently so charmed with the company of each other, politely invited the Abbé to England, intending to oblige his friend, who, instead of thanking, reprimanded him severely before the man, for such a sudden burst of tenderness towards a person he could know nothing at all of, and thus put a sudden finish to all his own, and Mr. Thrale's entertainment, from the company of the Abbé Roffette.'

The 'Piozzi Letters' contain allusions to more than one disagreement in France. On May 1, 1780, he wrote to Mrs. Thrale: 'The exhibition, how will you do, either to see or not to see? The exhibition is eminently splendid. There is contour, and keeping, and grace, and expression, and all the varieties of artificial excellence.'* She answers: 'When did I ever plague you about contour, and grace, and expression? I have dreaded them all three since that hapless day at Compiegne, when you teased me so, and Mr. Thrale made what I hoped would have proved a lasting peace; but French ground is unfavourable to fidelity, perhaps, and so now you begin again; after having taken five years' breath, you might have done more than this. Say another word and I will bring up afresh the history of your exploits at St. Denis, and how cross you were for nothing—but somehow or other our travels never make any part either of our conversation or correspondence.'†

Johnson, however, had gained in health by the tour,

* 'Piozzi Letters,' ii. 111. † *Ibid.*, ii. 116.

and was in high good-humour after his return. He had provided himself with a Paris-made 'wig of handsome construction,' and his journal shows that he had bought other articles of dress. The close of the year found him living on the usual terms with the Thrales.

The Ode written in Skye was not the only poetical compliment addressed by Johnson to his mistress. He gave a personal turn to some Italian verses by Baretti, in an improvised paraphrase:

> 'Long may live my lovely Hetty!
> Always young and always pretty;
> Always pretty, always young,
> Live my lovely Hetty long!
> Always young and always pretty,
> Long may live my lovely Hetty!'

She inserted these lines in the 'Anecdotes,' and on a copy of that book presented by her to Sir James Fellowes in 1816, added a marginal note: 'I heard these verses sung at Mr. Thomas's by three voices not three weeks ago.'

'On another occasion,' she says in the 'Anecdotes,' 'I can boast verses from Dr. Johnson. As I went into his room the morning of my birthday once, I said to him: "Nobody sends me any verses now, because I am five-and-thirty years old; and Stella was fed with them till forty-six, I remember." My being just recovered from illness and confinement will account for the manner in which he burst out suddenly, for so he did, without the least previous hesitation whatsoever, and without having entertained the smallest intention towards it half a minute before:

> 'Oft in danger, yet alive,
> We are come to thirty-five;
> Long may better years arrive,
> Better years than thirty-five.
> Could philosophers contrive
> Life to stop at thirty-five,
> Time his hours should never drive

> O'er the bounds of thirty-five.
> High to soar, and deep to dive,
> Nature gives at thirty-five.
> Ladies, stock and tend your hive,
> Trifle not at thirty-five ;
> For howe'er we boast and strive,
> Life declines from thirty-five.
> He that ever hopes to thrive
> Must begin by thirty-five :
> And all who wisely wish to wive
> Must look on Thrale at thirty-five.'

'" And now," said he, as I was writing them down, " you may see what it is to come for poetry to a dictionary-maker ; you may observe that the rhymes run in alphabetical order exactly." And so they do.'

Mrs. Thrale omitted in the 'Anecdotes' to mention the year in which these verses were written. In 'Thraliana' she says they were made in 1777, but in one of her memorandum-books she refers them to the correct date—1776.

Now and then she would try her own hand at impromptu versifying. 'Mrs. Aston,' said Johnson once of his first love, 'was a beauty and a scholar, and a wit, and a Whig, and she talked all in praise of liberty, and so I made this epigram upon her. She was the loveliest creature I ever saw :

> ' Liber ut esse velim, suasisti, pulchra Maria,
> Ut maneam liber, pulchra Maria, vale.'

' Will it do this way in English, sir ?' said Mrs. Thrale :

> ' Persuasions to freedom fall oddly from you,
> If freedom we seek, fair Maria, adieu."*

In 1776 Boswell reached London, on March 15, and, calling next morning on Dr. Johnson, found that 'he was removed from Johnson's Court, No. 7, to Bolt Court, No. 8, still keeping to his favourite Fleet Street.' The house in Bolt Court was his last habitation ; it was burnt down in 1819.† Being informed that he was at Mr.

* Anec., p. 157.   † *Notes and Queries*, S. 1, v. 233.

Thrale's, in the Borough, the caller hastened thither, and found Mrs. Thrale and him at breakfast. The hours of the family were not early. Burney tells how Johnson came down one morning to the breakfast-room, and was a considerable time by himself before anybody appeared, and how, on a subsequent day, being twitted by Mrs. Thrale for being late, he defended himself by alluding to the morning when he had been too early: 'Madam, I do not like to come down to vacuity!'

Boswell continues: 'I was kindly welcomed. In a moment he was in a full glow of conversation; and I felt myself elevated, as if brought into another state of being. Mrs. Thrale and I looked to each other while he talked, and our looks expressed our congenial admiration and affection for him. I shall ever recollect this scene with great pleasure. I exclaimed to her, "I am now, intellectually, *Hermippus redivivus*—I am quite restored by him, by transfusion of mind." "There are many," she replied, "who admire and respect Mr. Johnson; but you and I *love* him!"

'He seemed very happy in the near prospect of going to Italy with Mr. and Mrs. Thrale. "But," said he, "before leaving England I am to take a jaunt to Oxford, Birmingham, my native city Lichfield, and my old friend Dr. Taylor's at Ashbourne in Derbyshire. I shall go in a few days, and you, Boswell, shall go with me." I was ready to accompany him, being willing even to leave London to have the pleasure of his conversation.'

Four days later Boswell accompanied Johnson to Oxford, whence they proceeded to Birmingham and Lichfield, intending afterwards to make a long stay with Dr. Taylor; but this visit was cut short, and the projected journey to Italy was destined not to take place. As the travellers were on the point of leaving

Lichfield for Derbyshire, a letter reached Johnson from Mr. Perkins, announcing the death of Thrale's only son Henry, and concluding with the words, ' I need not say how much they wish to see you in London.' The boy, a lad of ten, had died suddenly on March 23, before his father's door. So much we learn from a notice published at the time,* but no further particulars appear to have been preserved.

' One of the most dreadful things that have happened in my time!' was Johnson's exclamation on reading the news. ' This,' he added, ' is a total extinction to their family, as much as if they were sold into captivity.' In vain Boswell suggested that Mr. Thrale had daughters who might inherit his wealth. ' Daughters!' cried the moralist warmly, ' he'll no more value his daughters than——' ' I was going to speak,' says Boswell. ' Sir,' said he, ' don't you know how you yourself think? Sir, he wishes to propagate his name. . . . I would have gone to the extremity of the earth to have preserved this boy.'

It was to little purpose, therefore, that on Tuesday, March 26, there came for the pair of friends what Boswell calls ' an equipage properly suited to a wealthy well-beneficed clergyman,† Dr. Taylor's large, roomy post-chaise, drawn by four stout, plump horses, and driven by two steady, jolly postilions, which conveyed them to Ashbourne. The second evening after their arrival found them on the road to London. On March 29 their chaise deposited them in the Poultry, whence Johnson hurried away in a hackney-coach to the Borough, and found Mrs. Thrale, her eldest daughter, and Baretti on the point of

---
* *Gent. Mag.*, 1776, p. 142.
† ' Dr. Taylor had a good estate of his own, and good preferment in the Church, being a Prebendary of Westminster and Rector of Bosworth.'— BOSWELL.

setting out for Bath. Baretti says that Mrs. Thrale had abruptly proposed this journey from a wish to avoid the sight of the funeral.* She did not delay her departure on seeing Johnson, who, Boswell thought, was in no good humour at this want of ceremony; but the letters which he addressed to Mrs. Thrale at Bath do not indicate any feeling of displeasure.

On March 30 he wrote: 'Do not indulge your sorrow; try to drive it away, by either pleasure or pain; for, opposed to what you are feeling, many pains will become pleasures. Remember the great precept: "*Be not solitary; be not idle.*"† . . . . That I feel what friendship can feel, I hope I need not tell you.‡ I loved him as I never expect to love any other little boy; but I could not love him as a parent. I know that such a loss is a laceration of the mind. I know that a whole system of hopes, and designs, and expectations is swept away at once, and nothing left but bottomless vacuity. What you feel I have felt,§ and hope that your disquiet will be shorter than mine.'‖

* At the foot of the fine inscription on Thrale's monument in St. Leonards' Church, Streatham, are the words: 'Consortes tumuli habet Rodolphum patrem, strenuum fortemque virum, et Henricum filium unicum, quem spei parentum mors inopina decennem præripuit. Ita domus felix et opulenta quam erexit avus, auxitque pater, cum nepote decidit. Abi viator! et vicibus rerum humanarum perspectis, æternitatem cogita.' 'In the same tomb lie interred his father, Ralph Thrale, a man of vigour and activity, and his only son, Henry, who died before his father, aged ten years. Thus a fortunate and opulent family, raised by the grandfather and augmented by the father, became extinguished with the grandson. Go, reader, and reflecting on the vicissitudes of all human affairs, meditate on eternity.' Johnson here breaks his own rule against addressing epitaphs to the passer-by.

† Burton, in the last lines of 'The Anatomy of Melancholy,' says: 'Only take this for a corollary and conclusion: as thou tenderest thine own welfare in this and all other melancholy, thy good health of body and mind, observe this short precept, Give not way to solitariness and idleness, "Be not solitary, be not idle."'

‡ He had written of the boy in the previous summer: 'Pray give my service to my dear friend Harry, and tell him that Mr. Murphy does not love him better than I do.'—'Piozzi Letters,' i. 262.

§ He is referring, of course, to the death of his wife.

‖ 'Piozzi Letters,' i. 310.

Again, on April 1 : 'When you were gone, Mr. Thrale soon sent me away. I came next day, and was made to understand that when I was wanted I should be sent for ; and therefore I have not gone yesterday or to-day ; but I will soon go again, whether invited or not.'*

On Good-Friday, which this year was April 5, Boswell, having attended morning service at St. Clement's Church, walked home with Johnson, and records that in the afternoon Thrale called, appearing, he adds, to bear the loss of his son with a manly composure, but seeming to hesitate as to the intended Italian tour. Johnson's entry in his diary is : ' My design was to pass part of the day in exercises of piety, but Mr. Boswell interrupted me ; of him, however, I could have rid myself; but poor Thrale, *orbus et exspes*, came for comfort, and sat till seven, when we all went to church.'

By Easter Tuesday the tour had been given up, and Johnson wrote to his mistress : ' Mr. Thrale's alteration of purpose is not weakness of resolution ; it is a wise man's compliance with the change of things, and with the new duties which the change produces. Whoever expects me to be angry, will be disappointed. I do not even grieve at the effect ; I grieve only at the cause.' Mrs. Thrale's fugitive visit to Bath had been a short one, for on Wednesday, April 10, she was again at home to receive Murphy, Johnson, and Boswell at dinner. It appears to have been now determined that a visit of the whole family to Bath should be substituted for foreign travel ; the weak state of Queeney's health was assigned as one motive for the change of plan, and Johnson expressed to Boswell his conviction of its reasonableness. The party appears to have been confined to familiar friends, and Mrs. Thrale took her usual share in the conversation, showing her

* 'Piozzi Letters,' i. 311.

knowledge of English literature by the remark that Pope's 'Dying Christian to his Soul' was partly borrowed from Flatman.*

The downfall of the hopes which the Thrales had built upon their son divided the attention of their circle with a topic of more general interest. Since the beginning of the year, their old acquaintance Garrick had withdrawn from Drury Lane Theatre, and had been succeeded there by a body of new proprietors, of whom Sheridan was the most important member. The retired manager, half sorry to be released, talked freely in all companies about himself and his past career with the pleasant vanity which distinguished him. Boswell tells us that on April 11 he dined with Johnson at General Paoli's, and mentioned his having that morning introduced to Garrick a Flemish nobleman of great rank and fortune, to whom Garrick spoke of Abel Drugger † as *a small part*, adding, with an appearance of grave recollection: 'If I were to begin life again, I think I should not play those low characters.' 'Upon which,' says Boswell, 'I observed: "Sir, you would be in the wrong, for your great excellence is your variety of playing, your representing so well characters so very different." JOHNSON: "Garrick, sir, was not in earnest in what he said, for, to be sure, his peculiar excellence is his variety, and, perhaps, there is not any one character which has not been as well acted by somebody else, as he could do it." BOSWELL: "Why then, sir, did he talk so?" JOHNSON: "Why, sir, to make you answer as you did."

* The lines borrowed from are :
> 'When on my sick bed I languish,
> Full of sorrow, full of anguish ;
> Fainting, gasping, trembling, crying,
> Panting, groaning, speechless, dying—
> Methinks I hear some gentle spirit say,
> Be not fearful ; come away.'
>
> Campbell's 'Brit. Poets,' p. 301.

† Abel Drugger is a character in Ben Jonson's 'Alchemist.'

BOSWELL: " I don't know, sir; he seemed to dip deep into his mind for the reflection." JOHNSON: " He had not far to dip, sir; he had said the same thing probably twenty times before." '

Murphy writes that Hogarth saw Garrick in Richard III., and on the following night in Abel Drugger, and was so struck that he said to him: 'You are in your element when you are begrimed with dirt, or up to your elbows in blood.'* Cooke, in his ' Memoirs of Macklin,' says that a Lichfield grocer, who came to London with a letter of introduction to Garrick from Peter Garrick, saw him act Abel Drugger, and returned without calling on him. He said to Peter Garrick: ' I saw enough of him on the stage. He may be rich, as I dare say any man who lives like him must be; but by ——, though he is your brother, Mr. Garrick, he is one of the shabbiest, meanest, most pitiful hounds I ever saw in the whole course of my life.'†

Soon after the dinner at General Paoli's, the Thrales and Johnson went to Bath, where, on April 26, they were joined by Boswell, who visited them at his own request. On the arrival of the latter, he found that Mr. and Mrs. Thrale were gone to the Rooms, leaving Johnson alone to entertain the new-comer for the evening. On this Dr. Birkbeck Hill exclaims: ' To the Rooms! and their only son dead three days over one month!' Yet it is clear that Dr. Johnson did not consider their behaviour at all heartless. On the contrary, he had advised Mrs. Thrale to return to her usual amusements as soon as possible, and Boswell, though charmed with Bath, did not find its pleasures very exciting; for in a letter to his friend Temple he quotes Quin's description of it as 'the cradle of age, and a fine slope to the grave.' He presently

* Murphy's 'Garrick,' p. 21.   † *Ibid.*, p. 110.

returned to London, 'to eat commons in the Inner Temple,' and was soon followed by Johnson, who came up to assist his friend Taylor in some law business which had brought the clergyman to town. After Johnson's departure, Mrs. Thrale wrote to him : ' Baretti said you would be very angry because this dreadful event made us put off our Italian journey, but I know you better. Who knows even now that 'tis deferred for ever ? Mr. Thrale says he shall not die in peace without seeing Rome, and I am sure he will go nowhere that he can help without you.'* Yet Johnson had more than once treated Mrs. Thrale rather roughly during his stay in Bath, checking one of her flights with the injunction, 'When you are calculating, calculate,' and another with a caution to beware of getting her wings clipped.

He wrote to her repeatedly from London. On May 16 he says: 'This is my third letter. Well, sure I shall have something to-morrow. Our business stands still. The doctor says I must not go ; and yet my stay does him no good. His solicitor says he is sick ; but I suspect he is sullen. The doctor, in the meantime, has his head as full as yours at an election. Livings and preferments, as if he were in want, with twenty children, run in his head. But a man must have his head on something small or great.†

In the same letter he describes the dinner with Wilkes, at Messrs Dilly's :

'For my part, I begin to settle and keep company with grave Aldermen. I dined yesterday in the Poultry with Mr. Alderman Wilkes,‡ and Mr. Alderman Lee,

---

* 'Piozzi Letters,' i. 317.   † *Ibid.*, i. 325.
‡ In April, 1769, the Court of Aldermen by a majority decided that Wilkes was disqualified for election as a member of their body. On his release from prison, in April, 1770, he was, however, admitted without a division. The Livery returned him for Lord Mayor at the head of the list in

and Councillor Lee, his brother. There sat you the while, so sober, with your W——s, and your H——s, and my aunt and her turnspit; and, when they are gone, you think by chance on Johnson, what is he doing? What should he be doing? He is breaking jokes with Jack Wilkes upon the Scots. Such, madam, are the vicissitudes of things. And there was Mrs. Knowles, the Quaker, that works the sutile* pictures, who is a great admirer of your conversation. She saw you at Mr. Shaw's, at the election time. She is a Staffordshire woman, and I am to go and see her. Staffordshire is the nursery of art; here they grow up till they are transplanted to London.†

'Yet it is strange that I hear nothing from you; I hope you are not angry or sick. Perhaps you are gone without me, for spite, to see places. That is natural enough, for evil is very natural; but I shall vex, unless it does you good.'

On the same day the lady was writing to her correspondent:

'I had no notion of your staying away from us so long, or you should not surely have wanted a letter; you might reasonably expect, and claim indeed, my best thanks for the sweet visit paid five days ago to my babies: a most friendly action in you, and a most polite one in dear Dr. Taylor, and what I had never been hoping for. All unexpected pleasures are doubly precious.

'Grata superveniet quæ non sperabitur hora.'

1772 and 1773, but he was in each case passed over by the Aldermen. In 1774 his brethren, having to choose between him and the retiring Lord Mayor, reluctantly admitted the popular favourite to the civic chair. In 1775 Boswell was not a little elated at receiving a complimentary letter from Lord Mayor Wilkes.—' Letters of Boswell,' p. 209.

* Misprinted by Mrs. Piozzi *futile*. Mrs. Knowles was famous for some kind of needlework.

† He is alluding to the fact that he was a Staffordshire man.

'We have a flashy friend here already, who is much your adorer; I wonder how you will like *him?* An Irishman he is; very handsome, very hot-headed, loud and lively, and sure to be a favourite with you, he tells us, for he can live with a man of ever *so odd a temper.* My master laughs, but likes him, and it diverts me to think what you will do when he professes that he could clean shoes for you; that he could shed his blood for you; with twenty mere extravagant flights—and you say, *I* flatter! *Upon my honour, sir, and indeed now,* as Dr. C——l's phrase is, *I am but a twitter to him.*'

'Well, you hate Bath, and will be very uncomfortable when you come this time, I believe; for, after all, I *must* be civil to my aunt, who is exceedingly kind to me; and I must dress and go out, and do like other people, or you will be first to censure and condemn me; more than that, our dear master, who cannot be quiet without you for a week, will be always infallibly on your side, and encourage long lectures about the fit of a cap, which you will not give me a minute to put on as it should be—so I see my fate before it arrives. Come to Bath, though, and at least convince yourself that we are not noting infelicities from which you are cruelly excluded.'*

The Irishman referred to in this letter appears to have been a Mr. Musgrave, who is humorously described in Madame d'Arblay's Diary. Despite flattery, however, and solicitation, Johnson seems to have remained in town. He is able to requite his mistress by good news of the brewery: 'To-day I went to look into my places at the Borough. I called on Mr. Perkins in the counting-house. He crows and triumphs, "As we go on we shall double our business." . . . Surely I shall get down to you next week.'† He did not get down, for when Dr.

* 'Piozzi Letters,' i. 327. † *Ibid.*, i. 333.

Taylor's business was done with he was still detained by an attack of gout, until his friends had left Bath. Not long after their return to Streatham came the long-impending rupture between the Thrales and Baretti. We give the principal passages from an account of the quarrel which Mrs. Thrale states that she wrote at the time:

'*July* 6, 1776.—This day is made remarkable by the departure of Mr. Baretti, who has since October, 1773, been our almost constant inmate, companion, and I vainly hoped, our friend. On the 11th of November, 1773, Mr. Thrale let him have £50, and at our return from France £50 more, besides his clothes and pocket money; in return to all this, he instructed our eldest daughter—or thought he did — and puffed her about the town for a wit, a genius, a linguist, etc. At the beginning of the year 1776 we purposed visiting Italy under his conduct, but were prevented by an unforeseen and heavy calamity: that Baretti, however, might not be disappointed of money as well as of pleasure, Mr. Thrale presented him with a hundred guineas, which at first calmed his wrath a little, but did not, perhaps, make amends for his vexation; this I am the more willing to believe, as Dr. Johnson not being angry too, seemed to grieve him no little, after all our preparations made.

'Now Johnson's virtue was engaged; and he, I doubt not, made it a point of conscience not to increase the distresses of a family oppressed with affliction. Baretti, however, from this time grew sullen and captious; he went on as usual, notwithstanding, making Streatham his home, carrying on business there, when he thought he had any to do, and teaching his pupil at by-times when he chose so to employ himself; for he always took his choice of hours, and would often spitefully fix on such as were particularly disagreeable to me, whom he has now not liked a long while, if ever he did. He professed, however, a violent attachment to our eldest daughter; said if she had died instead of her poor brother, he should have destroyed himself, with many as wild expressions of fondness. Within these few days, when my back was turned, he would often be telling her that he would go away and stay a month, with other threats of the same nature; and she, not being of a caressing or obliging disposition, never, I suppose, soothed his anger or requested his stay. . . .

'My daughter kept on telling me that Mr. Baretti was grown very odd and very cross, would not look at her exercises, but said he would leave this house soon, for it was no better than Pandemonium. Accordingly, the next day he packed up his cloke-bag, which he had not done for three years, and sent it to town; and while we were wondering what he would say about it at breakfast, he was walking to London himself, without taking leave of any one person, except it may be the girl, who owns they had much talk, in the course of which he expressed great aversion to me, and even to her, who, he said, he once thought well of.'

'Since our quarrel,' afterwards wrote the lady, 'I had occasion to talk of him with Tom Davies, who spoke with horror of his ferocious temper. "And yet," says I, "there is great sensibility about Baretti: I have seen tears often stand in his eyes." "Indeed," replies Davies, "I should like to have seen that sight vastly, when—even butchers weep."'

In what she wrote later, Mrs. Thrale gives some further particulars of the affronts she had received from Baretti, accusing him, among other things, of having said to her eldest daughter, 'that if her mother died in a lying-in, which happened while he lived here, he hoped Mr. Thrale would marry Miss Whitbred, who would be a pretty companion for her, and not tyrannical and overbearing like me.' It has been said to be unlikely that he would say this to the girl, but his friends evidently thought that his rash and passionate temper was capable of anything.

Johnson's short account written to Boswell* does not contain anything to throw doubt upon Mrs. Thrale's statement. 'Baretti went away from Thrale's in some whimsical fit of disgust or ill-nature, without taking any leave. It is well if he finds in any other place as good an habitation, and as many conveniences.' And Baretti had little or nothing to allege in his own defence, when in 1788 he told his story in the *European Magazine*.† He said: 'When madam took it into her head to give herself airs, and treat me with some coldness and superciliousness, I did not hesitate to set down at breakfast my dish of tea not half drunk, go for my hat and stick that lay in the corner of the room, turn my back to the house *insalutato hospite*, and walk away to London without uttering a syllable.' In another place‡ he wrote that Johnson had led him to expect that Thrale would give him an annuity for his trouble, and that, after waiting six years and a half without receiving a shilling, he grew tired at last, and on some provocation from Mrs. Thrale left them abruptly. He had, in fact, been less than three years in the family, and the presents in money had to be admitted by the writer of a notice of Baretti, which his friends published after his death.§

Baretti appears to have afterwards made it up with the Thrales; he states that, at the end of four years, they met him at a house near Beckenham, and coaxed him into a

---
* In a letter dated December 21, 1776, which Boswell prints.
† Vol. xiii. 398.   ‡ In a marginal note on 'Piozzi Letters,' i. 338.
§ See *Gent. Mag.* for May, 1789. The paper was written by Dr. Vincent, Dean of Westminster.

reconciliation, 'which,' adds he, 'as almost all reconciliations prove, was not very sincere on her side or mine; so that there was a total end of it on Mr. Thrale's demise, which happened about three years after.'* That some sort of seeming peace was patched up is clear, as we shall see from statements made by Mrs. Thrale herself, but Baretti is wrong in his dates, at all events, for Thrale did not survive the rupture five years altogether.

No incident worth mentioning distinguished the remainder of this year, the autumn of which was spent by the Thrales and Johnson at Brighton.

Mr. Hayward tells us† that Mrs. Thrale kept a copious diary and note-book, called 'Thraliana,' from 1776 to 1809. 'It is now,' [1861] he continues, 'in the possession of Mr. Salusbury,‡ who deems it of too private and delicate a character to be submitted to strangers, but has kindly supplied me with some curious passages from it.' The first entry is in these words: 'It is many years since Doctor Samuel Johnson advised me to get a little book, and write in it all the little anecdotes which might come to my knowledge, all the observations I might make or hear, all the verses never likely to be published, and, in fine, everything that struck me at the time. Mr. Thrale has now treated me with a repository, and provided it with the pompous title of "Thraliana." I must endeavour to fill it with nonsense new and old.—15th September, 1776.'

On an early page occurs the following:

'As this is "Thraliana," I will now write Mr. Thrale's character in it. It is not because I am in good or ill

---

* *European Magazine*, 1788. † Hayward's 'Piozzi,' i. 6.
‡ The Rev. G. A. Salusbury, Rector of Westbury, Salop, from whom Mr. Hayward obtained much of his information. This gentleman was the eldest son of Sir John Piozzi Salusbury, nephew of Piozzi, and adopted son of Mrs. Piozzi.

humour with him, or he with me, for we are not capricious people, but have, I believe, the same opinion of each other at all places and times.

'Mr. Thrale's person is manly, his countenance agreeable, his eyes steady, and of the deepest blue; his look neither soft nor severe, neither sprightly nor gloomy, but thoughtful and intelligent; his address is neither caressive nor repulsive, but unaffectedly civil and decorous; and his manner more completely free from every kind of trick or particularity than I ever saw any person's. He is a man wholly, as I think, out of the power of mimicry. He loves money, and is diligent to obtain it; but he loves liberality too, and is willing enough both to give generously, and to spend fashionably. His passions either are not strong, or else he keeps them under such command that they seldom disturb his tranquillity or his friends; and it must, I think, be something more than common which can affect him strongly, either with hope, fear, anger, love, or joy. His regard for his father's memory is remarkably great, and he has been a most exemplary brother; though, when the house of his favourite sister was on fire, and we were all alarmed with the account of it in the night, I well remember that he never rose, but, bidding the servant who called us to go to her assistance, quietly turned about, and slept to his usual hour. I must give another trait of his tranquillity on a different occasion. He had built great casks holding a thousand hogsheads each, and was much pleased with their profit and appearance. One day, however, he came down to Streatham as usual to dinner, and after hearing and talking of a hundred trifles, "But I forgot," says he, "to tell you how one of my great casks is burst, and all the beer run out."

'Mr. Thrale's sobriety, and the decency of his conversation, being wholly free from all oaths, ribaldry, and profaneness, make him a man exceedingly comfortable to live with; while the easiness of his temper, and slowness to take offence add greatly to his value as a domestic man. Yet I think his servants do not much love him, and I am not sure that his children have much affection for him; low people, almost all indeed agree to abhor him, as he has none of that officious and cordial manner which is universally required by them, nor any skill to dissemble his dislike of their coarseness. With regard to his wife, though little tender of her person, he is very partial to her understanding; but he is obliging to nobody, and confers a favour less pleasing than many a man refuses to confer one. This appears to me to be as just a character as can be given of the man with whom I have now lived thirteen years: and though he is extremely reserved and uncommunicative, yet one must know something of him after so long acquaintance. Johnson has a very great degree of kindness and esteem for him, and says if he would talk more his manner would be very completely that of a perfect gentleman.'*

* Hayward's 'Piozzi,' ii. 188.

CHAPTER V.

Visit to Dr. Burney's—The Lives of the Poets—Progress of the Brewery—Advice about 'Thraliana'—Boswell at Ashbourne—Dr. Taylor's Cattle and Waterfall—Mrs. Thrale in Low Spirits—Letters from Johnson—Her Alleged Inaccuracy—A Lecture—Precept and Practice—Johnson and Lord Marchmont—Cornelius Ford—A Ghost Story—Thrale over-brews himself—'Evelina' Published—Miss Burney Introduced at Streatham—Kindly Received—Second Visit—Johnson as an Inmate—His Opinions on Dress—Family Life at Streatham—Johnson's Domestic Economy—Lady Lade—Johnson's Portrait—The Brewery Prospers—The Black Dog—Discord in Bolt Court—Sophy Streatfield—Dr. Collier—Mrs. Thrale Jealous—Tears at Command—The Thrales at Brighton—Mr. Thrale has a Fit—Johnson's Sympathy—Thrale's Health Improves—Mrs. Thrale's Dislike of the Borough.

On March 19, 1777, Johnson wrote to Mrs. Thrale: 'You are all young and gay and easy; but I have miserable nights, and know not how to make them better; but I shift pretty well a-days, and so have at you all at Dr. Burney's to-morrow. I never thought of meeting you at Sir Joshua's, nor knew that it was a great day. But things, as sages have observed, happen unexpectedly; and you thought little of seeing me this fortnight, except to-morrow. But go where you will, and see if I do not catch you. When I am away, everybody runs away with you, and carries you among the grisettes, or whither they will. I hope you will find the want of me twenty times before you see me.'*

This letter refers to the first visit paid to Dr. Burney's house in St. Martin's Street, by the Thrale party, of which we have given an account elsewhere.†

* 'Piozzi Letters,' i. 345. † 'Fanny Burney and her Friends,' p. 51.

A few days later, Johnson had an interview, of which Lord Macaulay has spoken in a memorable passage: 'On Easter-Eve, 1777, some persons, deputed by a meeting, which consisted of forty of the first booksellers in London, called upon him. Though he had some scruples about doing business at that season, he received his visitors with much civility. They came to inform him that a new edition of the English poets, from Cowley downwards, was in contemplation, and to ask him to furnish short biographical prefaces. He readily undertook the task, a task for which he was pre-eminently qualified. His knowledge of the literary history of England since the Restoration was unrivalled. That knowledge he had derived partly from books, and partly from sources which had long been closed; from old Grub Street traditions; from the talk of forgotten poetasters and pamphleteers who had long been lying in parish vaults; from the recollections of such men as Gilbert Walmesley, who had conversed with the wits of Button; Cibber, who had mutilated the plays of two generations of dramatists; Orrery, who had been admitted to the society of Swift; and Savage, who had rendered services of no very honourable kind to Pope. The biographer therefore sat down to his task with a mind full of matter. He had at first intended to give only a paragraph to every minor poet, and only four or five pages to the greatest name. But the flood of anecdote and criticism overflowed the narrow channel. The work, which was originally meant to consist only of a few sheets, swelled into ten volumes.'* This paragraph is an expansion of what Mrs. Piozzi had expressed in a couple of sentences: 'Johnson's knowledge of literary history was extensive and surprising. He knew every adventure of every book

* Lord Macaulay's Miscellaneous Works, vol. ii., p. 298.

you could name almost, and was exceedingly pleased with the opportunity which writing the Poets' Lives gave him to display it.'*

Our information respecting the Thrales in 1777 is almost entirely derived from the correspondence that passed between them and Johnson, and mainly from the Doctor's share of it. When the ' Letters to and from the late Samuel Johnson, LL.D.' were published by Mrs. Piozzi in 1788, Miss Burney wrote : ' The few she has selected of her own do her much credit; she has discarded all that were trivial and merely local, and given only such as contain something instructive, amusing, and ingenious.'† At the present day we would willingly exchange most of these studied letters for a few of the discarded ones; the former, which show some awe of the writer's correspondent, exhibit less ease of style than her later productions; the latter would at least have thrown more light on her life and doings.

In the summer of 1777 Johnson made his usual journey into the Midlands, taking Oxford on his way. At the beginning of August he writes to Mrs. Thrale from University College that he has picked up some small materials for his Lives at the library, and he mentions a proposal of Boswell's to meet him during his excursion. ' Bozzy, you know,' he says, ' makes a huge bustle about all his own motions and all mine. I have enclosed a letter to pacify him, and reconcile him to the uncertainties of human life.' ‡

But Johnson's principal topic on his route is the prospects of the harvest, which the rapid growth of their business had made more than usually interesting and important to his master and mistress. Referring to a

* 'Anecdotes.'   † Madam d'Arblay's 'Diary.'
‡ 'Piozzi Letters,' i. 349, 350.

pool which Thrale was then making at Streatham, he says: 'My master may plant and dig till his pond is an ocean, if he can find water, and his parterre a down. I have no doubt of a most abundant harvest, and it is said that the produce of barley is particularly great. We are not far from the great year of a hundred thousand barrels, which, if three shillings be gained upon each barrel, will bring us fifteen thousand pounds a year. . . . But suppose we shall get but two shillings a barrel, that is ten thousand a year.'* Again, a few days later: 'But amidst all these little things there is one great thing. The harvest is abundant, and the weather *à la merveille*. No season ever was finer. Barley, malt, beer, and money. There is the series of ideas. The deep logicians call it a *sorites*. I hope my master will no longer endure the reproach of not keeping me a horse.'†

On September 6 he writes: 'As you have now little to do, I suppose you are pretty diligent at the "Thraliana," and a very curious collection posterity will find it. Do not remit the practice of writing down occurrences as they arise, of whatever kind, and be very punctual in annexing the dates. Chronology, you know, is the eye of history, and every man's life is of importance to himself. Do not omit painful casualties, or unpleasing passages; they make the variegation of existence; and there are many transactions of which I will not promise with Æneas, *et hæc olim meminisse juvabit*—yet that remembrance which is not pleasant may be useful.'‡

On September 13, from Ashbourne: 'Boswell, I believe, is coming. He talks of being here to-day. I shall be glad to see him. But he shrinks from the Baltick expedition, which I think is the best scheme in our power. What we shall substitute, I know not. He wants to see

---

* 'Piozzi Letters,' i. 357.   † *Ibid.*, i. 360.   ‡ *Ibid.*, i. 362.

Wales, but except the woods of Bâch y Graig, what is there in Wales? What that can fill the hunger of ignorance, or quench the thirst of curiosity? We may, perhaps, form some scheme or other, but, in the phrase of Hockley-in-the-Hole,* it is pity he has not a better bottom.' 'It appears,' says Boswell, 'that Johnson, now in his sixty-eighth year, was seriously inclined to realize the project of our going up the Baltick, which I had started when we were in the Isle of Skye.'

Again, on September 15:

'Do you call this punctual correspondence? There was poor I writing, and writing, and writing, on the 8th, on the 11th, on the 13th; and on the 15th I looked for a letter, but I may look and look. Instead of writing to me you are writing the "Thraliana." But—*he must be humble who would please.*

'Last night came Boswell. I am glad that he is come. He seems to be very brisk and lively, and laughs a little at . . . .

'You talk of pine-apples and venison. Pine-apples, it is sure, we have none; but venison, no forester that lived under the greenwood-tree ever had more frequently upon his table. We fry, and roast, and bake, and devour in every form.

'We have at last fair weather in Derbyshire, and everywhere the crops are spoken of as uncommonly exuberant. Let us now get money and have it. All that is paid is saved, and all that is laid out in land or malt. But I long to see twenty thousand pounds in the bank, and to see my master visiting this estate and that, as purchases

---

* Hockley-in-the-Hole was in Clerkenwell. In the *Spectator*, No. 436, Hockley-in-the-Hole is described as a place of no small renown for the gallantry of the lower order of Britons. In *The Beggar's Opera*, act i., Mrs. Peachum says to Filch: 'You should go to Hockley-in-the-Hole, and to Marylebone, child, to learn valour. These are the schools that have bred so many brave men.'

are advertised. But perhaps all this may be when Colin's forgotten and gone. Do not let me be forgotten before I am gone, for you will never have such another as,

'Dearest dear madam, your most humble servant.'*

On the 18th he wrote: 'Boswell is with us, in good humour, and plays his part with his usual vivacity.'† On this Baretti noted in his copy: 'That is, he makes more noise than anybody in company, talking and laughing loud.'‡

It was no doubt Dr. Taylor at whom Boswell laughed. That bucolic clergyman was, 'in his usual way, very busy with his cattle and his dogs.' He made Boswell ride with him over his farm, and showed him one cow which he had sold for a hundred and twenty guineas, and another for which he had been offered a hundred and thirty! Johnson in his letters from Ashbourne has frequent jokes about his host's cattle.§ He took more interest in an artificial cascade, which Dr. Taylor had formed by building a strong dyke of stone across the river behind his garden.

On October 1 Mrs. Thrale writes to him from Brighton in a fit of low spirits:

'In some letter lately you wonder at my using black

---

* 'Piozzi Letters,' i. 368. † *Ibid.*, i. 370.

‡ On p. 216 in vol i. he noted: 'Boswell is not quite right-headed, in my humble opinion.'

§ '*July* 23, 1770.—I have seen the great bull, and very great he is. I have seen, likewise, his heir apparent, who promises to inherit all the bulk, and all the virtues of his sire. I have seen the man who offered an hundred guineas for the young bull, while he was yet little better than a calf.' 'Piozzi Letters,' i. 33. '*July* 3, 1771.—The great bull has no disease but age. I hope in time to be like the great bull; and hope you will be like him, too, a hundred years hence. *Ibid.*, p. 39. '*July* 10, 1771.—There has been a man here to-day to take a farm. After some talk he went to see the bull, and said that he had seen a bigger. Do you think he is likely to get a farm?' *Ibid.*, p. 43. '*October* 31, 1772.—Our bulls and cows are all well; but we yet hate the man that had seen a bigger bull. Our waterfall at the garden makes a great roaring this wet weather.' *Ibid.*, p. 61.

wax—for the paper was only not gilt—as if you had forgotten my numberless reasons for *mourning*, because you are not perpetually hearing me recall them to your memory. Affliction, however, is very good for us all, I doubt not, or it would hardly be bestowed so liberally. The flower of an aloe tree is, I am told, so peculiarly sweet that bees, best judges in such a case, seek it from an immense distance; we know how bitter the stem is, and how rarely we are indulged with the blossom. . . .

'I cannot guess how long we are to stay here; Mr. Thrale does not tell me, and I am, as you say, no good *winder*. . . .

'When are we likely to meet? If the doctor's waterfall roars happily, I think there is little chance, for a month, of your quitting Ashbourne, except to show its environs to Mr. Boswell.'*

Mrs. Thrale certainly had abundant cause for sorrow. She had lost child after child, including both her sons. At this time she had borne eleven children, and had only four daughters living.

On October 6 Johnson wrote to her:

'Methinks you are now a great way off; and if I come, I have a great way to come to you; and then the sea is so cold, and the rooms are so dull; yet I do love to hear the sea roar, and my mistress talk—For when she talks, ye gods! how she will talk. I wish I were with you, but we are now near half the length of England asunder. It is frightful to think how much time must pass between writing this letter and receiving an answer, if any answer were necessary.

'Taylor is now going to have a ram; and then, after Aries and Taurus, we shall have Gemini. His oats are now in the wet; here is a deal of rain. . . .

* 'Piozzi Letters,' i. 391-4.

'When I come to town, I am to be very busy about my Lives. Could not you do some of them for me? ... I am glad master unspelled you, and run you all on rocks, and drove you about, and made you stir. Never be cross about it. Quiet and calmness you have enough of—a little hurry stirs life—and,

> '"Brushing o'er adds motion to the pool."
> DRYDEN.

'Now *pool* brings my master's excavations into my head. I wonder how I shall like them; I should like not to see them till we all see them together. He will have no waterfall to roar like the doctor's. I sat by it yesterday and read Erasmus's *Militis Christiani Enchiridion*. Have you got that book?

'Make my compliments to dear Queeney. I suppose she will dance at the Rooms; and your heart will go one knows not how.'*

A few days later he wrote: 'I cannot but think on your kindness and my master's. Life has, upon the whole, fallen short, very short, of my early expectation; but the acquisition of such a friendship, at an age when new friendships are seldom acquired, is something better than the general course of things gives man a right to expect. I think on it with great delight, I am not very apt to be delighted.'†

At the end of November Johnson wrote to Boswell: 'Mrs. Thrale is in hopes of a young brewer. They got by their trade last year a very large sum, and their expenses are proportionate.' The lady's hopes, as we shall see, were not destined to be fulfilled.

Boswell made a visit to Streatham at the end of March, 1778, his account of which illustrates his constant desire to depreciate Mrs. Thrale: 'I had before dinner

* 'Piozzi Letters,' ii. 2.   † *Ibid.*, ii. 7.

repeated a ridiculous story told me by an old man who had been a passenger with me in the stage-coach to-day. Mrs. Thrale, having taken occasion to allude to it in talking to me, called it "the story told you by the old *woman*." "Now, madam," said I, "give me leave to catch you in the fact; it was not an old *woman*, but an old *man*, whom I mentioned as having told me this." I presumed to take an opportunity, in presence of Johnson, of showing this lively lady how ready she was, unintentionally, to deviate from exact authenticity of narration.'

A more modest man than James would not have held his hostess bound to treasure up every syllable that had fallen from him while bestowing all his tediousness on the company.* The lady, moreover, would not admit that she had been guilty of any mistake. She wrote on the margin of the page containing Boswell's reflection: 'Mrs. Thrale knew there was no such thing as an old man; when a man gets superannuated they call him an old woman.' Boswell certainly had his full share of that extreme literalness which, according to Charles Lamb, incapacitates Scotchmen for understanding any indirect expression.

The biographer continues his attack: 'Next morning, while we were at breakfast, Johnson gave a very earnest recommendation of what he himself practised with the utmost conscientiousness: I mean a strict attention to truth, even in the most minute particulars. "Accustom your children," said he, " constantly to this; if a thing happened at one window, and they, when relating it, say that it happened at another, do not let it pass, but instantly

---

* Beauclerk wrote to Lord Charlemont in 1773: 'If you do not come here, I will bring all the club over to Ireland to live with you, and that will drive you here in your own defence. Johnson shall spoil your books, Goldsmith pull your flowers, and Boswell *talk to you*: stay then if you can.'—Charlemont's Life, i. 347.

check them; you do not know where deviation from truth will end." BOSWELL: "It may come to the door: and when once an account is at all varied in one circumstance, it may by degrees be varied so as to be totally different from what really happened." Our lively hostess, whose fancy was impatient of the rein, fidgeted at this, and ventured to say: "Nay, this is too much. If Mr. Johnson should forbid me to drink tea, I would comply, as I should feel the restraint only twice a day; but little variations in narrative must happen a thousand times a day, if one is not perpetually watching." JOHNSON: "Well, madam, and you *ought* to be perpetually watching. It is more from carelessness about truth than from intentional lying that there is so much falsehood in the world."'

Yet that the severe moralist did not, even in his published writings, invariably maintain the high standard of truth which he enforced upon others, Boswell himself bears witness. 'Dr. Johnson,' he says, 'was by no means attentive to minute accuracy in his "Lives of the Poets;"' and he mentions two instances of misstatements in the first impression of that work, which, though pointed out to the author, were continued by him in subsequent editions.* 'Johnson,' says Mr. Hayward, 'could be lax when it suited him; as, speaking of epitaphs: "The writer of an epitaph should not be considered as saying nothing but what is strictly true. Allowance must be made for some degree of exaggerated praise. In lapidary inscriptions a man is not upon oath." Is he upon oath in relating an anecdote? or could he do more than swear to the best of his recollection and belief if he was?'†

At the visit to Streatham just mentioned, Johnson, according to Boswell's account, had joined him in

* Boswell's 'Johnson' (Dr. Birkbeck Hill's edition), iii. 359, note 2; iv. 51, note 2.
† Hayward's 'Piozzi,' i. 278.

lecturing Mrs. Thrale; on the next occasion of his dining there, the Scotchman had accompanied Johnson on the invitation of the latter alone, a sufficient proof of the lady's good nature. Yet if we may believe the biographer, Johnson on their way down talked to him of 'a certain female friend's laxity of narration, and inattention to truth,' saying: 'Do talk to her of it: I am weary!' Of course, Mrs. Thrale is meant, and of course Boswell, though he printed this story in his book, was prudent enough to avoid a quarrel while good dinners were to be enjoyed at Streatham. He tells us that, on their arrival, Johnson was occupied for a considerable time in reading the 'Memoirs of Fontenelli,' leaning and swinging upon the low gate into the Court without his hat. We cannot wonder that, after reading what her revered friend was reported to have said of her behind her back, the lady should have had the malice to write opposite to this passage in her copy of Boswell's Life: 'I wonder how he liked the story of the asparagus'—a palpable hit at Johnson's selfishness at table. This time, however, Johnson, instead of crushing his hostess, turned upon the North Briton. At dinner Mrs. Thrale magnanimously expressed a wish to go and see Scotland. JOHNSON: 'Seeing Scotland, madam, is only seeing a worse England. It is seeing the flower gradually fade away to the naked stalk. Seeing the Hebrides, indeed, is seeing quite a different scene.'

Mrs. Thrale, on her part, was not afraid to hint her displeasure even to the great man himself when his behaviour appeared to be unreasonable. Thus, in the May following, officious Boswell had obtained from Lord Marchmont a promise to furnish information for the life of Pope, which Johnson was then about to write. 'Elated,' writes the biographer, 'with the success of my spontaneous exertion, I hastened down to Mr. Thrale's at Streatham, where he now was, that I might insure his being at home next day, and after dinner, when I thought he would receive the good news in the best humour, I announced it eagerly: "I have been at work for you to-day, sir. I have been with Lord Marchmont. He bade me tell you he has a great respect for you, and will call on you to-morrow at one o'clock, and communicate all he knows about Pope." JOHNSON: "I shall not be in town to-morrow. I don't care to know about Pope." Mrs. THRALE (surprised, and a little angry): "I suppose, sir, Mr. Boswell thought that, as you are to write Pope's life, you would wish to know about him." JOHNSON: Wish! why yes! If it rained knowledge I'd hold out my hand; but I would not give myself the trouble to go in quest of it." There was no arguing with him at the moment. Some time afterwards he said: "Lord Marchmont will call upon me, and then I shall call on Lord Marchmont." Mrs. Thrale was uneasy at this unaccountable caprice, and told me that if I did not take care to bring about a meeting between Lord Marchmont and him, it would never take place, which would be a great pity.'

'Of Johnson's pride,' says Northcote, 'I have heard Reynolds observe that if any man drew him into 'a state of obligation without his own consent, that man was the first he would affront by way of clearing off the account.'* On this afternoon, having duly snubbed his patient admirer, he recovered his temper, and fell into conversation on a licentious stanza attributed to Pope, and other matters, some of which would be deemed too delicate to be handled at a modern dinner-party.

During this talk, Boswell suddenly introduced a fresh topic. 'Among the numerous prints,' he says, 'pasted

* Northcote's 'Reynolds,' i. 71.

on the walls of the dining-room at Streatham, was Hogarth's "Modern Midnight Conversation."' Dr. Birkbeck Hill wonders whether the word *pasted* is here strictly used, and thinks it likely that the wealthy brewer, who had a taste for the fine arts, afforded Hogarth at least a frame. 'I asked him,' continues Boswell, 'what he knew of Parson Ford, who makes a conspicuous figure in the riotous group. . . . Was there not a story of his ghost having appeared?' An appeal of this kind was never addressed in vain to Johnson. It turned out that he knew a great deal about the parson, and all that there was to be known respecting his ghost. The Reverend Cornelius Ford was a cousin of Johnson, who had heard that he was 'a man of great parts, very profligate, but not impious.' He died at the Hummums* in Covent Garden, a place whither people resorted in those days to get themselves cupped. A waiter at the house, who had been absent when the death occurred, returned without knowing what had happened, and in his visits to the cellar met Ford twice. Learning that Ford was dead, he was seized with a fever, on recovering from which he said that he had a message to deliver to some women from the deceased. He went out to deliver it, and when he came back said that he had performed his errand, and that the women had exclaimed, 'Then we are all undone!' Dr. Pellet, continued Johnson, who was not a credulous man, inquired into the truth of this story, and he said the evidence was irresistible. The sage added that his own wife went to the Hummums to investigate the matter, and came away satisfied that it was true; but, he cautiously observed, the supernatural part of the narrative rested entirely on the word of the waiter.

* Baths are called Hummums in the East, and hence these hotels in Covent Garden, where there were baths, were called by that name.

These things to hear from their revered friend did Boswell and Mrs. Thrale seriously incline on that May evening. On the following day Johnson talked a great deal in very good humour. The history of these two days at Streatham, as told by Boswell, sets some of the peculiarities of the sage's temper and conversation in a very clear light, but we cannot afford space for illustrations unconnected with the place or the family. A few days afterwards Boswell returned to Scotland, where he heard from Johnson, under date of July 3: 'Mrs. Thrale, poor thing! has a daughter. Mr. Thrale dislikes the times, like the rest of us.' The lady is pitied because she has been disappointed of the young brewer, who had been hoped for; the cause of the brewer's discontent is explained in an entry made shortly after in 'Thraliana':

'*July* 18, 1778.—Mr. Thrale over-brewed himself last winter, and made an artificial scarcity of money in the family, which has extremely lowered his spirits. Mr. Johnson endeavoured last night, and so did I, to make him promise that he would never brew a larger quantity of beer in one winter than 80,000 barrels; but my Master, mad with the noble ambition of emulating Whitbread and Calvert, two fellows that he despises, could scarcely be prevailed on to promise even *this*, that he will not brew more than four score thousand barrels a year for five years to come. He did promise that much, however; and so Johnson bade me write it down in the "Thraliana"; and so the wings of speculation are clipped a little—very fain would I have pinioned her, but I had not strength to perform the operation.'*

In the summer of this year, the world was talking largely of a new novel by an anonymous writer. Succesful novels were much less common in those days than

---

* Hayward's 'Piozzi,' i. 74.

they are now; and great was the interest when it became known that the author of 'Evelina' was a child of Dr. Burney, historian of music, and a popular professor of the art. Being a constant visitor at Streatham Park, where he gave lessons to Queeney, the Doctor was at once invited to introduce the daughter who had suddenly become an object of curiosity. In the early part of August, 1778, Fanny Burney entered in her Diary an account of her first visit to Streatham, which had taken place a few days before:

"Our journey to Streatham was the least pleasant part of the day, for the roads were dreadfully dusty, and I was really in the fidgets for thinking what my reception might be, and from fearing they would expect a less awkward and backward kind of person than I was sure they would find.

"Mr. Thrale's house is white, and very pleasantly situated in a paddock. Mrs. Thrale was strolling about, and came to us as we got out of the chaise.

"She there received me, taking both my hands, and with mixed politeness and cordiality welcomed me to Streatham. She led me into the house, and addressed herself almost wholly for a few minutes to my father, as if to give me an assurance she did not mean to regard me as a show, or to distress or frighten me by drawing me out. Afterwards she took me upstairs, and showed me the house, and said she had very much wished to see me at Streatham, and should always think herself much obliged to Dr. Burney for his goodness in bringing me, which she looked upon as a very great favour.

"But though we were some time together, and though she was so very civil, she did not hint at my book, and I love her much more than ever for her delicacy in avoiding a subject which she could not but see would have greatly embarrassed me.

"When we returned to the music-room, we found Miss Thrale was with my father. Miss Thrale is a very fine girl, about fourteen years of age, but cold and reserved, though full of knowledge and intelligence.

"Soon after, Mrs. Thrale took me to the library: she talked a little while upon common topics, and then, at last, she mentioned 'Evelina.' . . .

"I now prevailed upon Mrs. Thrale to let me amuse myself, and she went to dress. I then prowled about to choose some book, and I saw upon the reading table 'Evelina.' I had just fixed upon a new translation of Cicero's 'Lælius,' when the library door was opened, and Mr. Seward* entered. I instantly put away my book, because I dreaded being thought studious and affected. He offered his service to find anything for me, and then, in the same breath, ran on to speak of the book with which I had myself 'favoured the world.'

"The exact words he began with I cannot recollect, for I was actually confounded by the attack, and his abrupt manner of letting me know he was *au fait* equally astonished and provoked me.† How different from the delicacy of Mr. and Mrs. Thrale!" After giving an account of the conversation at dinner, the Diary proceeds: "We left Streatham at about eight o'clock, and Mr. Seward, who handed me into the chaise, added his interest to the rest, that my father would not fail to bring me again next week to stay with them for some time."‡

---

* William Seward, F.R.S., author of 'Anecdotes of some Distinguished Persons' and 'Biographiana,' a sequel to the same. He was an intimate friend of the Thrales, and is not to be confounded with the Rev. Mr. Seward of Lichfield.

† 'Few people do him justice,' said Mrs. Thrale of Seward, 'because, as Dr. Johnson calls him, he is an abrupt young man; but he has excellent qualities, and an excellent understanding.'—Mme. d'Arblay's 'Diary,' new edition, i. 85.

‡ Mme. d'Arblay's 'Diary,' i. 21-25.

This second visit took place as proposed, and Miss Burney wrote of it:

"Our journey was charming. The kind Mrs. Thrale would give courage to the most timid. She did not ask me questions, or catechize me upon what I knew, or use any means to draw me out, but made it her business to draw herself out: that is, to start subjects, to support them herself, and take all the weight of the conversation, as if it behoved her to find me entertainment. But I am so much in love with her that I shall be obliged to run away from the subject, or I shall write of nothing else.

"When we arrived here, Mrs. Thrale showed me my room, which is an exceeding pleasant one, and then conducted me to the library, there to divert myself while she dressed.

"Miss Thrale soon joined me, and I began to like her. Mr. Thrale was neither well, nor in spirits all day. Indeed, he seemed not to be a happy man, though he has every means of happiness in his power. But I think I have rarely seen a very rich man with a light heart and light spirits.

"After dinner I had a delightful stroll with Mrs. Thrale, and she gave me a list of all her 'good neighbours' in the town of Streatham, and said she was determined to take me to see Mr. ——, the clergyman, who was a character I could not but be diverted with, for he had so furious and absurd a rage for building, that in his garden he had as many temples, and summer-houses, and statues as there are in the gardens of Stowe; though he had so little room for them, that they all seemed tumbling one upon another. In short, she was all unaffected drollery and sweet good humour.

"At tea we all met again, and Dr. Johnson was gaily sociable. He gave a very droll account of the children of Mr. Langton, 'who,' he said, 'might be very good children if they were let alone; but the father is never easy when he is not making them do something which they cannot do: they must repeat a fable, or a speech, or the Hebrew alphabet; and they might as well count twenty for what they know of the matter. However, the father says half, for he prompts every other word. But he could not have chosen a man who would have been less entertained by such means.'

"'I believe not!' cried Mrs. Thrale; 'nothing is more ridiculous than parents cramming their children's nonsense down other people's throats. I keep mine as much out of the way as I can.'

"'Yours, madam,' answered he, 'are in nobody's way; no children can be better managed, or less troublesome; but your fault is a too great perverseness in not allowing anybody to give them anything. Why should they not have a cherry, or a gooseberry, as well as bigger children?' . . .

"Indeed, the freedom with which Dr. Johnson condemns whatever he disapproves is astonishing; and the strength of words he uses would, to most people, be intolerable; but Mrs. Thrale seems to have a sweetness of disposition that equals all her other excellences, and far from making a point of vindicating herself, she generally receives his admonitions with the most respectful silence. . . .*

"*Saturday morning.*—Dr. Johnson was again all himself, and so civil to me—even admiring how I dressed myself. Indeed, it is well I have so much of his favour, for it seems he always speaks his mind concerning the dress of ladies, and all ladies who are here obey his injunctions implicitly, and alter whatever he disapproves. This is a part of his character that much surprises me; but notwithstanding he is sometimes so absent, and always so

* Mme. d'Arblay's 'Diary,' i. 29-31.

near-sighted, he scrutinizes into every part of almost everybody's appearance. . . .

"We had been talking of colours, and of the fantastic names given to them, and why the palest lilac should be called a *soupir étouffé.*

"'Why, madam,' said he, with wonderful readiness, 'it is called a stifled sigh because it is checked in its progress, and only half a colour.'

"I could not help expressing my amazement at his universal readiness upon all subjects, and Mrs. Thrale said to him:

"'Sir, Miss Burney wonders at your patience with such stuff; but I tell her you are used to me, for I believe I torment you with more foolish questions than anybody else dares do.'

"'No, madam,' said he, 'you don't torment me—you tease me, indeed, sometimes.'

"'Ay, so I do, Dr. Johnson, and I wonder you bear with my nonsense.'

"'No, madam, you never talk nonsense; you have as much sense, and more wit, than any woman I know!'

"'Oh,' cried Mrs. Thrale, blushing, 'it is my turn to go under the table this morning, Miss Burney!'*

"*Streatham, August* 26.—My opportunities for writing grow less and less, and my materials more and more. After breakfast, I have scarcely a moment that I can spare all day. Mrs. Thrale I like more and more. Of all the people I have ever seen since I came into this "gay and gaudy world," I never before saw the person who so strongly resembles our dear father. I find the likeness perpetually; she has the same natural liveliness, the same general benevolence, the same rare union of gaiety and of feeling in the disposition.

* Mme. d'Arblay's 'Diary,' i. 40, 41.

"And so kind is she to me! She told me, at first, that I should have all my mornings to myself, and therefore I have actually studied to avoid her, lest I should be in her way; but since the first morning she seeks me, sits with me, saunters with me in the park, or compares notes over books in the library; and her conversation is delightful; it is so entertaining, so gay, so enlivening, when she is in spirits, and so intelligent and instructive when she is otherwise, that I almost as much wish to record all she says as all Dr. Johnson says. Proceed—no! Go back, my muse, to Thursday. Dr. Johnson came home to dinner.

"In the evening, he was as lively, and full of wit and sport as I have ever seen him, and Mrs. Thrale and I had him quite to ourselves, for Mr. Thrale came in from giving an election dinner (to which he sent two bucks and six pine-apples) so tired that he neither opened his eyes nor his mouth, but fell fast asleep. Indeed, after tea he generally does.

"Dr. Johnson was very communicative concerning his present work of the 'Lives of the Poets'; Dryden is now in the press, and he told us he had been just writing a dissertation upon 'Hudibras.'"*

Miss Burney made another visit to Streatham in September. On her arrival Dr. Johnson was absent, having gone to stay with his friend Bennet Langton, who was a captain in the Lincolnshire Militia, and then stationed with his regiment at Warley Camp.† Three days later, however, he returned, to her great joy. "At

---

* Mme. d'Arblay's 'Diary,' i. 44.
† A threat of invasion by the united forces of France and Spain, at the time when we were at war with America, had caused the militia to be called out. 'We shall at least not doze as we used to do in summer. The Parliament is to have only short adjournments; and our senators, instead of retiring to horse-races (*their* plough), are all turned soldiers, and disciplining militia. Camps everywhere.'—Horace Walpole to Mann, May 31, 1778.

tea-time," she writes, "the subject turned upon the domestic economy of Dr. Johnson's own household.

"Mr. Thrale: 'And pray who is clerk of your kitchen, Sir?'"

"Dr. Johnson: 'Why, Sir, I am afraid there is none. A general anarchy prevails in my kitchen, as I am told by Mr. Levet, who says it is not now what it used to be.'

"Mrs. Thrale: 'Mr. Levet, I suppose, Sir, has the office of keeping the hospital in health?—for he is an apothecary.'

"Dr. Johnson: 'Levet, Madam, is a brutal fellow, but I have a good regard for him; for his brutality is in his manners, not his mind.'

"Mr. Thrale: 'But how do you get your dinners dressed?'

"Dr. Johnson: 'Why, Desmoulins has the chief management of the kitchen; but our roasting is not magnificent, for we have no jack.'

"Mr. Thrale: 'No jack! Why, how do they manage without?'

"Dr. Johnson: 'Small joints, I believe, they manage with a string, and larger are done at the tavern. I have some thoughts' (with a profound gravity) 'of buying a jack, because I think a jack is some credit to a house.'

"Mr. Thrale: 'Well, but you'll have a spit, too?'

"Dr. Johnson: 'No, Sir, no; that would be superfluous; for we shall never use it; and if a jack is seen, a spit will be presumed.'

"Mrs. Thrale: 'But pray, Sir, who is the Poll you talk of?—she that you used to abet in her quarrels with Mrs. Williams, and call out, "At her again, Poll! Never flinch, Poll!"'

"Dr. Johnson: 'Why, I took to Poll very well at first, but she won't do upon a nearer examination.'

"MRS. THRALE: 'How came she among you, Sir?'

"DR. JOHNSON: 'Why, I don't rightly remember, but we could spare her very well from us. Poll is a stupid slut. I had some hopes of her at first; but when I talked to her tightly and closely, I could make nothing of her; she was wiggle-waggle, and I could never persuade her to be categorical.'"*

During this visit Miss Burney met another member of the Thrale family, of whom she gives no very flattering account. In describing the guests at a dinner-party, she writes: "Lady Lade—I ought to have begun with her. I beg her ladyship a thousand pardons—though if she knew my offence I am sure I should not obtain one. She is own sister to Mr. Thrale. She is a tall and stout woman; has an air of mingled dignity and haughtiness, both of which wear off in conversation. She dresses very youthful and gaily, and attends to her person with no little complacency. She appears to me uncultivated in knowledge, though an adept in the manners of the world, and all that. She chooses to be much more lively than her brother; but liveliness sits as awkwardly upon her as her pink ribbons. . . . . Lady Lade has been very handsome, but is now, I think, quite ugly—at least, she has a sort of face I like not."†

At another time, when finding fault with a bandeau then in fashion, Johnson said: 'The truth is, women, take them in general, have no idea of grace. Fashion is all they think of. I don't mean Mrs. Thrale and Miss Burney, when I talk of women!—they are goddesses! and therefore I except them.'

"MRS. THRALE: 'Lady Lade never wore a bandeau, and said she never would, because it is unbecoming.'

"DR. JOHNSON (laughing): 'Did not she? Then is

* Mme. d'Arblay's 'Diary,' i. 63. † *Ibid.*, i. 86.

Lady Lade a charming woman, and I have yet hopes of entering into engagements with her!'

"MRS. THRALE: 'Well, as to that, I can't say; but, to be sure, the only similitude I have yet discovered in you, is in size; there you agree mighty well.'

"DR. JOHNSON: 'Why, if anybody could have worn the bandeau, it must have been Lady Lade; for there is enough of her to carry it off; but you are too little for anything ridiculous; that which seems nothing upon a Patagonian, will become very conspicuous upon a Lilliputian; and of you there is so little in all, that one single absurdity would swallow up half of you.'"*

Mrs. Thrale and Madame d'Arblay paint Johnson at Streatham in very different colours from those which he usually wears in Boswell's pages. When his biographer met him in London, he was for the most part either at home, or in the company of men only. In October, 1778, he was at Bolt Court ill, and wrote thence in low spirits to his mistress, who was at Brighton:—

"You that are among all the wits, delighting and delighted, have little need of entertainment from me, whom you left at home unregarded and unpitied, to shift in a world to which you have made me so much a stranger. Yet I know you will pretend to be angry if I do not write a letter, which, when you know the hand, you will perhaps lay aside to be read when you are dressing to-morrow; and which, when you have read it, if that time ever comes, you will throw away into the drawer and say—'stuff'! . . . . I have sat twice to Sir Joshua, and he seems to like his own performance. He has projected another, in which I am to be busy; but we can think on it at leisure. . . . .

"Now miss has seen the camp, I think she should

* Mme. d'Arblay's 'Diary,' i. 67.

write some account of it. A camp, however familiarly we may speak of it, is one of the great scenes of human life. War and peace divide the business of the world. Camps are the habitation of those who conquer kingdoms, or defend them.

"But what are wits, and pictures, and camps, and physick? There is still a nearer concern to most of us.—Is my master come to himself? Does he talk, and walk, and look about him, as if there were yet something in the world for which it is worth while to live? Or does he yet sit and say nothing? He was mending before he went, and surely he has not relapsed."*

Nine days later he wrote: "You appear to me to be now floating on the spring-tide of prosperity, on a tide not governed by the moon, but as the moon governs your heads; on a tide, therefore, which is never likely to ebb but by your own faults. I think it very probably in your power to lay up eight thousand pounds a year for every year to come, increasing all the time, what needs not be increased, the splendour of all external appearance. And surely such a state is not to be put into yearly hazard for the pleasure of *keeping the house full*, or the ambition of *outbrewing Whitbread*. Stop now, and you are safe—stop a few years, and you may go safely on thereafter, if to go on shall seem worth the while."†

Again, on October 31 :—"Long live Sir John Shelley that lures my master to hunt. I hope he will soon shake off the black dog, and come home as light as a feather. And long live Mrs. G——, that downs my mistress. I hope she will come home as flexible as a rush. . . . Sir Joshua has finished my picture, and it seems to please everybody, but I shall wait to see how it pleases you."‡

---

* 'Piozzi Letters,' ii. 20. † *Ibid.*, ii. 24. ‡ *Ibid.*, ii. 26.

The picture here referred to is the familiar portrait of Johnson, which was one of the Streatham portraits to be presently mentioned.

Mrs. Thrale says in reply: '*I* have lost what made my happiness in all seasons of the year; but the black dog shall not make prey of both my master and myself. My master swims now, and forgets the black dog.'*

Thrale, having surmounted the temporary embarrassment caused by his over-brewing in the previous winter, recovered a portion of his spirits; but his sorrow for the loss of his male heir was more deep-seated and corroding than his wife's. Baretti, in a marginal note on the 'Piozzi Letters,' says: 'Mr. Thrale, who was a worldly man, and followed the direction of his own feelings with no philosophical or Christian distinctions, having lost the strong hope of being one day succeeded in the profitable brewery by the only son he had left, gave himself silently up to his grief, and fell in a few years a victim to it.' In a later note he says: 'The poor man could never subdue his grief on account of his son's death.'

Johnson, while seeking to rouse his friend, was suffering from domestic troubles of his own. His letters speak of scolds between Mrs. Williams and Mrs. Desmoulins, and of Levet standing at bay, *fierce as ten furies*. At length, on November 14, he writes:—

"I really think I shall be very glad to see you all safe at home. I shall easily forgive my master his long stay, if he leaves the dog behind him. We will watch, as well as we can, that the dog shall never be let in again, for when he comes, the first thing he does is to worry my master. This time he gnawed him to the bone. Content, said Rider's almanack, makes a man richer than the Indies. But surely he that has the Indies

* 'Piozzi Letters,' ii. 32.

in his possession, may, without very much philosophy, make himself content. So much for my master and his dog, a vile one it is, but I hope if he is not hanged, he is drowned; with another lusty shake he will pick my master's heart out. . . . Mr. Macbean has no business. We have tolerable concord at home, but no love. Williams hates everybody. Levet hates Desmoulins, and does not love Williams. Desmoulins hates them both. Poll loves none of them. . . .

"Mrs. Queeney might write to me, and do herself no harm; she will neglect me till I shall take to Susy, and then Queeney may break her heart, and who can be blamed? I am sure I have stuck to Queeney as long as I could."*

Shortly before she made acquaintance with Miss Burney, Mrs. Thrale had grown intimate with another young lady, who, like herself, had been a pupil of Dr. Collier. Sophia Streatfield, the beautiful daughter of a handsome and wealthy widow, had studied Greek under the learned Civilian. Though growing infirm from age when they first met, the preceptor inspired his fair scholar with an attachment even warmer than that which had subsisted between him and Hester Salusbury. At the end of several years, he died in her house, and was buried at her expense. She and Mrs. Thrale were afterwards thrown together at Brighton, and having often heard of each other, at once became fast friends. The elder at first had nothing but praise for the younger, and was never tired of listening to her stories of their old master. Presently, however, jealousy arose between the two ladies. The matron observed, or fancied she observed, that Sophy, not contented with her legitimate succession to the heart of Dr. Collier, was endeavouring to supplant herself in the

* 'Piozzi Letters,' ii. 37.

esteem of Mr. Thrale. 'No wonder,' she wrote,* 'that Mr. Thrale, whose mind wanted some new object since he has lost his son, and lost besides the pleasure he had taken in his business, encouraged a sentimental attachment to Sophia Streatfield, who became daily more and more dear to him, and almost necessary.' Her husband, she complained, absented himself from home, and spent his time in Clifford Street, where the Streatfields lived. 'Miss Browne,' she adds, 'who sang enchantingly, and had been much abroad, and Miss Burney, whose powers of amusement were many and various, were *my* companions then at Streatham Park, with Dr. Johnson; who wanted me to be living in the Borough, because less inconvenient to him, and so said that I passed my winter in Surrey, feeding my chickens and starving my understanding.'†

In January, 1779, she made the following entry in 'Thraliana': 'Mr. Thrale is fallen in love, really and seriously, with Sophy Streatfield; but there is no wonder in that; she is very pretty, very gentle, soft, and insinuating; hangs about him, dances round him, cries when she parts from him, squeezes his hand slyly, and with her sweet eyes full of tears looks so fondly in his face—and all for love of me as she pretends—that I can hardly sometimes help laughing in her face.'‡

The fair S. S., as Sophy Streatfield was familiarly called at Streatham Park, was first seen there by Miss Burney in February, 1779, and is frequently mentioned by the latter in her Diary: "I find her a very amiable girl, and extremely handsome; not so wise as I expected, but very well; however, had she not chanced to have had so uncommon an education, with respect to literature or

* In a note on a copy of the 'Piozzi Letters.' † Hayward's 'Piozzi,' ii. 36.
‡ *Ibid.*, i. 111.

learning, I believe she would not have made her way among the wits by the force of her natural parts.

"Mr. Seward, you know, told me that she had tears at command, and I begin to think so too, for when Mrs. Thrale, who had previously told me I should see her cry, began coaxing her to stay, and saying, 'If you go, I shall know you don't love me so well as Lady Gresham,' she did cry—not loud, indeed, nor much, but the tears came into her eyes, and rolled down her fine cheeks.

"'Come hither, Miss Burney,' cried Mrs. Thrale, 'come and see Miss Streatfield cry!'

'I thought it a mere badinage. I went to them, but when I saw real tears I was shocked, and saying, 'No, I won't look at her,' ran away frightened, lest she should think I laughed at her, which Mrs. Thrale did so openly, that, as I told her, had she served me so, I should have been affronted with her ever after.

"Miss Streatfield, however, whether from a sweetness not to be ruffled, or from not perceiving there was any room for taking offence, gently wiped her eyes, and was perfectly composed."*

Miss Burney mentions another scene of the same kind as having occurred a little later:

"'Seward,' said Mrs. Thrale, 'had affronted Johnson, and then Johnson affronted Seward, and then S. S. cried.' . . .

"SIR PHILIP CLERKE: 'Well, I have heard so much of these tears, that I would give the universe to have a sight of them.'

"MRS. THRALE: 'Well, she shall cry again, if you like it.'

"S. S.: 'No, pray, Mrs. Thrale.'

"SIR PHILIP: 'Oh, pray do! pray let me see a little of it.'

---

* Mme. d'Arblay's 'Diary,' i. 135.

"MRS. THRALE : 'Yes, do cry a little, Sophy' (in a wheedling voice), 'pray do! Consider, now, you are going to-day, and it's very hard if you won't cry a little; indeed, S. S., you ought to cry.'

"Now for the wonder of wonders. When Mrs. Thrale, in a coaxing voice, suited to a nurse soothing a baby, had run on for some time—while all the rest of us, in laughter, joined in the request—two crystal tears came into the soft eyes of the S. S. and rolled gently down her cheeks! Such a sight I never saw before, nor could I have believed. She offered not to conceal or dissipate them; on the contrary, she really contrived to have them seen by everybody. She looked, indeed, uncommonly handsome; for her pretty face was not, like Chloe's, blubbered; it was smooth and elegant, and neither her features nor complexion were at all ruffled; nay, indeed, she was smiling all the time.

"'Look, look!' cried Mrs. Thrale; 'see if the tears are not come already.'

"Loud and rude bursts of laughter broke from us all at once. How, indeed, could they be restrained?"*

In the last days of May, 1779, the Thrales, accompanied by Miss Burney, went to their house at Brighton, where they were joined by Arthur Murphy. Miss Burney writes :—

" Just before we went to dinner a chaise drove up to the door, and from it issued Mr. Murphy. He met with a very joyful reception, and Mr. Thrale, for the first time in his life, said he was 'a good fellow,' for he makes it a sort of rule to salute him with the title of 'scoundrel' or 'rascal.' They are very old friends, and I question if Mr. Thrale loves any man so well. . . . Mr. Murphy was the life of the party; he was in good spirits, and extremely entertaining; he told a million of stories admirably well.'

* Mme. d'Arblay's ' Diary,' i. 154.

A day or two afterwards: "We had a very grand dinner to-day (though nothing to a Streatham dinner) at the Ship Tavern, where the officers mess, to which we were invited by the Major and Captain." As the Major was a man of at least £8,000 a year, and the Captain of £4,000 or £5,000, the dinner was likely to be grand enough. "The supper was very gay; Mrs. Thrale was in high spirits, and her wit flashed with incessant brilliancy. Mr. Murphy told several stories with admirable humour, and the Bishop of Peterborough was a worthy third in contributing towards general entertainment."*

After a few days' stay the party returned to Streatham, and at the beginning of June Mr. Thrale had his first attack of apoplexy. He had slept at Streatham Park, and left it after breakfast looking as usual. His sister's husband, Mr. Nesbitt, had recently died, and he had gone to the widow's house to hear the will read. There he was taken ill during dinner; his head sank upon the table, and as soon as he was able to raise it, he was found to be unconscious; his speech was confused, and he seemed to know nobody. Mrs. Nesbitt and her lady companion thought he was delirious; 'instead of calling help, they called their carriage, and brought him five or six miles out of town in that condition—was it not enough to enrage one?' says Mrs. Thrale indignantly. Dr. Burney and his daughter seem to have been at Streatham when the sick man arrived, and to have at once proceeded to London in search of medical aid. Fanny, who returned immediately afterwards, reports that he was much better before the physician came, though he was not himself again for three days. 'At dinner,' she writes, 'everybody tried to be cheerful; but a dark and gloomy cloud hangs over the head of poor Mr. Thrale, which no flashes of merriment

* Mme. d'Arblay's 'Diary,' i. 144.

or beams of wit can pierce through; yet he seems pleased that everybody should be gay, and desirous to be spoken to and of as usual.'*

Johnson had started for Lichfield and Ashbourne before the Thrales went to Brighton, and did not return to London till the close of June. On May 29 he wrote: 'It is good to wander a little, lest one should dream that all the world was Streatham, of which one may venture to say, *none but itself can be its parallel*.' After hearing the bad news he wrote again: 'I am the more alarmed by this violent seizure, as I can impute it to no wrong practices or intemperance of any kind. . . . What can he reform? or what can he add to his regularity and temperance? He can only sleep less.' Baretti, in a note on this, says: 'Dr. Johnson knew that Thrale would eat like four, let physicians preach. . . . Maybe he did not know it, so little did he mind what people were doing. Though he sat by Thrale at dinner, he never noticed whether he eat much or little. A strange man!'

But Johnson's want of observation certainly did not arise from indifference. On June 24 he wrote to Mrs. Thrale:

'You really do not use me well in thinking that I am in less pain on this occasion than I ought to be. There is nobody left for me to care about but you and my master, and I have now for many years known the value of his friendship and the importance of his life too well not to have him very near my heart. I did not at first understand his danger, and when I knew it, I was told likewise that it was over—and over I hope it is for ever. . . . Do what you can, however, to keep my master cheerful and slightly busy till his health is confirmed; and if we can be sure of that, let Mr. Perkins go to Ireland

* Mme. d'Arblay's 'Diary,' i. 149.

and come back as opportunity offers, or necessity requires, and keep yourself airy, and be a sunny little thing.'*

On July 30 Miss Burney wrote to her friend Crisp: 'I have the pleasure to tell you that Mr. Thrale is as well as ever he was in health, though the alarming and terrible blow he so lately received has, I fear, given a damp to his spirits that will scarce ever be wholly conquered. Yet he grows daily rather more cheerful; but the shock was too rude and too cruel to be ever forgotten.'†

At the time of the brewer's seizure, his wife was expecting to become a mother for the thirteenth time. 'A quarrel among the clerks,' she wrote afterwards, 'which I was called to pacify, made a complete finish of the child, and nearly of me. The men were reconciled, though, and my danger accelerated their reconcilement.'

Early in October the family went to their house at Brighton, taking Fanny Burney with them, and stopping to visit Sevenoaks and Tunbridge Wells by the way. Johnson remained in London, in better spirits than usual, though suffering a little from gout, and harassed by the dissensions in his household. On October 28 he wrote: 'I eat meat seldom, and take physic often, and fancy that I grow light and airy. A man that does not begin to grow light and airy at seventy is certainly losing time, if he intends ever to be light and airy.'‡ The news from Sussex helped to keep him cheerful: 'I hear from everybody that Mr. Thrale grows better. He is *columen domus*; and if he stands firm, little evils may be overlooked.'§ He wrote to Mrs. Thrale on November 7: 'My master, I hope, hunts and walks and courts the belles, and shakes Brighthelmstone. When he comes back, frolic and active, we

---

* 'Piozzi Letters,' ii. 56.   † Mme. d'Arblay's 'Diary,' i. 167.
‡ 'Piozzi Letters,' ii. 73.
§ *Ibid.*, ii. 77. Mrs. Thrale was suffering from toothache.

will make a feast, and drink his health, and have a noble day. . . . Have you any assemblies at this time of the year? And does Queeney dance? And does Burney dance too? I would have Burney dance with C——,* and so make all up. Discord keeps her residence in this habitation, but she has for some time been silent. We have much malice, but no mischief. Levet is rather a friend to Williams, because he hates Desmoulins more. A thing that he should hate more than Desmoulins is not to be found.'† Again nine days later he says: 'At home we do not much quarrel; but perhaps the less we quarrel the more we hate. There is as much malignity amongst us as can well subsist, without any thoughts of daggers or poisons.'‡

His correspondent wrote after his death: 'He really was oftentimes afraid of going home, because he was so sure to be met at the door with numberless complaints; and he used to lament pathetically to me that they made his life miserable from the impossibility he found of making theirs happy, when every favour he bestowed on one was wormwood to the rest. If, however, I ventured to blame their ingratitude, and condemn their conduct, he would instantly set about softening the one and justifying the other, and finished commonly by telling me that I knew not how to make allowances for situations I had never experienced.'§

The improvement in Thrale's health appears to have continued to the end of the year, but there were occasional fluctuations which caused his wife much uneasiness. At one moment she conceived the idea of inducing her husband to vest his business in trustees, and to remove

---

* Cumberland, who was then at Brighton, and of course jealous of the author of 'Evelina.'
† 'Piozzi Letters,' ii. 79.   ‡ *Ibid.*, ii. 93.   § 'Anecdotes.'

with his family to the West-end. One motive which she assigned for these proposals was fear of embarrassment from expensive additions which the sick brewer was tempted to make to his premises. In the letter last quoted from, Johnson comments on her scheme with his customary freedom of language:

"I do not see who can be trustee for a casual and variable property, for a fortune yet to be acquired. The trade must be carried on by somebody who must be answerable for the debts contracted. This can be none but yourself; unless you deliver up the property to some other agent, and trust the chance both of his prudence and his honesty. Do not be frighted; trade could not be managed by those who manage it, if it had much difficulty. Their great books are soon understood, and their language—

> 'If speech it may be call'd, that speech is none
> Distinguishable in number, mood, or tense'—

is understood with no very laborious application... What Mr. Scrase says about the Borough is true, but is nothing to the purpose. A house in the square will not cost so much as building in Southwark; but buildings are more likely to go on in Southwark if your dwelling is at St. James's. Everybody has some desire that deserts the great road of prosperity, to look for pleasure in a bye-path. I do not view with so much indignation Mr. Thrale's desire of being the first Brewer, as your despicable dread of living in the Borough.... Of this folly let there be an end—at least, an intermission.'*

This plain-speaking had its effect for the time; and the Thrales spent the winter in Southwark as usual.

Meanwhile the lady continued to be vexed by jealousy

* 'Piozzi Letters,' ii. 92.

of the fair S. S. 'Here is Sophy Streatfield again,' she wrote, 'handsomer than ever, and flushed with new conquests; the Bishop of Chester* feels her power, I am sure; she showed me a letter from him. I repeated to her out of Pope's Homer: " Very well, Sophy," cried I :

> '" Range undisturbed among the hostile crew,
> But touch not Hinchcliffe,† Hinchcliffe is my due."

'Miss Streatfield,' says my master, 'could have quoted these lines in the Greek; his saying so piqued me, and piqued me because it was true. I wish I understood Greek! Mr. Thrale's preference of her to me never vexed me so much as my consciousness—or fear, at least —that he has reason for his preference. She has ten times my beauty, and five times my scholarship; wit and knowledge she has none.'‡

'This incomprehensible girl,' as Mrs. Thrale called her, harassed the latter down to the time of her husband's death, and afterwards. Thrale fondled her when he was well; she sat by his sick-bed; when he was gone she teased the widow with tales of his passion for her; and then went in quest of fresh admirers. No one ever impugned Sophy's character; she was engaged for many years to a clergyman; but she finally died an old maid. She was everybody's admiration, and nobody's choice.

* Dr. Porteous, afterwards Bishop of London.
† For Hector. Hinchcliffe was Bishop of Peterborough.
‡ Hayward's 'Piozzi,' i. 113.

CHAPTER VI.

Mr. Thrale has a Second Fit—Recruits at Bath—Anxiety about him—Society at Bath—Melmoth—An Election in Prospect—Mrs. Thrale visits Southwark—Her Activity—Johnson Flattered—The Life of Congreve—The Gordon Riots—Alarm at Bath—The Brewery Saved—Address of Perkins—The Thrales Flee from Bath—Quiet Restored in London—Zeal of John Wilkes—Anecdotes—Perkins Rewarded—Johnson and Queeney—Mrs. Cholmondely—Seventy-Two—Bolt Court—Thrale Loses his Seat—His Health Declines—The Streatham Portraits—Verses on Them by Mrs. Thrale—The Library at Streatham Park—Grosvenor Square—Conversazione—Other Entertainments—A Foreign Tour Projected—Signs of Danger—Voracious Appetite—Sudden Death—Johnson's Grief—He Comforts the Widow—The Will—The Executors—Distress of Mrs. Thrale—The Trade to be Carried on—Johnson's Mercantile Ardour—The Brewery Sold—The Barclays—The Summer at Streatham—Johnson and Pepys—Piozzi and Sacchini—Mrs. Thrale and Fanny Burney.

MR. THRALE never completely recovered from his first attack of apoplexy. His appetite, at all times immoderate, became morbidly voracious.

'Cibus omnis in illo
Causa cibi est; semperque locus fit inanis edendo,'*

was the quotation, more apt than feeling, by which his wife afterwards described his state at this time. He was incapable of self-control, and would suffer no remonstrance. 'Nobody,' says Baretti, 'ever had spirit enough to tell him that his fits were apoplectic: such is the blessing of being rich, that nobody dares to speak out.' He had a second seizure at his house in the Borough, towards the end of February, 1780: was bled till he fainted; and after a prolonged struggle, rallied, contrary

* Ovid, Met., viii. 841, 842.

to the expectation of his physicians, who, as soon as possible, sent him to recruit at Bath with his family.

The party were accompanied by Fanny Burney; and her diary, coupled with the correspondence between Mrs. Thrale and Johnson, who remained in town, furnishes a full account of all that happened during the visit. On April 6 Johnson wrote:

"If health and reason can be preserved by changing three or four meals a week, or if such change will best increase the chances of preserving them, the purchase is surely not made at a very high price. Death is dreadful, and fatuity is more dreadful, and such strokes bring both so near, that all their terrors ought to be felt. I hope that to our anxiety for him Mr. Thrale will add some anxiety for himself. . . . . Now one courts you, and another caresses you, and one calls you to cards, and another wants you to walk; and amidst all this, pray try to think now and then a little of me, and write often."*

The writer having published the first four volumes of his 'Lives of the Poets' in the spring of the preceding year, was now engaged on the composition of the remaining six. On April 11 he writes again: 'Do you go to the house where they write for the Myrtle?† You are at all places of high resort, and bring home hearts by dozens; while I am seeking for something to say about men of whom I know nothing but their verses, and sometimes very little of them. Now I have begun, however, I do not despair of making an end.'‡

On April 28 Mrs. Thrale wrote: "I had a very kind letter from you yesterday, dear sir, with a most circum-

---

* 'Piozzi Letters,' ii. 97.
† Lady Miller's, at Batheaston, where a vase was kept dressed with pink ribbons and myrtles, into which competitors for prizes offered by the mistress of the house were invited to put copies of verses.
‡ 'Piozzi Letters,' ii. 100.

stantial date.* You took trouble with my circulating letter,† Mr. Evans writes me word, and I thank you sincerely for so doing; one might do mischief else, not being on the spot.

"Yesterday evening was passed at Mrs. Montagu's. There was Mr. Melmoth.‡ I do not like him, though, nor he me. It was expected we should have pleased each other. He is, however, just Tory enough to hate the Bishop of Peterborough for Whiggism, and Whig enough to abhor you for Toryism.

"Mrs. Montagu flattered him finely; so he had a good afternoon on't. This evening we spent at a concert. Poor Queeney's sore eyes have just released her; she had a long confinement, and could neither read nor write; so my master treated her very good-naturedly with the visits of a young woman in this town, a tailor's daughter, who professes music, and teaches so as to give six lessons a day to ladies, at five and threepence a lesson. Miss Burney says she is a great performer; and I respect the wench for getting her living so prettily: she is very modest and pretty-mannered, and not seventeen years old.

"You live in a fine whirl indeed; if I did not write

---

* Johnson, who often complained that his correspondent was careless in dating her letters, had dated his letter, 'London, April 25, 1780,' and added: 'Now there is a date; look at it.'—' Piozzi Letters,' ii. 109. In his reply he wrote: 'London, May 1, 1780. Mark that—you did not put the year to your last.'—*Ibid.*, ii. 112.

† An Address to the Electors of Southwark.

‡ The author of the Fitzosborne Letters. Miss Burney has thus described this evening: 'We were appointed to meet the Bishop of Chester at Mrs. Montagu's. This proved a very gloomy kind of grandeur; the Bishop waited for Mrs. Thrale to speak, Mrs. Thrale for the Bishop; so neither of them spoke at all. Mrs. Montagu cared not a fig, as long as she spoke herself, and so she harangued away. Meanwhile Mr. Melmoth, the Pliny Melmoth, as he is called, was of the party, and seemed to think nobody half so great as himself. He seems intolerably self-sufficient—appears to look upon himself as the first man in Bath, and has a proud conceit in look and manner, mighty forbidding!'—Mme. d'Arblay's ' Diary,' i. 249.

regularly, you would half forget me, and that would be very wrong, for I *felt* my regard for you in my *face* last night, when the criticisms were going on.

"This morning it was all connoisseurship; we went to see some pictures painted by a gentleman artist, Mr. Taylor, of this place; my master makes one everywhere, and has got a dawling companion to ride with him now. . . . He looks well enough, but I have no notion of health for a man whose mouth cannot be sewed up. Burney and I and Queeney tease him every meal he eats, and Mrs. Montagu is quite serious with him, but what *can* one do? He will eat, I think, and if he does eat I know he will not live; it makes me very unhappy, but I must bear it. Let me always have your friendship."*

In the following month a General Election was in prospect, and Johnson pressed Mrs. Thrale to come to London for a week, and show herself to the electors of Southwark, talking in confident terms of her husband's recovery, lest his illness and withdrawal from business should be turned to his disadvantage by opponents. 'Be brisk,' he wrote, 'be splendid, and be public. The voters for the Borough are too proud and too little dependent to be solicited by deputies; they expect the gratification of seeing the candidate bowing or curtseying before them. If you are proud, they can be sullen. Such is the call for your presence; what is there to withhold you? I see no pretence for hesitation. Mr. Thrale certainly shall not come; and yet somebody must appear whom the people think it worth the while to look at.'†

Such a summons was no mean tribute to the lady's ability and adroitness. She answers on May 9: 'I am willing to show myself in Southwark, or in any place, for my master's pleasure or advantage; but have no present

* Boswell's Johnson, Hill's edition, iii. 421. † 'Piozzi Letters,' ii. 115.

conviction that to be re-elected would be advantageous, so shattered a state as his nerves are in just now. Do not you, however, fancy for a moment that I shrink from fatigue, or desire to escape from doing my duty; spiting one's antagonist is a reason that never ought to operate, and never does operate with me. I care nothing about a rival candidate's innuendos, I care only about my husband's health and fame; and if we find that he earnestly wishes to be once more member for the Borough ... he *shall* be member, if anything done or suffered by me will help make him so.'*

Meanwhile Johnson became quite impatient for her arrival. Roused to an unusual pitch of gallantry, he said or sang:

> 'Cette Anne si belle,
> Qu'on vante si fort,
> Pourquoi ne vient elle?
> Vraiment elle a tort.'

The lady came, and for a week or more was involved in business, electioneering, canvassing, and letter-writing without intermission. After her return to Bath, he wrote: 'You have had, with all your adulations, nothing finer said of you than was said last Saturday night of Burke and me. We were at the Bishop of ——'s, and towards twelve we fell into talk, to which the ladies listened, just as they do to you, and said, as I heard, *There is no rising unless somebody will cry "Fire!"* ... You cannot think how doggedly I left your home on Friday morning, and yet Mrs. Abbess gave me some mushrooms; but what are mushrooms without my mistress?'†

His mistress repaid him in kind: " Here is everything in this pretty town of Bath—everything possible; good and bad, for what I see. Did we tell you, when we were in London the other day, how Miss Burney picked up

* 'Piozzi Letters,' ii. 117. † *Ibid.*, ii. 127.

a female infidel one morning, and bid her read Rasselas; and how I lighted on a fanatic, and bid *her* read Rasselas? Perhaps not, for you only call such intelligence flattery; though the London wits beat us at that too, when they talk of crying 'Fire' in the street that they may break up a conversation which would otherwise engage them till next day. All this, however, we set on one side during the election hurry. My master will stand to his hand-bill; he likes it: and I like exceedingly your sullen removal from the *round tower*, where mushrooms would almost grow of themselves now, the weather is getting so hot. Our flagstones upon the South Parade burn one's feet through one's shoes; but the Bath belles, fearless of fire ordeal, trip about, secure in cork soles and a clear conscience. I wish, though, that you would put in a word of your own to Mr. Thrale about eating less; for he will mind you more than us, and his too great spirits just at this moment fright me. . . . .

"How does Congreve's life turn out? Tell me all the news. I would not wish you to be *too much* flattered; milk itself, when injected into the veins, is poison, the wise men say; so if adulation should be forced upon you, cry out, or run away to me, or anything; but I expect these Lives to be very clever things, after all; take as little pains with them as you can. We will have all the great prose-writers some time, and then I shall be zealous for Bacon.

"Meantime, Heaven send this Southwark election safe, for a disappointment would half kill my husband; and there is no comfort in tiring every friend to death in such manner, and losing the town at last."*

The Doctor was fully equal to the occasion. He responds:

* 'Piozzi Letters,' ii. 129.

"Congreve, whom I despatched at the Borough, while I was attending the election, is one of the best of the little Lives; but then I had your conversation.

"You seem to suspect that I think you too earnest about the success of your solicitation; if I gave you any reason for that suspicion, it was without intention. It would be with great discontent that I should see Mr. Thrale decline the representation of the Borough, and with much greater should I see him ejected. To sit in Parliament for Southwark is the highest honour that his station permits him to attain; and his ambition to attain it is surely rational and laudable. . . . The expense, if it was more, I should wish him to despise. Money is made for such purposes as this. And the method to which the trade is now brought will, I hope, save him from any want of what he shall now spend. . . .

"Do not I tell you everything? What wouldst thou more of man? It will, I fancy, be necessary for you to come up once again, at least, to fix your friends and terrify your enemies. Take care to be informed, as you can, of the ebb and flow of your interests; and do not lose at Capua the victory of Cannæ. I hope I need not tell you, dear madam, that I am, etc.

"*Thursday, May 25, 1780.* No. 8, Bolt Court, Fleet Street, London.—Look at this and learn."*

The Thrales remained at Bath until a local disturbance, excited by the Gordon Riots in London, drove them away. In a letter written on Friday, June 9, after mentioning the destruction of Lord Mansfield's house, the burning of Newgate and other prisons, besides several outrages more, including the demolition of what he called 'two mass-houses,' Johnson wrote to Mrs. Thrale: 'What has happened at your house you will know.

* 'Piozzi Letters,' ii. 137.

The harm is only a few butts of beer; and I think you may be sure that the danger is over.' He added, with much composure: 'Pray tell Mr. Thrale that I live here, and have no fruit, and if he does not interpose, am not likely to have much; but I think he might as well give me a little, as give all to the gardener. Pray make my compliments to Queeney and Burney.'*

Meanwhile, the friends for whom he wrote were enduring an agony of suspense. The mob on that evening rose at Bath, broke into a Roman Catholic chapel, and set it on fire. 'Mrs. Thrale and I,' says the Burney diary, 'sat up till four o'clock, and walked about the parades, and at two we went with a large party to the spot, and saw the beautiful new building consuming.' On their return Mrs. Thrale sat down to begin a letter to Bolt Court:

"Bath, 3 o'clock on Saturday morning,
June 10, 1780.

Oh, my dear Sir! was I ever particular in dating a letter before? And is this a time to begin to be particular, when I have been up all night in trembling agitation, and only write now to drive time forward till the post comes in? . . . . Miss Burney is frighted; but she says better times will come. She made me date my letter so, and persists in hoping that ten years hence we shall all three read it over together, and be merry. Oh, no, no, no! Here is poor prospect of merriment. The flames of the Romish chapel are not yet extinguished, and the rioters are going to Bristol to burn that. Their shouts are still in my ears; and I do not believe a dog or cat in the town sleeps this night. Mr. Thrale seems thunder-stricken, he don't mind anything; and Queeney's curiosity is stronger than her fears. But perhaps you

* 'Piozzi Letters,' ii. 145.

will ask, *Who is consternated?* as you did about the French invasion.... The mob had always an idea of my husband's being a concealed Papist, and they used to say that we kept a priest in the house....

'Here come the letters; safe, safe, safe! Sir Philip, kind creature, has been more than charming; he has saved us all by his friendly activity—God bless him! Do go to his house, and thank him; pray do; and tell him how I love him—he loves *you;* and a visit from Doctor Johnson will be worth forty letters from me, though I shall write instantly.

'Perkins has behaved like an Emperor; and it is my earnest wish and desire—command, if you please to call it so—that you will go over to the brewhouse and express *your* sense of his good behàviour.'*

'Nothing,' she wrote in 'Thraliana,' 'but the astonishing presence of mind shewed by Perkins in amusing the mob, with meat and drink and huzzas, till Sir Philip Jennings Clerke could get the troops, and pack up the counting-house bills, bonds, etc., and carry them, which he did, to Chelsea College for safety, could have saved us from actual undoing. The villains *had* broke in, and our brewhouse would have blazed in ten minutes, when a property of £150,000 would have been utterly lost, and its once flourishing possessors quite undone.'†

On that same Saturday morning a Bath and Bristol paper asserted that Mr. Thrale was a Papist.‡ This malicious attack alarmed Mrs. Thrale for her husband's personal safety, and determined her to leave Bath at once, and travel by easy stages, and a devious route, to Brighton, where peace and quiet reigned.

On the same day Johnson was writing to her: 'The

* 'Piozzi Letters,' ii. 146.   † Hayward's 'Piozzi,' i. 128.
‡ Mme. d'Arblay's 'Diary,' i. 292.

soldiers are stationed so as to be everywhere within call; there is no longer any body of rioters, and the individuals are hunted to their holes, and led to prison; the streets are safe and quiet; Lord George was last night sent to the Tower. Mr. John Wilkes was this day with a party of soldiers in my neighbourhood, to seize the publisher of a seditious paper.'*

On the 12th he wrote: 'All is well, and all is likely to continue well. The streets are quiet, and the houses are all safe. . . . The public has escaped a very heavy calamity. The rioters attempted the Bank on Wednesday night, but in no great number, and, like other thieves, with no great resolution. Jack Wilkes headed the party that drove them away. . . . Jack, who was always zealous for order and decency, declares that if he be trusted with power, he will not leave a rioter alive. There is, however, now no longer any need of heroism or bloodshed; no blue riband is any longer worn.† . . . Thus far I had written when I received your letter of battle and conflagration. You certainly do right in retiring: for who can guess the caprice of the rabble? My master and Queeney are dear people for not being frighted, and you and Burney are dear people for being frighted. I wrote to you a letter of intelligence and consolation, which, if you stayed for it, you had on Saturday; and I wrote another on Saturday, which perhaps may follow you from Bath, with some achievement of John Wilkes.'‡

Wilkes had by this time sown his wild oats. On the 28th of the previous November Horace Walpole had written to Sir Horace Mann: 'That old meteor, Wilkes, has again risen above the horizon, when he had long

* 'Piozzi Letters,' ii. 152.
† Lord George Gordon and his followers, during these outrages, wore blue ribands in their hats.—MALONE.
‡ 'Piozzi Letters,' ii. 154.

seemed virtually extinct. The citizens, revolted from the Court on the late disgraces, have voted him into the post of Chamberlain of London, a place of fifteen hundred pounds a year. How Masaniello and Rienzi and Jack Cade would stare at seeing him sit down as comfortably as an Alderman of London! If he should die of a surfeit of custards at last!'*

On June 14, 1780, Walpole wrote to the same correspondent: 'Wilkes has very sensibly ridden home on Lord George, and distinguished himself by zeal and spirit.'†

George III. told Lord Eldon that at a levee he asked Wilkes after his friend Serjeant Glynne. '*My* friend, sir?' says Wilkes to the King; 'he is no friend of mine.' 'Why,' said the King, 'he *was* your friend and your counsel in all your trials.' 'Sir,' rejoined Wilkes, 'he *was* my *counsel*—one *must* have a counsel; but he was no *friend:* he loves sedition and licentiousness, which I never delighted in. In fact, sir, he was a Wilkite, which I never was.' The King said the confidence and humour of the man made him at the moment forget his impudence!‡

Samuel Rogers, who was born in 1763, remembered Wilkes well. 'He was quite as ugly,' said the poet, 'and squinted as much, as his portraits make him; but he was very gentlemanly in appearance and manners. I think I see him at this moment, walking through the crowded streets of the City, as Chamberlain, on his way to Guildhall, in a scarlet coat, military boots, and a bag-wig —the hackney-coachmen in vain calling out to him: " A coach, your honour?"'§

Having placed her husband in security at Brighton,

---

* Walpole's 'Letters,' vii. 283. † *Ibid.*, vii. 401.
‡ Twiss's 'Eldon,' ii. 356. § Rogers' 'Table-Talk,' p. 43.

Mrs. Thrale hastened to London to take any farther precautions that might be needed for the preservation of his property and business. 'We have now got arms,' she wrote, 'and mean to defend ourselves by force, if further violence is intended. Sir Philip comes every day at some hour or another—good creature, how kind he is, and how much I ought to love him! God knows I am not in this case wanting to my duty. I have presented Perkins, with my master's permission, with two hundred guineas, and a silver urn for his lady, with his own cipher on it, and this motto: Mollis responsio iram avertit.'* She did not, however, obtain the brewer's sanction to this liberal gift until after her return to Brighton, for on June 29 she writes thence to Miss Burney, who was now at home: 'My master is quite in rosy health—he is indeed—and jokes Peggy Owen for her want of power to flash. He made many inquiries for you; and was not displeased that I had given Perkins two hundred guineas instead of one—a secret I never durst tell before, not even to Johnson, not even to you—but so it was.'†

On July 27 Johnson wrote to her: "And thus it is, madam, that you serve me. After having kept me a whole week, hoping and hoping, and wondering and wondering what could have stopped your hand from writing, comes a letter to tell me that I suffer by my own fault. As if I might not correspond with my Queeney, and we might not tell one another our minds about politics or morals, or anything else. Queeney and I are both steady, and may be trusted. We are none of the giddy gabblers; we think before we speak.

"I am afraid that I shall hardly find my way this summer into the country, though the number of my Lives

---

* Hayward's 'Piozzi,' i. 128. † Mme. d'Arblay's 'Diary,' i. 300.

now grows less. I will send you two little volumes in a few days.* . . .

"I dined yesterday at Sir Joshua's, with Mrs. Cholmondely, and she told me I was the best critic in the world; and I told her that nobody in the world could judge like her of the merit of a critic."†

Again, on August 14: "I hope you have no design of stealing away to Italy before the election, nor of leaving me behind you: though I am not only seventy, but seventy-one. Could not you let me lose a year in round numbers? Sweetly, sweetly sings Dr. Swift:

> 'Some dire misfortune to portend,
> No enemy can match a friend.'

But what if I am seventy-two? I remember Sulpitius says of St. Martin (now that's above your reading), 'Est animus victor annorum, et senectuti cedere nescius.' Match me that among your young folks. If you try to plague me, I shall tell you that, according to Galen, life begins to decline from *Thirty-five*.

"But as we go off, others come on. Queeney's last letter was very pretty. What a hussey she is to write so seldom! She has no events? Then let her write sentiment, as you and I do; and sentiment, you know, is inexhaustible.

"If you want events, here is Mr. Levet just come in, at four-score, from a walk to Hampstead, eight miles, in August. This, however, is all that I have to tell you, except that I have three bunches of grapes on a vine in my garden; at least, this is all that I will now tell of my garden.

"Both my females are ill—both very ill: Mrs. Desmoulins thought that she wished for Dr. Turton; and I sent for him, and then took him to Mrs. Williams; and he prescribes

---

* He means volumes of proof-sheets.   † 'Piozzi Letters,' ii. 169.

for both, though without much hope of benefiting either. Yet physic has its powers: you see that I am better; and Mr. Shaw* will maintain that he and I saved my master. But if he is to live always away from us, what did we get by saving him? If we cannot live together, let us hear; when I have no letter from Brighthelmstone, think how I fret, and write oftener."†

On September 1 came the long-expected dissolution of Parliament. Thrale's friends could no longer flatter themselves that he was in rosy health. His state had begun again to occasion great anxiety; and though he was once more a candidate for Southwark, and seems to have come to town for the election, he was unable to be present on the hustings. Johnson wrote his address to the electors, in which an apology was made for his absence, on the ground that his 'recovery from a very severe distemper was not yet perfect.'

The plea proved fruitless. The invalided brewer, never very popular, was superseded by a more active rival, whom Johnson had ridiculed as 'Hotham the Hatmaker.' Some time after Thrale's death the Borough was canvassed on behalf of Mr. Henry Thornton. His agent waited on Mrs. Thrale, who promised her support. 'I wish your friend success,' she said, 'and think he will have it. He may probably come in for two Parliaments; but,' she added bitterly, 'if he tries for a third, were he an angel from heaven, the people of Southwark would cry, "Not this man, but Barabbas."' ‡

In October Johnson wrote to Boswell: 'Mr. Thrale's loss of health has lost him the election. He is now going to Brighton, and expects me to go with him; and how

---

* Mr. Shaw was the surgeon who had bled Thrale in the winter.
† 'Piozzi Letters,' ii, 177.
‡ 'Memoirs of Letitia Matilda Hawkins,' i. 66, note.

long I shall stay I cannot tell. I do not much like the place, but yet I shall go, and stay while my stay is desired.' ' Our master is in good spirits and good humour,' wrote Miss Burney about the end of the same month, ' but I think he looks sadly; so does our Mrs. T., who agitates herself into an almost perpetual fever.'* On his way home from Brighton Thrale was seized with alarming symptoms, but the attack passed off for the time. Yet we hear that after dinner he was only to be kept from heavy and profound sleep by cards; and Fanny, though ill herself, was compelled to join in the evening rubber. On December 14, having left Streatham three days before, she writes to her friend : ' Does the card system flourish? Does Dr. Johnson continue gay and good-humoured, and "valuing nobody" in a morning? Is Miss Thrale steady in asserting that all will do perfectly well? But most I wish to hear, whether our dear master is any better in spirit?—and whether my sweet Dottoressa perseveres in supporting and exerting her own?'

Mrs. Thrale in her reply assumes a tone of cheerfulness which she can scarcely have felt. Mr. Thrale, she says, makes all the haste to be well that mortal man can make. On Thursday, January 4, 1781, she writes : ''Tis now high time to tell you that the pictures are come home, all but *mine*—which my master don't like. He has *ordered* your father hither to sit to-morrow in his peremptory way; and I shall have the dear Doctor every morning at breakfast. I took ridiculous pains to tutor him to-day, and to insist in *my* peremptory way on his forbearing to write or read late this evening, that my picture might not have bloodshot eyes.'†

---

* Mme. d'Arblay's ' Diary,' i. 316.
† *Ibid.*, i. 323. Thursday was the day of Dr. Burney's weekly attendance at Streatham.

Characters.

The pictures here referred to are the collection of portraits which Sir Joshua Reynolds had been for some time engaged in painting for the library at Streatham. Mrs. Thrale and her eldest daughter were at full length, in one piece, which was placed over the fireplace. The rest of the pictures were all three-quarter lengths. Mr. Thrale's likeness hung over the door leading to his study. Above the bookcases were his friends: Lord Sandys, Lord Westcote, Murphy, Goldsmith, Reynolds himself, Sir Robert Chambers, Garrick, Baretti, Burney, Burke, Johnson.

On the characters of the various personages portrayed in this gallery Mrs. Thrale amused herself with writing descriptive verses, some of which possess considerable merit; we give a few specimens:

> 'A manner so studied, so vacant a face,
> These features the mind of our Murphy disgrace;
> A mind unaffected, soft, artless, and true,
> A mind which, though ductile, has dignity too.
> Where virtues ill-sorted are huddled in heaps,
> Humanity triumphs, and piety sleeps;
> A mind in which mirth may with merit reside,
> And Learning turns Frolic, with Humour, his guide.
> Whilst wit, follies, faults, its fertility prove,
> Till the faults you grow fond of, the follies you love;
> And corrupted at length by the sweet conversation,
> You swear there's no honesty left in the nation.
> An African landscape thus breaks on the sight,
> Where confusion and wildness increase the delight;
> Till in wanton luxuriance indulging our eye,
> We faint in the forcible fragrance, and die.
> *   *   *   *
> Of Reynolds all good should be said, and no harm,
> Tho' the heart is too frigid, the pencil too warm;
> Yet each fault from his converse we still must disclaim,
> As his temper 'tis peaceful, and pure as his fame.
> Nothing in it o'erflows, nothing ever is wanting,
> It nor chills like his kindness, nor glows like his painting.
> When Johnson by strength overpowers our mind,
> When Montagu dazzles, and Burke strikes us blind;
> To Reynolds well-pleas'd for relief we must run,
> Rejoice in his shadow, and shrink from the sun.
> *   *   *   *

See Thrale from intruders defending his door,
While he wishes his house would with people run o'er;
Unlike his companions, the make of his mind,
In great things expanded, in small things confined.
Yet his purse at their call, and his meat to their taste,
The wits he delighted in lov'd him at last;
And finding no prominent follies to fleer at,
Respected his wealth and applauded his merit:
Much like that empirical chemist was he,
Who thought Anima Mundi the grand panacea.
Yet when every kind element help'd his collection,
Fell sick while the med'cine was yet in projection.

* * * * *

Baretti hangs next; by his frowns you may know him,
He has lately been reading some new-published poem;
He finds the poor author a blockhead, a beast,
A fool without sentiment, judgment, or taste.
Ever thus let our critic his insolence fling,
Like the hornet in Homer, impatient to sting.
Let him rally his friends for their frailties before 'em,
And scorn the dull praise of that dull thing, decorum;
While tenderness, temper, and truth he despises,
And only the triumph of victory prizes.
Yet let us be candid, and where shall we find
So active, so able, so ardent a mind?
To your children more soft, more polite with your servant,
More firm in distress, or in friendship more fervent?
Thus Ætna enraged her artillery pours,
And tumbles down palaces, princes, and towers;
While the fortunate peasantry, fix'd at its foot,
Can make it a hot-house to ripen their fruit.

* * * * *

See next, happy contrast! in Burney combine
Every power to please, every talent to shine.
In professional science a second to none,
In social, if second, thro' shyness alone.
So sits the sweet violet close to the ground,
Whilst holy-oaks and sunflow'rs flaunt it around.
His character form'd free, confiding, and kind,
Grown cautious by habit, by station confin'd:
Tho' born to improve and enlighten our days,
In a supple facility fixes his praise:
And contented to soothe, unambitious to strike,
Has a faint praise from all men, from all men alike.
While thus the rich wines of Frontiniac impart
Their sweets to our palate, their warmth to our heart,
All in praise of a liquor so luscious agree,
From the monarch of France to the wild Cherokee.'

In 1780 Reynolds had raised the price of his portraits, of the three-quarter size, from thirty-five to fifty guineas.

Sir Joshua Reynolds.

Thrale died without having discharged his debt for the Streatham portraits, and they had to be paid for by his widow at the increased price, which was more than several of them fetched when the collection was sold by auction in 1816.

The room in which these pictures were hung was regarded by visitors to Streatham Park with something like the fondness which the remembrance of 'the venerable chamber' at Holland House, celebrated by Macaulay, inspired in the heart of the historian. 'While the Lives of the Poets was in progress,' says Madame d'Arblay, 'Dr. Johnson would frequently produce one of the proof-sheets to embellish the breakfast-table, which was always in the library, and was certainly the most sprightly and agreeable meeting of the day. These sheets Mrs. Thrale was permitted to read aloud, and the discussions to which they led were in the highest degree entertaining.'*

At the end of January, 1781, the Thrales, instead of making the Borough their place of abode as usual, removed from Streatham to Grosvenor Square, where the sick man had hired a furnished house for the season. Boswell, in mentioning this change of residence, attributes it to the solicitation of Mrs. Thrale. She wrote opposite the passage: 'Spiteful again; he went by direction of his physicians where they could easiest attend him.' Yet it appears that her personal inclinations counted for something in the matter. In 'Thraliana,' after expressing a fear that the world would accuse her of tempting her husband in his weakness to take a fine house for her at the fashionable end of town, she wrote: 'I cannot be sorry, for it will doubtless be comfortable to see one's friends commodiously . . . I will make myself comfortable

* 'Memoirs of Dr. Burney,' ii. 177.

in my new habitation, and be thankful to God and my husband.'*

Johnson had a room in the new house. 'Think,' wrote Hannah More, 'of Johnson's having apartments in Grosvenor Square; but he says it is not half so convenient as Bolt Court.'†

On February 6 Mrs. Thrale writes to Miss Burney:

'Yesterday I had a conversazione. Mrs. Montagu was brilliant in diamonds, solid in judgment, critical in talk. Sophy smiled, Piozzi sang, Pepys panted with admiration, Johnson was good-humoured, Lord John Clinton attentive, Dr. Bowdler lame, and my master not asleep. Mrs. Ord looked elegant, Lady Rothes dainty, Mrs. Davenant dapper, and Sir Philip's curls were all blown about by the wind. Mrs. Byron rejoices that her Admiral and I agree so well; the way to his heart is connoisseurship, it seems, and for a background and contorno, who comes up to Mrs. Thrale, you know.'‡

Notwithstanding the precarious condition of Thrale's health, the hospitalities at his house this winter were more frequent and on a larger scale than ever. On March 18 his wife wrote in 'Thraliana': 'Well! Now I have experienced the delights of a London winter, spent in the bosom of flattery, gaiety, and Grosvenor Square; 'tis a poor thing, however, and leaves a void in the mind, but I have had my compting-house duties to attend, my sick master to watch, my little children to look after, and how much good have I done in any way? Not a scrap, that I can see; the pecuniary affairs have gone on perversely; how should they do otherwise, when the sole proprietor is incapable of giving orders, yet not so far incapable as to be set aside? Distress, fraud, folly, meet me at every turn,

---

* Hayward's 'Piozzi,' i. 130.   † H. More's 'Memoirs,' i. 207.
‡ Mme. d'Arblay's 'Diary,' i. 325.

and I am not able to fight against them all, though endued with an iron constitution, which shakes not by sleepless nights or days severely fretted. . . . Mr. Thrale talks now again of going to Spa and Italy ; how shall we drag him thither—a man who cannot keep awake four hours at a stroke ? Well! this will indeed be a trial of one's patience ; and who must go with us on this expedition ?'*

On the day on which this scheme of foreign travel was announced, Miss Burney dined in Grosvenor Square. Her feelings were divided between disapproval of the project and disappointment at finding that she herself was not to be included in the party. In the evening, she tells us, there was a great rout. The company was very brilliant ; it included several peers ; the greatest beauty in the room, except the S. S., was Mrs. Gwynn, lately Miss Horneck ; and the greatest fright was Lord Sandys. The novelist spent the following day also in the Square with a smaller number of guests : and on Thursday, March 22, she was there again, when there was a very gay party to dinner.'

How much of this incessant round of entertainments was due to the restlessness of the invalid, and how much to that of his wife, is not quite clear. The latter, perhaps, unconscious of her own state of mind, imputed the whole to her husband. ' Dinners and company,' she says, ' engrossed all his thoughts ; he talked of the lamprey season and the Ranelagh season ;' meanwhile, the condition of the patient went from bad to worse. Before the end of March his physicians had declared against his going abroad. ' It is settled,' writes Miss Burney, ' that a great meeting of his friends is to take place before he actually prepares for the journey, and they are to encircle him in a body, and endeavour, by representations and

* Hayward's ' Piozzi,' i. 130.

entreaties, to prevail with him to give it up; and I have little doubt myself but, amongst us, we shall be able to succeed.'*

The execution of this design was prevented by his sudden death.

"On Sunday, the 1st of April," wrote Mrs. Thrale, "I went to hear the Bishop of Peterborough preach at May Fair Chapel, and though the sermon had nothing in it particularly pathetic, I could not keep my tears within my eyes. I spent the evening, however, at Lady Rothes', and was cheerful. Found Sir John Lade, Johnson, and Boswell with Mr. Thrale, at my return to the Square. On Monday morning Mr. Evans came to breakfast: Sir Philip and Dr. Johnson to dinner; so did Baretti. Mr. Thrale eat voraciously—so voraciously that, encouraged by Jebb and Pepys, who had charged me to do so, I checked him rather severely, and Mr. Johnson added these remarkable words: 'Sir, after the denunciation of your physicians this morning, such eating is little better than suicide.' He did not, however, desist, and Sir Philip said that he eat apparently in defiance of control, and that it was better for us to say nothing to him. Johnson observed that he thought so too; and that he spoke more from a sense of duty than a hope of success. Baretti and these two spent the evening with me, and I was enumerating the people who were to meet the Indian Ambassadors on the Wednesday. I had been to Negri's and bespoke an elegant entertainment."†

On Tuesday occurred the catastrophe: "Mr. Thrale came home so well, and in such spirits! He had invited more people to my concert, or conversazione, or musical party of the next day, and was delighted to think what a show we should make. He eat, however, more than

* Mme. d'Arblay's 'Diary,' i. 330. † Hayward's 'Piozzi,' i. 132.

voraciously...." In the course of the evening he was found by his eldest daughter on the floor in a fit of apoplexy, and died early in the morning of Wednesday, the 4th. 'Mrs. Garrick and I,' wrote Hannah More, 'were invited to an assembly at Mrs. Thrale's. There was to be a fine concert, and all the fine people were to be there. Just as my hair was dressed, came a servant to forbid our coming, for that Mr. Thrale was dead.'*

On April 13, which was Good-Friday, Johnson wrote in his 'Meditations': 'On Wednesday, 11th, was buried my dear friend Thrale, who died on Wednesday, 4th; and with him were buried many of my hopes and pleasures. On Sunday, 1st, the physician warned him against full meals; on Monday I pressed him to observance of his rules, but without effect; on Tuesday I was absent, but his wife pressed forbearance upon him again, unsuccessfully. At night I was called to him, and found him senseless, in strong convulsions. I stayed in the room, except that I visited Mrs. Thrale twice. About five, I think, on Wednesday morning, he expired. I felt almost the last flutter of his pulse, and looked for the last time upon the face that for fifteen years had never been turned upon me but with respect and benignity. Farewell! May God, that delighteth in mercy, have had mercy on thee. I had constantly prayed for him some time before his death. The decease of him from whose friendship I had obtained many opportunities of amusement, and to whom I turned my thoughts as to a refuge from misfortunes, has left me heavy.'†

It was the seventh anniversary of Goldsmith's death.

On the following day Johnson wrote to the widow:

---

* 'Memoirs,' i. 208.

† On the same paper is a note: 'My first knowledge of Thrale was in 1765. I enjoyed his favours for about a fourth part of my life.'

'I am not without my part of the calamity. No death since that of my wife has ever oppressed me like this. .... We read the will to-day; but I will not fill my first letter with any other account than that, with all my zeal for your advantage, I am satisfied; and that the other executors, more used to consider property than I, commended it for wisdom and equity. Yet why should I not tell you that you have five hundred pounds for your immediate expenses, and two thousand pounds a year, with both the houses and all the goods?'*

On the 7th he says: "I hope you begin to find your mind grow clearer. My part of the loss hangs upon me. I have lost a friend of boundless kindness at an age when it is very unlikely that I should find another."†

On the 9th: "That you are gradually recovering your tranquillity is the effect to be humbly expected from trust in God. Do not represent life as darker than it is. Your loss has been very great, but you retain more than almost any other can hope to possess. You are high in the opinion of mankind; you have children from whom much pleasure may be expected; and that you will find many friends, you have no reason to doubt. Of my friendship, be it worth more or less, I hope you think yourself certain, without much art or care. It will not be easy for me to repay the benefits that I have received; but I hope to be always ready at your call. Our sorrow has different effects: you are withdrawn into solitude, and I am driven into company. I am afraid of thinking what I have lost. I never had such a friend before. Let me have your prayers, and those of my dear Queeney.

"The prudence and resolution of your design to return so soon to your business and your duty deserves great praise. I shall communicate it on Wednesday to the

* 'Piozzi Letters,' ii. 192. † *Ibid.*, ii. 193.

other executors. Be pleased to let me know whether you would have me come to Streatham to receive you, or stay here till the next day."*

The executors were Mr. John Cator,† Mr. Jeremiah Crutchley,‡ Mr. Henry Smith, and Dr. Johnson; and Mrs. Thrale herself was executrix.§ The four gentlemen had each a legacy of £200. 'Everybody says,' wrote Dr. Beattie, 'that Mr. Thrale, should have left Johnson £200 a year, which, from a fortune like his, would have been a very inconsiderable deduction.'‖ Boswell tells us that the same opinion was generally entertained by the members of the Club. The Doctor, however, accepted the trust in a more hearty spirit than any of his colleagues.

On April 11 he wrote to his mistress: "Mr. Perkins pretends that your absence produces a thousand difficulties, which I believe it does not produce. He frights Mr. Cator. Mr. Crutchley is of my mind, that there is no need of hurry. I would not have this importunity give you any alarm or disturbance; but to pacify it, come as soon as you can prevail upon your mind to mingle with business. I think business the best remedy for grief as soon as it can be admitted.

"We met to-day, and were told of mountainous difficulties, till I was provoked to tell them that if there were really so much to do and suffer, there would be no

---

* 'Piozzi Letters,' ii. 195.

† Cator was M.P. for Ipswich in 1784. Johnson described him as having 'much good in his character, and much usefulness in his knowledge.' Elsewhere he says: 'Cator has a rough, manly, independent understanding, and does not spoil it by complaisance.' Johnson used to visit Cator at his seat at Beckenham. Miss Burney, as we shall see, formed a much lower opinion of him.

‡ M.P. for Horsham in 1784. He was believed by Mrs. Thrale to be a natural son of Thrale, whom, she says, he resembled in many things, though not in person, as he was both ugly and awkward.

§ Hayward's 'Piozzi,' ii. 47.

‖ Beattie's 'Life,' ed. 1824, p. 190.

executors in the world. Do not suffer yourself to be terrified.

"I comfort you, and hope God will bless and support you; but I feel myself like a man beginning a new course of life. I had interwoven myself with my dear friend."*

On April 29 Miss Burney wrote from Streatham to her friend Mr. Crisp: 'Mrs. Thrale flew immediately upon this misfortune to Brighthelmstone to Mr. Scrase—*her* Daddy Crisp—both for consolation and counsel; and she has but just quitted him, as she deferred returning to Streatham till her presence was indispensably necessary upon account of proving the will. . . . I am now here with her, and endeavour by every possible exertion to be of some use to her. She looks wretchedly indeed, and is far from well; but she bears up, though not with calm intrepidity, yet with flashes of spirit that rather, I fear, spend than relieve her. Such, however, is her character; and were this exertion repressed, she would probably sink quite. Miss Thrale is steady and constant, and very sincerely grieved for her father.

'The four executors have all behaved generously and honourably, and seem determined to give Mrs. Thrale all the comfort and assistance in their power. She is to carry on the business jointly with them. Poor soul! it is a dreadful toil and worry to her.'†

In 'Thraliana' the widow wrote:

"*Streatham, May* 1, 1781.—I have now appointed three days a week to attend at the counting-house.

"If an angel from heaven had told me twenty years ago that the man I knew by the name of *Dictionary Johnson* should one day become partner with me in a great trade, and that we should jointly or separately sign notes, drafts,

---

* 'Piozzi Letters,' ii. 196.
† Mme. d'Arblay's 'Diary and Letters,' i. 334.

etc., for three or four thousand pounds of a morning, how unlikely it would have seemed ever to happen! Unlikely is no word, though—it would have seemed *incredible*, neither of us then being worth a groat, God knows, and both as immeasurably removed from commerce as birth, literature, and inclination could get us. Johnson, however, who desires above all other good the accumulation of new ideas, is but too happy with his present employment; and the influence I have over him, added to his own solid judgment and a regard for truth, will at last find it in a small degree difficult to win him from the delight of seeing his name, in a new character, flaming away at the bottom of bonds and leases."*

But the scheme of continuing the business was not destined to be of long duration, even though Johnson gave his valuable assistance. On returning to Streatham in May, after a short absence, Miss Burney wrote: 'Miss Owen and I arrived here without incident, which, in a journey of six or seven miles, was really marvellous. Mrs. Thrale came from the Borough with two of the executors, Dr. Johnson and Mr. Crutchley, soon after us. She had been badly worried, and in the evening frightened us all by again fainting away. Dear creature! she is all agitation of mind and body; but she is now wonderfully recovered, though in continual fevers about her affairs, which are mightily difficult and complicated.'† She alone among the executors understood anything of the business and the whole five together could not carry it on without the advice of the manager Perkins, who was bent on being taken into partnership.

It was therefore presently determined to dispose of a trade by which, says Mrs. Thrale, in some years £15,000

---

* Hayward's 'Piozzi,' i. 139.
† Mme. d'Arblay's 'Diary,' i. 336.

or £16,000 had undoubtedly been got,* but by which in some years its possessor had suffered agonies of terror, and tottered twice upon the verge of bankruptcy. 'Among all my fellow-executors,' she says elsewhere, 'none but Johnson opposed selling the concern. Cator, a rich timber merchant, was afraid of implicating his own credit as a commercial man. Crutchley hated Perkins, and lived upon the verge of a quarrel with him every day, while they acted together. Smith cursed the whole business, and wondered what his relation, Mr. Thrale, could mean by leaving him £200, he said, and such a burden on his back to bear for it. All were well pleased to find themselves secured, and the brewhouse decently, though not very advantageously, disposed of, except dear Doctor Johnson, who found some odd delight in signing drafts for hundreds and for thousands, to him a new, and as it appeared, delightful, occupation. When all was nearly over, however, I cured his honest heart of its incipient passion for trade, by letting him into some, and only some, of its mysteries.'

Mrs. Thrale's account of Johnson's mercantile ardour is confirmed by Boswell: 'I could not but be somewhat diverted by hearing Johnson talk in a pompous manner of his new office, and particularly of the concerns of the brewery, which it was at last resolved should be sold. Lord Lucan tells a very good story, which, if not precisely exact, is certainly characteristical—that when the sale of Thrale's brewery was going forward, Johnson appeared bustling about, with an ink-horn and pen in his buttonhole, like an excise man; and on being asked what he really considered to be the value of the property which was to be disposed of, answered: "We are not here

---

* Baretti, in a MS. note on the 'Piozzi Letters,' i. 369, says that 'the two last years of Thrale's life his brewery brought him £30,000 a year net profit.' But on this point Mrs. Thrale is a better authority.

to sell a parcel of boilers and vats, but the potentiality of growing rich beyond the dreams of avarice." '

Miss Burney thus writes of the day of the sale: 'Mrs. Thrale went early to town, to meet all the executors, and Mr. Barclay, the Quaker, who was the bidder. She was in great agitation of mind, and told me, if all went well, she would wave a white handkerchief out of the coach-window. Four o'clock came, and dinner was ready, and no Mrs. Thrale. Queeney and I went out upon the lawn, where we sauntered in eager expectation till near six, and then the coach appeared in sight, and a white handkerchief was waved from it. I ran to the door of it to meet her, and she jumped out of it, and gave me a thousand embraces while I gave my congratulations. She went instantly to her dressing-room, where she told me in brief how the matter had been transacted, and then we went down to dinner. Dr. Johnson and Mr. Crutchley had accompanied her home.'*

The brewery was bought by David Barclay, a descendant of Robert Barclay, the celebrated apologist of the Quakers. This gentleman, who was then the head of the banking firm of Barclay and Co., placed at the head of the brewhouse his nephew from America, Robert Barclay, and Perkins, who had been Thrale's manager, and thus became the founder of the world-renowned house of Barclay, Perkins and Co.

The sale was thus announced to Langton by Johnson, in a letter dated June 16, 1784:

'You will perhaps be glad to hear that Mrs. Thrale is disencumbered of her brewhouse; and that it seemed to the purchaser so far from an evil, that he was content to give for it £135,000. Is the nation ruined?' Mrs. Thrale mentions that four years were allowed for payment of the

* Mme. d'Arblay's 'Diary,' i. 346.

purchase-money. She adds that she never regretted the sale, as it was certainly best for herself and her daughters at the time, though the Quaker obtained the brewhouse a prodigious bargain, and the place became doubled in value within a very few years.

The widow and her daughters spent the summer at Streatham. Miss Burney was a guest during the greater part of the season, while Johnson came and went according to his wont. In the early part of the time Fanny describes the Doctor as charming both in spirits and humour. 'I really think,' she says, 'he grows gayer and gayer daily, and more ductile and pleasant.' 'I have very often,' she wrote a little later, 'long and melancholy discourses with Dr. Johnson about our dear deceased master, whom indeed he regrets incessantly.'* It is plain that Johnson was exerting himself to be agreeable. But the restraining influence which he most respected was now removed, and the result was not long in showing itself.

Miss Burney gives an account of an attack made by Johnson, at a dinner-party, on Mr. Pepys, a Master in Chancery, and a man of social distinction. 'Never before,' she writes, ' have I seen Dr. Johnson speak with so much passion. "Mr. Pepys," he cried in a voice the most enraged, "I understand you are offended by my *Life of Lord Lyttelton!* What is it you have to say against it? Come forth, man! Here am I, ready to answer any charge you can bring." . . . One happy circumstance, however, attended the quarrel, which was the presence of Mr. Cator, who would by no means be prevented talking himself, either by reverence for Dr. Johnson, or ignorance of the subject in question; on the contrary, he gave his opinion, quite uncalled for, upon everything that was said

---

* Mme. d'Arblay's 'Diary,' i. 337, 368.

by either party, and that with an importance and pomposity that rendered the whole dispute, when in his hands, nothing more than ridiculous, and compelled even the disputants themselves, all inflamed as they were, to laugh.' After the contention had been carried even into the drawing-room, 'Mrs. Thrale, with great spirit and dignity, said she should be very glad to hear no more of it. Everybody was silenced; and Dr. Johnson, after a pause, said, " Well, madam, you *shall* hear no more of it; yet I will defend myself in every part and in every atom."' Next morning, 'Dr. Johnson went to town for some days, but not before Mrs. Thrale read him a very serious lecture upon giving way to such violence, which he bore with a patience and quietness that even more than made his peace with me.'* Thrale would have arrested the dispute at once by a few decisive words. The effect of the lady's lecture soon wore away.

The Burney diary of the doings at Streatham this year is continued till the middle of September. Dr. Burney's daughter knew all the Italian musicians of note who were then in England, and under date July 10 we read :—' You will believe I was not a little surprised to see Sacchini. He is going to the Continent with Piozzi; and Mrs. Thrale invited them both to spend the last day at Streatham, and from hence proceed to Margate.'

The friendship between Mrs. Thrale and Fanny Burney was not always perfectly free from clouds. Johnson once observed that his mistress showed the insolence of wealth as well as the conceit of parts; the latter, he said, had some foundation, but the former was a wretched thing. In like manner, Miss Burney sometimes felt that Mrs. Thrale was inclined to treat her as a dependent, while the elder lady thought that her many kindnesses did not

* Mme. d'Arblay's 'Diary,' ii. 355.

invariably meet with due acknowledgment. The latter tells how she nursed the young writer through an illness; 'and now,' she adds, 'with the true gratitude of a wit, she tells me that the world thinks the better of me for my civilities to her.' At another time we read: 'Not an article of dress, not a ticket for public places, not a thing in the world that she could not command from me: yet always insolent, always pining for home, always preferring her mode of life in St. Martin's Street to all I could do for her. She is a saucy-spirited little puss, to be sure, but I love her dearly for all that; and I fancy she has a real regard for me, if she did not think it beneath the dignity of a wit, or of what she values more—the dignity of Dr. Burney's daughter—to indulge it.' In 1781, she writes with still greater irritation: "What a blockhead Dr. Burney is to be always sending for his daughter home so. Is she not better and happier with me than she can be anywhere else? Dr. Johnson is enraged at the silliness of their family conduct; I confess myself provoked excessively, but I love the girl dearly, and the Doctor, too, for that matter, only he has such odd notions."

CHAPTER VII.

Introduction to Piozzi — Account of him — He goes Abroad — Second Sight — Piozzi Returns — Beginning of Uneasiness — Good Resolutions — Harley Street — The Widow Watched — Fears for Johnson — Death of Levet — Verses on him — Johnson's Emotion — Social Comforts — Mrs. Thrale has an Assembly — Literary Women — Mrs. Thrale Described — Rumours of her Marrying Again — Johnson Ill and Dispirited — A Lecture on Peevishness — Dr. Lee — Modern Refinement — Burton on Melancholy — Johnson and the Quakers — His Position at Streatham — A Disastrous Lawsuit — Reasons for Quitting Streatham — The Park Let to Lord Shelburne — The Last Summer there — Madame d'Arblay's Recollections — Johnson's Farewell to Streatham — He Accompanies Mrs. Thrale to Brighton — His Severity — Mrs. Thrale confesses her Attachment — Conduct of her Daughters and Miss Burney — Her Mental Struggles — Piozzi Dismissed — Embarrassments — Argyll Street — Resolution to leave London — Removal to Bath — The Parting with Piozzi — Mrs. Thrale loses her Youngest Daughter — Resentment.

MRS. THRALE's acquaintance with Piozzi commenced in 1780. Their first meeting had been in 1777. Madame d'Arblay tells how one evening at Dr. Burney's house, when Signor Piozzi was accompanying himself on the piano, Mrs. Thrale, stealing on tip-toe behind him, began ludicrously imitating his airs and gestures. Burney whispered to her: 'Because, madam, you have no ear yourself for music, will you destroy the attention of all who in that one point are otherwise gifted.'* The lady took this reproof in excellent part, but such an introduction was not likely to lead to further intercourse. While, however, the Thrales were at Brighton, after the Gordon Riots, Piozzi came thither also, for the benefit of his health, and was followed by a letter from Miss Burney, recommending him to her friend as a man who, though he had

* 'Memoirs of Dr. Burney,' ii. 110.

lost his fine voice, was still possessed of enchanting musical powers, and able to lighten the burthen of existence. According to notes written by Mrs. Thrale, some at the time and some at later dates, both she and Mr. Thrale took to their new acquaintance at once. In spite of weakened tones, his style of singing remained exquisite, while his performance on the piano was unrivalled. 'He wants nothing from us,' wrote the lady in August, 1780; 'I see nothing ail the man but pride. The newspapers yesterday told what all the musical folks gained, and set Piozzi down at £1,200 a year.'

'Mr. Piozzi,' she writes later on, 'was the son of a gentleman of Brescia, who meant him for the Church, and educated him accordingly; but he resisted the celibat, escaped from those who would have made him take the vows, and as his uncle said: "Ah, Gabrielli, thou wilt never get nearer the altar than the organ-loft," so it proved. He ran from the Venetian state to Milan, where the Marchese d' Araciel proved his constant friend and protector, and encouraged him in his fancy for trying Paris and London, instead of being a burthen to his parents, who had fourteen children, a limited income, and many pecuniary uneasinesses. Whilst here his fame reached the Queen of France, who sent for him and Sacchini, the great opera composer.'*

It was in obedience to this summons that Piozzi and Sacchini were quitting England, when they came to Streatham to take leave, as mentioned in our last chapter.

Piozzi returned from France before the end of the year, 'loaded with presents, honours, and emoluments.' So far his attentions to Mrs. Thrale had been observed by Johnson without any apparent displeasure. At the beginning of November he was in Lichfield, and she wrote to him:

* Hayward's 'Piozzi,' ii. 49.

'Instead of trying the *Sortes Virgilianæ* for our absent friends, we agreed after dinner to-day to ask little Harriet* what they were doing now who used to be our common guests at Streatham. "Dr. Johnson," says she, "is very rich and wise; Sir Philip is drowned in the water, and Mr. Piozzi is very sick and lame, poor man!" What a curious way of deciding! All in her little soft voice.' . . . 'Adieu, dear sir, and be as cheerful as you can this gloomy season. I see nobody happy hereabouts but the Burneys; they love each other with uncommon warmth of family affection, and are beloved by the world as much as if their fondness were less concentrated. The Captain has got a fifty-gun ship now, and we are all so rejoiced. Once more farewell, and do not forget Streatham nor its inhabitants, who are all much yours.'†

On the 24th Johnson wrote from Ashbourne: 'Piozzi I find is coming, in spite of Miss Harriet's prediction, or second sight, and when *he* comes and *I* come, you will have two about you that love you; and I question if either of us heartily care how few more you have. But how many soever they may be, I hope you keep your kindness for me, and I have a great mind to have Queeney's kindness too.'‡

On the following day the widow entered in her Diary: 'I have got my Piozzi home at last; he looks thin and battered, but always kindly upon me, I think.' He was more prudent than she, however, for after she had translated an Italian sonnet written in his praise, he insisted on her burning the verses, and she was fain to content herself with writing her version into 'Thraliana.'§

On December 3rd Johnson wrote: 'You have got Piozzi again, notwithstanding pretty Harriet's dire denunciations. . . . Pray contrive a multitude of good

* Her youngest child.
† 'Piozzi Letters,' ii. 217.
‡ *Ibid.*, ii. 227.
§ Hayward's 'Piozzi,' i. 162.

things for us to do when we meet. Something that may *hold all together*, though if anything makes me love you more, it is going from you.'*

The first note of uneasiness seems to be audible in the last sentence. We hear it a second time in a letter written five days later from Birmingham:

'I am come to this place on my way to London and Streatham. I hope to be in London on Tuesday or Wednesday, and at Streatham on Thursday, by your kind conveyance. I shall have nothing to relate either wonderful or delightful. But remember that you sent me away, and turned me out into the world, and you must take the chance of finding me better or worse. This you may know at present, that my affection for you is not diminished, and my expectation from you is increased. Do not neglect me, nor relinquish me. Nobody will ever love you better, or honour you more.'†

The extracts which have been published from 'Thraliana' show that its author began the new year with good resolutions for the present, and vague schemes for the future. If, she wrote, for her sins, God should take from her her monitor, her friend, her inmate, her dear Dr. Johnson; if neither she should marry, nor the purchasers of the brewery should fail; if no change in public affairs interrupted communications with the Continent; and if Piozzi did not take a wife and settle in England, she would, at the end of the four years from the sale of the business, set out for Italy with her eldest girls, and see what the world could show her.‡ On January 4, 1782, she wrote:

'I have taken a house in Harley Street for three months, and hope to have some society—not company

---

* 'Piozzi Letters,' ii. 229.   † *Ibid.*, ii. 230.
‡ Hayward's 'Piozzi,' i. 163.

though; crowds are out of the question, but people will not come hither [to Streatham] on short days, and 'tis too dull to live all alone so. The world will watch me at first, and think I come a husband-hunting for myself or my fair daughters, but when I have behaved prettily for a while, they will change their mind.'*

Ten days later: '*Harley Street, 14th January*, 1782.—The first seduction comes from Pepys. I had a letter to-day desiring me to dine in Wimpole Street, to meet Mrs. Montagu and a whole *army of blues*, to whom I trust my refusal will afford very pretty speculation, and they may settle my character and future conduct at their leisure. Pepys is a worthless fellow at last; he and his brother run about the town, spying and inquiring what Mrs. Thrale is to do this winter; what friends she is to see; what men are in her confidence; how soon she will be married. The brother, the Medico, as we call him, lays wagers about me, I find; God forgive me, but they'll make me hate them both.'†

'*1st February*, 1782.—Here is Mr. Johnson ill, very ill indeed, and I do not see what ails him. 'Tis repelled gout, I fear, fallen on the lungs, and breath of course. What shall we do for him? If I lose *him* I am more than undone: friend, father, guardian, confidant! God give me health and patience! What shall I do?'‡

This year opened sadly for Johnson with the loss of his old friend, Robert Levet, who died suddenly and unexpectedly in his sleep on the morning of January 17. Johnson was in Harley Street when the event occurred. Relating it two months later to Langton, he wrote: 'At night as at Mrs. Thrale's I was musing in my chamber, I thought with uncommon earnestness, that however I might alter my mode of life, or whithersoever I might remove, I would endeavour to retain Levet about me.

* Hayward's 'Piozzi,' i. 165.   † *Ibid.*, i. 165.   ‡ *Ibid.*, i. 167.

In the morning my servant brought me word that Levet was called to another state, a state for which, I think, he was not unprepared, for he was very useful to the poor. How much soever I valued him, I now wish that I had valued him more.'*

Thackeray, when lecturing on the Four Georges, asked his audience if they remembered the verses—'the sacred verses'—which Johnson wrote on this occasion:

> 'Condemned to Hope's delusive mine,
>   As on we toil from day to day;
> By sudden blasts, or slow decline,
>   Our social comforts drop away.
>
> 'Well tried through many a varying year,
>   See Levet to the grave descend;
> Officious, innocent, sincere,
>   Of every friendless name the friend. †
>
> 'In Misery's darkest cavern known,
>   His useful care was ever nigh,
> Where hopeless Anguish poured his groan,
>   And lonely Want retired to die.
>
> 'No summons mocked by chill delay,
>   No petty gain disdained by pride;
> The modest wants of every day
>   The toil of every day supplied.
>
> 'His virtues walked their narrow round,
>   Nor made a pause, nor left a void;
> And sure the Eternal Master found
>   The single talent well employed.' ‡

---

* Boswell's 'Johnson,' Hill's edition, iv. 145. This letter was written on March 20, 1782; and Dr. Birkbeck Hill (iv. 158, note 4) refers to it as showing that, so early as that date, the writer foresaw that a change was coming. But the musing of which Johnson speaks was not in March, but on January 16, by which time he cannot have begun seriously to apprehend the loss of his mistress. Was he musing on something more agreeable? Separation from Levet would not have followed from his being thrown back on Bolt Court, as he ultimately was; it would, unless provided against, have followed from his taking up his abode entirely with Mrs. Thrale. The widow was certain to marry again; and when she smiled on Johnson, it is quite possible that, despite his years and infirmities, the old man may have dreamed of checkmating Piozzi, and carrying off the prize himself.

† Mrs. Piozzi ('Synonymy,' ii. 79), quoting this stanza under *officious*, says: 'Johnson, always thinking neglect the worst misfortune that could befall a man, looked on a character of this description with less aversion than I do.' This is rather a strange remark to be made by a learned lady. The writer, of course, used 'officious' in the sense of kind, doing good offices, which is the first meaning assigned to the word in his dictionary.

‡ Johnson's 'Works,' i. 342, where the poem is printed with the heading,

Johnson repeated these verses to Boswell 'with an emotion which gave them full effect.' Miss Palmer, Sir Joshua's niece, was present, at another time, when he repeated them, with the water running down his face. Though but little used to the melting mood, the rugged old dictator's sensibility is not to be judged solely by his performances on those colloquial evenings, of which he used to say to his biographer, 'Well, we had good talk'; and that faithful henchman would make answer, 'Yes, Sir; you tossed and gored several persons.' When he would inveigh against devotional poetry, and protest that all religious verses were cold and feeble, his mistress would remind him how, as often as he attempted to go through the ' *Dies iræ dies illa*,' his voice invariably choked at the words :

> ' Quærens me sedisti lassus,
> Redemisti crucem passus ;
> Tantus labor ne sit cassus.' *

'When he read his own satire,' says Mrs. Piozzi, 'in which the life of a scholar is painted, with the various obstructions thrown in his way to fortune and fame, he burst into a passion of tears. The family and a certain Mr. Scott only were present, who in a jocose way clapped him on the back, and said, " What's all this, my dear Sir ? Why, you and I and Hercules, you know, were all troubled with melancholy." He was a very large man, this Mr. Scott, and made out the triumvirate with Johnson and Hercules comically enough. The Doctor was so delighted at his odd sally that he suddenly embraced him, and the subject was immediately changed.'†

' On the Death of Mr. Robert Levet, a practiser in physic.' It was first published in the *Annual Register* for 1783, p 189, where the subject is called Dr. Robert Levet. On the next page is printed *John Gilpin*.
 * In the familiar modern English version :
> ' Faint and weary Thou hast sought me,
> On the cross of suffering bought me ;
> Shall such grace be vainly brought me ?'

† ' Anecdotes, p. 50.

So far as Johnson's social comforts depended on Mrs. Thrale, they dropped away very gradually. He passed almost the whole of this year 'in a succession of ailments,' which did not tend to soften his temper or his manners, nor in any way assist him to make head against the growing favour of a rival. His letters mark the slow progress of his decline, as well as the fluctuations of his health. On February 16 he writes:

'Dearest Lady, I am better, but not yet well; but hope springs eternal. As soon as I can think myself not troublesome you may be sure of seeing me, for such a place to visit nobody ever had. Dearest Madam, do not think me worse than I am; be sure, at least, that whatever happens to me, I am with all the regard that admiration of excellence and gratitude for kindness can excite, your,' etc.*

On the 21st: 'I hope to try again this week whether your house is yet so cold, for to be away from you, if I did not think our separation likely to be short, how could I endure? You are a dear, dear lady, and your kind attention is a great part of what life affords to your,' etc.†

At the end of the same month he wrote to Malone, that he went in a coach as far as Mrs. Thrale's, where he could use all the freedom that sickness required; and some time later to other correspondents, that he had been living much with Mrs. Thrale, and had all the care from her that she could take, or could be taken.

On February 20, Mrs. Thrale writes to Fanny Burney:

'Wednesday night, Going to bed.

'MY DEAREST BURNEY,

'May I venture, do you think, to call a little company about me on St. Taffy's day? Or will the world in general, and the Pepyses in particular, feel

---

* 'Piozzi Letters,' ii. 231.   † *Ibid.*, ii. 236.

shocked at my "dissipation" and my "haste to be married?" They came last night, and found me alone with Murphy. There was an epoch! The Bishop of Peterborough came in soon after. Queeney was gone to Miss Davenant's, with Miss Owen and Dr. Delap. What dangers we do go through! But I have not gone out to meet mine half-way, at least.

'Pray come on Friday se'nnight, if you never come again.

'I went to dear Dr. Johnson's, *rassegnarlo la solita servitù*, but at one o'clock he was not up, and I did not like to disturb him. I am very sorry about him—exceeding sorry! When I parted from you on Monday, and found him with Dr. Lawrence, I put my nose into the old man's wig and shouted; but got none except melancholy answers—so melancholy, that I was forced to crack jokes for fear of crying. . . .

'This morning I was with him again, and this evening Mrs. Ord's conversation, and Piozzi's *cara voce* have kept away care pretty well. Mr. Selwyn helped us to be comfortable. . . .

'Good-night, sweetest, I am tired and want to go to bed. Good-night once more, through the door at Streatham, for thither imagination carries your affectionate

'H. L. T.'*

The assembly—the first large party which the widow had given—took place, and included, besides a fair Greek who captivated Miss Burney, 'the Hales, Mr. Jenkinson,† Lord and Lady Sandys, the Burgoynes, Mr. Seward, Mr. Murphy, Dr. Delap, Mrs. Byron, and fifty more at least.'‡

In a letter written a few days later, Miss Burney

---

* Mme. d'Arblay's 'Diary,' i. 414.   † Afterwards Earl of Liverpool.
‡ Mme. d'Arblay's 'Diary,' i. 420.

mentions some verses on the literary women of the time, which appeared in the *Morning Herald* of March 12, 1782, and in which she and Mrs. Thrale were introduced in company with several other ladies of their acquaintance. Fanny supposed the anonymous author of these lines to be Mr. (afterwards Sir) W. W. Pepys, but they seem to have been the production of Dr. Burney.[*] They exhorted the *Herald* to desist from celebrating frail beauties, and to proclaim instead:

> 'Hannah More's pathetic pen,
> Painting high the impassioned scene;
> Carter's piety and learning,
> Little Burney's quick discerning;
> Cowley's[†] neatly pointed wit,
> Healing those her satires hit;
> Smiling Streatfield's ivory neck,
> Nose, and notions—*à la Grècque!*
> Let Chapone retain a place,
> And the mother of her Grace,
> Each art of conversation knowing,
> High-bred, elegant Boscawen;[‡]
> Thrale, in whose expressive eyes
> Sits a soul above disguise,
> Skilled with wit and sense t' impart
> Feelings of a generous heart.
> Lucan, Leveson, Greville, Crewe;
> Fertile-minded Montagu,
> Who makes each rising art her care,
> And brings her knowledge from afar.'

The writer did not intend this description of Mrs. Thrale to be unmixed flattery. Evidently he intended to convey what his daughter plainly expressed when she wrote of her friend: 'Mrs. Thrale is a most dear

---

[*] See Mme. d'Arblay's 'Diary,' i. 422, note by the editor.

[†] Author of 'The Belle's Stratagem,' and other less successful dramatic works, and also of some long poetical pieces. Born 1743; died 1809.

[‡] 'The Honourable Mrs. Boscawen,' wrote Boswell, 'widow of the Admiral, and mother of the present Viscount Falmouth; of whom, if it be not presumptuous in me to praise her, I would say that her manners are the most agreeable, and her conversation the best of anybody with whom I ever had the happiness to be acquainted.' She was also the mother of the Duchess of Beaufort and Mrs. Leveson-Gower.

> 'All Leveson's sweetness and all Beaufort's grace.'
> H. More's 'Sensibility.'

creature, but never restrains her tongue in anything. She laughs, cries, scolds, sports, reasons, makes fun—does everything she has an inclination to do, without any study of prudence, or thought of blame ; and pure and artless as is this character it often draws both herself and others into scrapes, which a little discretion would avoid.'

But though the newspapers were willing to insert compliments to Mrs. Thrale, they were equally ready to publish gossip to her disadvantage. She laid aside her weeds on the anniversary of her husband's death, and the town was at once full of rumours that she was preparing to replace them by a bridal veil. 'Lord Loughborough,' she wrote at the end of a week,* 'Sir Richard Jebb, Mr. Piozzi, Mr. Selwyn, Dr. Johnson, every man that comes to the house, is put in the papers for me to marry. In good time, I wrote to-day to beg the *Morning Herald* would say no more about me, good or bad.' Yet so far the public curiosity about her had inflicted no deep wounds on her vanity. Under date of April 17, she adds:

" I am returned to Streatham, pretty well in health, and very sound in heart, notwithstanding the watchers and the wager-layers, who think more of the charms of their sex by half than I, who know them better. . . . Somebody mentioned my going to be married t'other day, and Johnson was joking about it. 'I suppose, Sir,' said I, 'they think they are doing me honour with these imaginary matches, when perhaps the man does not exist who would do me honour by marrying me!' This, indeed, was said in the wild and insolent spirit of Baretti, yet 'tis nearer the truth than one would think for. A woman of passable person, ancient family, respectable character, uncommon talents, and three thousand a year, has a right to think herself any man's equal, and has

* In 'Thraliana,' Hayward's 'Piozzi,' i. 167.

nothing to seek but return of affection from whatever partner she pitches on. To marry for love would, therefore, be rational in me, who want no advancement of birth or fortune, and *till I am in love* I will not marry, nor perhaps then."*

Meanwhile Johnson, sick, out of spirits, and now fully conscious of losing ground, was in a much less placid temper. He appears to have accompanied his mistress to Streatham, but to have left her in dudgeon after a few days' stay. On April 25 he writes:

'Madam,—I have been very much out of order since you sent me away; but why should I tell you, who do not care, nor desire to know? I dined with Mr. Paradise on Monday, with the Bishop of St. Asaph yesterday, with the Bishop of Chester I dine to-day, and with the Academy on Saturday, with Mr. Hoole on Monday, and with Mrs. Garrick on Thursday, the 2nd of May, and then—what care you *what then?* .... Do not let Mr. Piozzi nor anybody else put me quite out of your head, and do not think that anybody will love you like your,' etc.†

On the last day of the month we find him begging to be sent for to Streatham; but he was not able to rest there; for on May 9 Mrs. Thrale wrote: 'To-day I bring home to Streatham my poor Dr. Johnson. He went to town a week ago by the way of amusing himself, and got so very ill that I thought I should never get him home alive.'‡

At the beginning of June, he is in Bolt Court again, and a little better. 'This day I dined upon skate, pudding, goose, and your asparagus, and could have eaten more, but was prudent. Pray for me, dear Madam; I hope the tide has turned. The change that I feel is more than I durst have hoped, or than I thought possible; but there

---

* In 'Thraliana,' Hayward's 'Piozzi,' i. 168.   † 'Piozzi Letters,' ii. 237.
‡ Hayward's 'Piozzi,' i. 159.

has not yet passed a whole day, and I may rejoice perhaps too soon. Come and see me ; and when you think best, upon due consideration, take me away.'*

On June 8 : 'I have this day taken a passage to Oxford for Monday. Not to " frisk," as you express it with very unfeeling irony, but to catch at the hopes of better health. The change of place may do something. To leave the house where so much has been suffered affords some pleasure.'† Four days later he apologizes for his ill-humour : ' My letter was perhaps peevish, but it was not unkind. I should have cared little about a wanton expression if there had been no kindness.'‡ At the University he met his devoted admirer, Hannah More. 'We do so gallant it about,' she writes. 'You cannot imagine with what delight he showed me every part of his own college.'§ Here, too, he received from his mistress a long, lively, and discursive letter :

"Streatham, June 14.

"DEAR SIR,

"I am glad you confess yourself peevish, for confession must precede amendment. Do not study to be more unhappy than you are ; and if you can eat and sleep well, do not be frighted, for there can be no real danger. Are you acquainted with Dr. Lee, the master of Baliol College ? And are you not delighted with his gaiety of manners and youthful vivacity now that he is eighty-six years old ? I never heard a more perfect or excellent pun than his, when some one told him how, in a late dispute among the Privy Councillors, the Lord Chancellor struck the table with such violence that he split it. 'No, no, no!' replied the master dryly, 'I can hardly

* 'Piozzi Letters,' ii. 242.
† *Ibid.*, ii. 251. This letter is misdated, and consequently misplaced in the correspondence.
‡ *Ibid.*, ii. 243.   § 'Memoirs,' i. 261.

persuade myself that he split the table, though I believe he divided the board.' Will you send me anything better from Oxford than this?—for there must be no more fastidiousness now; no more refusing to laugh at a good quibble, when you so loudly profess the want of amusement, and the necessity of diversion. How the people of this age do cry for rattles is indeed little to its credit; for knowledge is diffused most certainly, if not increased, and that ought to stand instead of perpetual variety, one would think. Apropos to general improvement: I was reading the 'Spectator' to Sophy, while my maid papered my curls yester-morning; it was vol. iii., p. 217, where the man complains of an indelicate mistress, who said, on some occasion, that 'her stomach ached,' and lamented how 'her teeth had got a seed stuck between them.' The woman that dressed me was so astonished at this grossness, though common enough in Addison's time one sees, that she cried out, 'Well, madam, surely that could never have been *a lady* who used expressions like those.'

"I much wonder whether this refinement has spread all over the Continent, or whether 'tis confined to our own island. When we were in France we could form but little judgment, as our time was passed chiefly among English; yet I recollect that one fine lady, who entertained us very splendidly, put her mouth to the teapot, and blew in the spout when it did not pour freely. My maid Peggy would not have touched the tea after such an operation. Was it convenient, and agreeable, and wise, and fine, I should like to see the world beyond sea very much:

"'But fate has fast bound her,
With Styx nine times round her.'

So your friend must look on the waves at Brighthelmstone without breathing a wish to cross them.

"Meantime, let us be as merry as reading Burton upon 'Melancholy' will make us. You bid me study that book in your absence; and now, What have I found? Why, I have found, or fancied, that he has been cruelly plundered; that Milton's first idea of 'L'Allegro' and 'Il Penseroso' was suggested by the verses at the beginning; that Savage's 'Speech of Suicide' in the 'Wanderer' grew up out of a passage you probably remember towards the 216th page; that Swift's 'tale of the woman that holds water in her mouth, to regain her husband's love by silence' had its source in the same farrago; and that there is an odd similitude between my lord's trick upon Sly the Tinker, in Shakspeare's 'Taming of the Shrew,' and some stuff I have been reading in Burton.

"And now, dear Sir, be as comfortable as you can, and do not dun me for that kindness which has never been withheld, only because it is cold weather and you want employment; but be gentle and tranquil like Dr. Adams,* or gay and flashy like Dr. Lee, and then—what then? Why then you will deserve Miss Adams's good-will, and Miss More's esteem, added to the humble service and attentive regard of your ever equally faithful

"H. L. T."†

This is the sort of letter which a clever woman addresses to a man her regard for whom is on the wane, but with whom she wishes to continue on friendly terms. He answers: 'Oxford has done, I think, what for the present it can do, and I am going slyly to take a place in the coach for Wednesday, and you or my sweet Queeney will fetch me on Thursday, and see what you can make of me.'‡

* The Master of Pembroke College. † 'Piozzi Letters,' ii. 245-248.
‡ *Ibid.*, ii. 249.

From this time until the establishment at Streatham was broken up in the following October, Johnson appears to have been almost constantly there with Mrs. Thrale. Neither his health nor his temper was in a state to endure the smallest strain. "It grew extremely perplexing and difficult," wrote the lady, "to live in the house with him when the master of it was no more; the worse, indeed, because his dislikes grew capricious, and he could scarce bear to have anybody come to the house whom it was absolutely necessary for me to see. Two gentlemen I perfectly well remember dining with us at Streatham in the summer of 1782, when Elliot's brave defence of Gibraltar was a subject of common discourse. One of these men naturally enough began some talk about red-hot balls thrown with surprising dexterity and effect, which Dr. Johnson having listened some time to, 'I would advise you, Sir,' said he, with a cold sneer, 'never to relate this story again. You really can scarce imagine how very poor a figure you make in the telling of it.' Our guest being bred a Quaker, and, I believe, a man of an extremely gentle disposition, needed no more reproofs for the same folly; so if he ever did speak again, it was in a low voice to the friend who came with him. The check was given before dinner, and after coffee I left the room. When in the evening, however, our companions were returned to London, and Mr. Johnson and myself were left alone, with only our usual family about us, 'I did not quarrel with those Quaker fellows,' said he very seriously. 'You did perfectly right,' replied I, 'for they gave you no cause of offence.' 'No offence,' returned he with an altered voice. 'And is it nothing, then, to sit whispering together when I am present, without ever directing their discourse towards me, or offering me a share in the conversation?' 'That was because you frighted him who spoke first about those hot balls.' 'Why, Madam, if a creature is neither capable of giving dignity to falsehood, nor willing to remain contented with the truth, he deserves no better treatment.' "*

The guests thus affronted were no doubt two of the Barclays, to whom, of course, their hostess wished to be especially civil.† Yet in spite of rudeness and ill-humour, Johnson had no thought of voluntarily leaving Streatham, nor any apprehension at that time of being dismissed by its owner. On August 24 he wrote to Boswell: 'Being uncertain whether I should have any call this autumn into the country, I did not immediately answer your kind letter. I have no call; but if you desire to meet me at Ashbourne, I believe I can come thither; if you had rather come to London, I can stay at Streatham—take your choice.' ‡

Meanwhile, Mrs. Thrale found herself embarrassed by a disastrous lawsuit, as well as enthralled by her growing attachment to Piozzi. She had become involved in a litigation with her uncle's widow,§ which all her friends appear to have deeply deplored. In August she wrote in her diary: 'The establishment of expense here at Streatham is more than my income will answer; my lawsuit with Lady Salusbury turns out worse in the event, and infinitely

---

* 'Anecdotes.'

† A few weeks before she had written to Miss Burney : 'David Barclay has sent me the "Apology for the Quakers," and thinks to convert me, I believe. I have often been solicited to change my religion by Papists. Why do all the people think me foolisher than I am?'—Mme. d'Arblay's 'Diary,' i. 427.

‡ Boswell's 'Johnson,' Hill's edition, iv. 153.

§ 'Lady Salusbury,' she told Sir James Fellowes, 'had threatened to seize upon my Welsh estate if I did not repay her money lent by Sir Thomas Salusbury to my father; money, in effect, which poor papa had borrowed to give *him* when he was a student at Cambridge, and your little friend just born. This debt, however, not having been cancelled, stood against me as heiress.'— Hayward's 'Piozzi,' ii. 57. But this can scarcely be a complete or correct account of the dispute between the two ladies. If it were, one does not see why the claim should have slept for so many years after the death of Sir Thomas.

more costly than I could have dreamed on. £8,000 is supposed necessary for the payment of it, and how am I to raise £8,000? ... I must go abroad and save money. To show Italy to my girls, and be showed it by Piozzi, has long been my dearest wish, but to leave Mr. Johnson shocked me, and to take him appeared impossible. His recovery, however, from an illness we all thought dangerous gave me courage to speak to him on the subject.' She goes on to say that she had just mustered resolution to tell him of her project, and that he had approved it, and advised her to put it into execution as soon as possible.* In the same, and a subsequent entry, she declares herself mortified at finding that the man she had so 'fondled in sickness and in health,' and who she 'really thought could not have existed without her *conversation*, forsooth, was not only prepared for her going abroad, but seemed not even anxious to go with her, and, indeed, glad to be rid of her.'

On August 12 Miss Burney wrote to her sister Susan: 'My dear Mrs. Thrale, the friend, though not the *most* dear friend of my heart, is going abroad for three years certain. This scheme has been some time in a sort of distant agitation, but it is now brought to a resolution. Much private business belongs to it relative to her detestable lawsuit; but much private inclination is also joined with it, relative to her long wishing to see Italy. ... Streatham, my other home, and the place where I have long thought my residence, dependent only upon my own pleasure, and where, indeed, I have received such as my father and you alone could make greater, is already let for three years to Lord Shelburne.'† Lord Shelburne, who as Prime Minister was negotiating peace with the

---
* Mr. Hayward ('Piozzi,' i. 168) quotes this entry from 'Thraliana' under date August 22; but Streatham had been let ten days before that time.
† Mme. d'Arblay's 'Diary,' i. 437.

United States, France, and Spain, had agreed to hire Streatham Park in order to be constantly near London.*

Meanwhile, the season dragged on wearily to its close. Cold and bad weather, even snow, helped to depress spirits that were already disturbed. Fanny had published 'Cecilia' shortly before the date of her last quoted letter, and about the same date she wrote to Mrs. Thrale: 'I have been kept in hot water, in defiance of snow, till I heard from my dearest Tyo;† and if you do like the book, I am gratified to my heart's content; and if you only say you do, to have it so said is very delightful, for your wish to give me pleasure would give it, if you hated all I ever wrote.... To-morrow I spend with Mrs. Ord. Friday, if there comes a dry frost,‡ to you will run your own F. B.'§

What she witnessed on her arrival is not written in F. B.'s diary. There she faithfully keeps the secret, with which no doubt she was already acquainted, of her Tyo's infatuation. But in the Memoirs of her father, published long after Mrs. Piozzi's death, Madame d'Arblay has described, with all the grandiosity of her latest style, the aspect of the place during the final period of her visiting there:

'Changed indeed was Streatham! Gone its chief, and changed his relict! unaccountably, incomprehensibly, indefinably changed! She was absent and agitated; not two minutes could she remain in a place; she hardly seemed to know whom she saw; her speech was so hurried that it was hardly intelligible; her eyes were

* Fitzmaurice's 'Shelburne,' iii. 242.
† A Tahitian word for 'friend,' which the Burneys had borrowed from Omai.
‡ On August 30 Horace Walpole wrote to Mann: 'We have had the most deplorably wet summer that ever I remember, after three hotter than any in my memory.'—'Letters,' viii. 273.
§ Mme. d'Arblay's 'Diary,' i. 440.

assiduously averted from those who sought them, and her smiles were faint and forced.'*

Dr. Burney and all others—Dr. Johnson not excepted—were cast into the same gulf of general neglect; all, that is, but Fanny, 'to whom, the fatal secret once acknowledged, Mrs. Thrale clung for comfort.' Finally we are told that, as the widow became more and more dissatisfied with her own situation, and impatient for its relief, she slighted Johnson's counsel, and avoided his society.† Madame d'Arblay remembered a scene in which her father, puzzled by what he saw, bade farewell to Streatham with tears in his eyes. She recalled another day on which Johnson accompanied her to London, and when they faced the windows, as the coach turned into Streatham Common, tremulously exclaimed: 'That house . . . is lost to me . . . for ever.'‡ We must not lay too much stress on these recollections. They were recorded after the lapse of nearly half a century, and are tinged, and perhaps distorted, by the thoughts and feelings with which the writer had been in the habit of regarding her friend's second marriage. If Dr. Johnson spoke of Streatham as lost to him for ever, he certainly did not mean that he was then in effect discarded by its owner, but only that he expected to have died, or lost his hold on her, before she resumed possession at the end of the three years' tenancy. Mrs. Thrale, however, has herself confirmed Madame d'Arblay's general account of the condition into which she had fallen before leaving her home. She says that she 'confessed her attachment to Piozzi and her eldest daughter together, with many tears and agonies, one day at Streatham; told them both that I wished I had two hearts for their sakes, but having only one, I would break it between them, and give them each *ciascheduno la metà!*'§

* 'Memoirs,' ii. 243. † *Ibid.*, ii. 250.
‡ *Ibid.*, ii. 252. § Hayward's 'Piozzi,' i. 189.

As old Michaelmas Day approached, and brought with it the necessity of giving place to Lord Shelburne, probably no one in the house regretted the prospect, except Johnson, who loved his old asylum, and disliked Brighton, whither he was to remove with the rest of the family.

On Sunday, October 6, Johnson entered into his 'Book of Meditations' a prayer which he composed on leaving Streatham; he went to church, and made a memorandum: *Templo valedixi cum osculo.* The following day he entered:

'I was called early. I packed up my bundles, and used the foregoing prayer with my morning devotions, somewhat, I think, enlarged. Being earlier than the family, I read St. Paul's farewell in the Acts, and then read fortuitously in the Gospels, which was my parting use of the library.'

Boswell, who suppresses the fact that Mrs. Thrale had let her house, and was leaving it at the same time with her guest, miscalls this a prayer 'on leaving Mr. Thrale's family,' and says that one cannot read it 'without some emotions not very favourable to the lady whose conduct occasioned it.' He would have his readers understand that in some way Johnson was cast off. Macaulay, and other writers, relying on Boswell, have followed suit. But where is the offence? Had not Mrs. Thrale the right to let her house? What could she do more for her old friend than carry him where she herself was going? The prayer certainly hints no reflection on her; it commends the family to the Divine protection; possibly this may have misled some writers into supposing that the author was being turned adrift. Croker, whom Macaulay so much despised, adds in a note: 'He seems to have taken leave of the kitchen as well as of the church in Latin.'

The note of his last dinner at Streatham, done into English, would run thus:

'*Sunday, October 6, 1782.*—I dined at Streatham on boiled leg of lamb, with spinach, the stuffing of flour and raisins; round of beef and turkey poult; and after the meat service, figs, grapes, not yet ripe in consequence of the bad season, with peaches, also hard. I took my place at table in no joyful mood, and partook of the food moderately, lest I should finish by intemperance. If I rightly remember, the banquet at the funeral of Hadon* came into my mind. When shall I revisit Streatham?'

Mrs. Thrale did not leave Streatham a day after nor a day before Johnson; she left the place, as he did, on October 7, 1782. She has mentioned this herself,† and he appears to have occupied a seat in the chaise which carried her to Brighton. At all events, we find him established there a few days after the removal. Boswell says that his friend Metcalfe was a good deal with him at Brighton this autumn, but omits the fact that Johnson was Mrs. Thrale's guest. Boswell's imitators have suggested that Johnson lived a kind of boarding-house life during this visit, and that 'he was not asked out into company with his fellow-lodgers.' But here again is a misrepresentation. Thrale, as we have seen, had a well-appointed house of his own at the Sussex watering-place; this now belonged to his daughters, but during their nonage was still presided over by their mother as mistress. If Johnson was not asked out, he had no one but himself to blame, as will be seen immediately.

Miss Burney joined the party on October 26, and on the 28th she writes: 'At dinner we had Dr. Delap and Mr. Selwyn, who accompanied us in the evening to a ball, as did also Dr. Johnson, to the universal amazement of

* We have not met with an explanation of this allusion.
† Hayward's 'Piozzi,' i. 188.

all who saw him there; but he said he had found it so dull being quite alone the preceding evening, that he determined upon going with us; ".for," he said, "it cannot be worse than being alone." Strange that he should think so! I am sure I am not of his mind.'*

On the 29th she describes a large party at home, in which Johnson fell upon Mr. Pepys, and fairly drove him from the house: 'Dr. Johnson was certainly right with respect to the argument and to reason; but his opposition was so warm, and his wit so satirical and exulting, that I was really quite grieved to see how unamiable he appeared, and how greatly he made himself dreaded by all, and by many abhorred.'† It is quite true that after this the Doctor was seldom included in invitations, but Miss Burney gives the reason: 'He is almost constantly omitted, either from too much respect or too much fear.'‡

'*November* 7.—Mr. Metcalfe called upon Dr. Johnson and took him out an airing. Mr. Hamilton is gone, and Mr. Metcalfe is now the only person out of this house that voluntarily communicates with the Doctor. He has been in a terrible severe humour of late, and has really frightened all the people, till they almost ran from him. To me only I think he is now kind, for Mrs. Thrale fares worse than anybody.'§

'*Wednesday, November* 20.—Mrs. Thrale and the three Miss Thrales‖ and myself all arose at six o'clock in the morning; and "by the pale blink of the moon" we went to the sea-side, where we had bespoke the bathing-women

---

* Mme. d'Arblay's 'Diary,' i. 445.
† *Ibid.*, i. 447.   ‡ *Ibid.*, i. 452.   § *Ibid.*, i. 459.
‖ Dr. Birkbeck Hill says, of her twelve children but these three were living, (iv. 157, note). There is a slight inaccuracy here. The three daughters referred to were Hester, Susan, and Sophia. But Mrs. Thrale at this time had two younger daughters, Cecilia and Harriet, whom she had left in a school at Streatham.—Hayward's 'Piozzi,' i. 192, note; ii. 53. 'Susan Thrale has just had her hair turned up and powdered, and taken to the womanly robe,' wrote Miss Burney in December, 1782.—Mme. d'Arblay's 'Diary,' i. 489.

to be ready for us, and into the ocean we plunged. It was cold, but pleasant. We then returned home, and dressed by candle-light, and as soon as we could get Dr. Johnson ready, we set out upon our journey, in a coach and a chaise, and arrived in Argyll Street at dinner-time. Mrs. Thrale has here fixed her tent for this short winter, which will end with the beginning of April, when her foreign journey takes place.'

The widow's passion had now passed beyond her control. Before she left Brighton she plainly confessed the state of her heart and mind to her eldest daughter, who, she says, must have known it already from a previous conversation at Streatham. She did this in order that the guardians might have ample time during the winter to take such steps as they might judge proper. Queeney, who inherited her father's temperament, showed herself cold, haughty, disdainful. Fanny Burney, on being taken into the conference, overflowed with tears and sympathy, but was more than ever determined to give no approval. Children, observed the writer of 'Cecilia,' religion,* situation, country, and character—to say nothing of the diminution of income by £800 a year, which was the penalty imposed by Thrale's will on a remarriage—were too much sacrifice to be made for any one man. Nevertheless, on her arrival in London, the enamoured lady proceeded to give her lover some hopes, while the guardians met to concert measures for preventing the three eldest girls from being carried out of England. It was not, however, deemed necessary or desirable to adopt any active proceedings. Mrs. Thrale took her full share in the ordinary engagements and employments of her London season. She gave parties, went to parties, was much

* It will be remembered that Miss Burney herself married a Roman Catholic.

with her Tyo, and paid an amount of attention to Johnson which proves anything rather than want of heart.

On December 20 the old man had been worse than usual, and wrote to her in his usual querulous tone: 'You can hardly think how bad I have been while you were in all your altitudes at the opera, and all the fine places, and thinking little of me. Queeney never sent me a kind word. I hope, however, to be with you again in a short time, and show you a man again.'* On the 27th Miss Burney writes: 'I dined with Mrs. Thrale and Dr. Johnson, who was very comic and good-humoured. . . . Mrs. Thrale, who was to have gone with me to Mrs. Ord's, gave up her visit in order to stay with Dr. Johnson. Miss Thrale, therefore, and I went together.'†

At this point a gap occurs in our materials. When the 'Thraliana' were examined, it was found that several pages were missing, and we have no letters to supply the deficiency. Beyond the information contained in the following extract, we know little, but evidently concerted efforts were made to influence the widow, about whose affairs so many persons busied themselves. Pressure was brought to bear, and eventually she was induced to dismiss Piozzi. The following is abridged from 'Thraliana': " January 29, 1783:

"The cold dislike of my eldest daughter I thought might wear away by familiarity with his merit, and that we might live tolerably together, or, at least, part friends—but no; her aversion increased daily, and she communicated it to the others. . . . By these means the notion of my partiality took air, and whether Miss Thrale sent him word slyly or not I cannot tell, but on the 25th January, 1783, Mr. Crutchley came hither to conjure me not to go to Italy; he had heard such things, he said, and by means

* 'Piozzi Letters,' ii. 252.   † Mme. d'Arblay's 'Diary,' i. 489.

next to miraculous. The next day, Sunday, 26th, Fanny Burney came, said I must marry him instantly or give him up; that my reputation would be lost else.

"I actually groaned with anguish, threw myself on the bed in an agony which my fair daughter beheld with frigid indifference. She had indeed never by one tender word endeavoured to dissuade me from the match, but said, coldly, that if I would abandon my children I must; that their father had not deserved such treatment from me; that I should be punished by Piozzi's neglect, for that she knew he hated me; and that I turned out my offspring to chance for his sake, like puppies in a pond, to swim or drown according as Providence pleased; that for her part, she must look herself out a place like the other servants, for my face would she never see more! 'Nor write to me?' said I. 'I shall not, Madam,' replied she with a cold sneer, 'easily find out your address; for you are going you know not whither, I believe.'

"Susan and Sophy said nothing at all, but they taught the two young ones to cry, 'Where are you going, mamma? will you leave us and die as our poor papa did?' There was no standing that, so I wrote my lover word that my mind was all distraction, and bid him come to me the next morning, 27th January—my birthday—and spent the Sunday night in torture not to be described. My falsehood to my Piozzi, my strong affection for him, the incapacity I felt in myself to resign the man I so adored, the hopes I had so cherished, inclined me strongly to set them all at defiance, and go with him to church to sanctify the promises I had so often made him; while the idea of abandoning the children of my first husband, who left me so nobly provided for, and who depended on my attachment to his offspring, awakened the voice of conscience, and threw me on my knees to pray for His direction who was hereafter to judge my conduct. His grace illuminated me, His power strengthened me, and I flew to my daughter's bed in the morning, and told her my resolution to resign my own, my dear, my favourite purpose, and to prefer my children's interest to my love. She questioned my ability to make the sacrifice; said one word from him would undo all my——[Here two pages are missing.]

"I told Dr. Johnson and Mr. Crutchley three days ago that I had determined—seeing them so averse to it—that I would not go abroad, but that, if I did not leave England, I *would* leave London, where I had not been treated to my mind, and where I had flung away much unnecessary money with little satisfaction; that I was greatly in debt, and somewhat distressed; that borrowing was always bad, but of one's children worst; that Mr. Crutchley's objection to their lending me their money when I had a mortgage to offer as security, was unkind and harsh; that I would go live in a little way at Bath till I had paid all my debts and cleared my income; that I would no more be tyrannized over by people who hated or people who plundered me; in short, that I would retire and save money, and lead this uncomfortable life no longer. They made little or no reply, and I am resolved to do as I declared."*

After raising every penny that could be made by cutting timber and other expedients, it appeared that a considerable sum over £7,000 had still to be provided for the settlement of the lawsuit, the payment of debts, and necessary expenses. It was at length arranged that the thousands should be advanced out of the children's fortunes on their mother giving the trustees a mortgage for that sum over her property in Denbighshire. Mr.

* Hayward's 'Piozzi,' i. 193.

Crutchley, a hard man, and suspected of wishing to marry Hester Thrale, found the remaining hundreds, and when the mortgage deeds were executed, bade the luckless borrower make her daughters her best curtsey, and thank them for keeping her out of gaol.*

When Boswell, having reached London on March 20, 1783, went next day to look for Johnson: 'I was glad,' he writes, 'to find him at Mrs. Thrale's house in Argyll Street, appearances of friendship between them being still kept up. . . . He sent a message to acquaint Mrs. Thrale that I was arrived. I had not seen her since her husband's death. She soon appeared, and favoured me with an invitation to stay to dinner, which I accepted. There was no other company but herself and three of her daughters, Dr. Johnson and I. She too said she was very glad I was come, for she was going to Bath, and would have been sorry to leave Dr. Johnson before I came. This seemed to be attentive and kind; and I, who had not been informed of any change, imagined all to be as well as formerly.'† On the following day, which was Saturday, Johnson was still at Mrs. Thrale's, when Boswell called, though he was going home in the afternoon, according to his custom before-mentioned. It is always to be remembered that, in the interval between taking his notes and publishing his book, the biographer quarrelled with the lady. Having chosen to represent the departure from Streatham as a rupture of old ties, he was obliged to treat the apparently cordial relations in Argyll Street as illusory. Yet it is clear, from his express testimony, that Johnson retained his quarters in Mrs. Thrale's house down to the time of her leaving London; and that she expressed affectionate anxiety as to what might become of him when she was gone.

* Hayward's 'Piozzi,' i. 175; ii. 57. † Boswell, iv. 166.

Yet Mrs. Thrale confessed in her 'Anecdotes' that the difficulty of keeping house with Johnson after her husband's death had something to do with her resolution to settle at Bath:

"When there was nobody to restrain his dislikes, it was extremely difficult to find anybody with whom he could converse, without living always on the verge of a quarrel, or of something too like a quarrel to be pleasing. I came into the room, for example, one evening, where he and a gentleman, whose abilities we all respected exceedingly, were sitting. A lady, who had walked in two minutes before me, had blown 'em both into a flame by whispering something to Mr. S——d, which he endeavoured to explain away, so as not to affront the Doctor, whose suspicions were all alive. 'And have a care, sir,' said he, just as I came in, 'the old lion will not bear to be tickled.'* The other was pale with rage, the lady wept at the confusion she had caused, and I could only say with Lady Macbeth:

"'So! you've displaced the mirth, broke the good meeting
With most admir'd disorder.'

"Such accidents, however, occurred too often; and I was forced to take advantage of my lost lawsuit, and plead inability of purse to remain longer in London or its vicinage. I had been crossed in my intentions of going abroad, and found it convenient, for every reason of health, peace, and pecuniary circumstances, to retire to Bath, where I knew Mr. Johnson would not follow me, and where I could for that reason command some little portion of time for my own use—a thing impossible while I remained at Streatham or at London, as my hours, carriage, and servants had long been at his command; who would not rise in the morning till twelve o'clock

---

* This must be the quarrel between Johnson and Seward at which Miss Streatfield cried.

perhaps, and oblige me to make breakfast for him till the bell rung for dinner, though much displeased if the toilet was neglected, and though much of the time we passed together was spent in blaming or deriding, very justly, my neglect of economy, and waste of that money which might make many families happy."*

On Sunday, April 6, she left town for Bath. The day previous Johnson made this entry in his diary: 'April 5. I took leave of Mrs. Thrale. I was much moved. I had some expostulations with her. She said that she was likewise affected. I commended the Thrales with great good will to God; may my petitions have been heard!'

On the morning of her departure she separated from Piozzi at a farewell breakfast. It had been arranged between them that he should quit England; their parting was of course a tender one. To prevent it from becoming too painful, she had secured the presence of a young Italian friend of her lover, and when all was over she flung herself into the arms of Fanny Burney.

She had requested Piozzi to return her letters, and leave the country. He agreed to do both. When he handed the packet of letters to Miss Thrale, he bade the girl take it to her mamma, and make of her a countess. 'It shall kill me,' he said, 'but it shall kill her too.' Queeney took the papers, and turned her back on the despised Italian. An unfounded report was spread that he had been bought off with the young ladies' money. Mrs. Thrale established herself in a house in Russell Street, Bath, on a plan of economy, with three daughters, three maids, and a man. But scarcely had she unpacked her trunks, when she was summoned to her two little girls, who had been seized with whooping-cough in the school where she had left them. Almost every ailment

* There is more of this passage, to which we shall recur later on.

proved fatal to her children. She wrote to Bolt Court: 'My health, my children, and my fortune, dear Sir, are coming fast to an end, I think: not so my sorrows. Harriet is dead, Cicely is dying.'* Cicely did not die, but recovered, and lived to grow up and marry. Johnson could always do himself justice with a pen ; he writes on May Day : ' I am glad that you went to Streatham, though you could not save the dear pretty little girl. I loved her, for she was Thrale's and yours, and by her dear father's appointment in some sort mine. I love you all, and therefore cannot without regret see the phalanx broken, and reflect that you and my other dear girls are deprived of one that was born your friend. To such friends, everyone that has them has recourse at last, when it is discovered, and discovered it seldom fails to be, that the fortuitous friendships of inclination or vanity are at the mercy of a thousand accidents. But we must still our disquiet with remembering that, where there is no guilt, all is for the best. I am glad to hear that Cicely is so near recovery.'†

A week after this Piozzi sailed for the Continent, having first lent his Dulcinea a thousand pounds, for which during his absence she remitted him interest to Italy. Perhaps the sense of loss gave something of sharpness to her next letter to Bolt Court.

* 'Piozzi Letters,' ii. 253.   † *Ibid.*, ii. 255.

CHAPTER VIII.

Discontent—Johnson has a Stroke — Mrs. Thrale's Situation—Sir Philip Jennings Clerk—An Old Friend—Mrs. Thrale's Health—Miss Burney's Sympathy—Repinings — Irritation—Want of Society—Piozzi Recalled—The News told to Johnson—Correspondence—Rupture—Farewell—Return of Piozzi—The Marriage—Baretti's Attack.

On June 15, 1783, Mrs. Thrale wrote to Johnson: "I believe it is too true, my dear Sir, that you think on little except yourself and your own health; but, then, they are subjects on which everyone else would think too—and that is a great consolation.

"I am willing enough to employ all my thoughts upon myself, but there is nobody here who wishes to think with or about me; so I am very sick and a little sullen, and disposed now and then to say, like King David, my lovers and my friends have been put away from me, and my acquaintance hid out of my sight. If the last letter I wrote showed some degree of placid acquiescence in a situation which, however displeasing, is the best I can get just now, I pray God to keep me in that disposition, and to lay no more calamity upon me which may again tempt me to murmur and complain. In the meantime assure yourself of my undiminished kindness and veneration; they have been long out of accident's power either to lessen or increase."*

On June 19 he writes: "I am sitting down in no

* 'Piozzi Letters,' ii. 264.

cheerful solitude to write a narrative which would once have affected you with tenderness and sorrow, but which you will perhaps pass over now with the careless glance of frigid indifference. For this diminution of regard, however, I know not whether I ought to blame you, who may have reasons which I cannot know, and I do not blame myself, who have for a great part of human life done you what good I could, and have never done you evil."

After describing a paralytic seizure by which two days before he had lost his speech for a time, he proceeds:

"How this will be received by you I know not. I hope you will sympathize with me; but perhaps

"'My mistress, gracious, mild, and good,
Cries, Is he dumb? 'Tis time he should.'

"But can this be possible? I hope it cannot. I hope that what, when I could speak, I spoke of you, and to you, will be in a sober and serious hour remembered by you; and surely it cannot be remembered but with some degree of kindness. I have loved you with virtuous affection; I have honoured you with sincere esteem. Let not all our endearments be forgotten, but let me have in this great distress your pity and your prayers. You see I yet turn to you with my complaints as a settled and unalienable friend; do not, do not drive me from you, for I have not deserved either neglect or hatred. . . . I am almost ashamed of this querulous letter, but now it is written, let it go."*

Mrs. Thrale's reply has not been preserved, but it appears to have contained a very practical proposal that she should go to town, and aid in nursing him. But neither did this please the fretful patient. He wrote: 'Your offer, dear Madam, of coming to me, is charmingly

* 'Piozzi Letters,' ii. 268.

kind; but I will lay it up for future use, and then let it not be considered as obsolete; a time of dereliction may come when I may have hardly any other friend; but in the present exigency, I cannot name one who has been deficient in civility and attention.'*

Perhaps he thought her safer at Bath. The trustees do not seem to have been quite at one as to the best course for her to pursue. Cator would have had her return to Streatham, but Johnson considered this to be undesirable, 'till the neighbourhood should have lost its habits of depredation.' He did not wish her to go back to be robbed by tradesmen and servants. It could not be said that her first attempts at governing herself and others had been very successful. She had mismanaged her affairs, incurred considerable debts, and involved herself in an attachment which displeased all her friends. It was better that she should remain in retirement until she had recovered herself, and retrieved her position.

Meanwhile, her friends seem to have been very attentive in inquiring after the patient in Bolt Court. Among the callers was Murphy, and a man of much higher position than Murphy, Sir Philip Jennings Clerk, who has been mentioned more than once in these pages as a confidential friend of the Thrale family. He was a Member of Parliament, and is thus described by Boswell: 'Sir Philip had the appearance of a gentleman of ancient family, well advanced in life. He wore his own white hair in a bag of goodly size, a black velvet coat, with an embroidered waistcoat, and very rich laced ruffles, which Mrs. Thrale said were old-fashioned, but which, for that reason, I thought the more respectable, more like a Tory, yet Sir Philip was in opposition in Parliament. "Ah, Sir," said Johnson, " ancient ruffles and modern principles

* 'Piozzi Letters,' ii. 278.

do not agree." Yet the two men were kept on good terms by Sir Philip's kindly nature, and his regard for Mrs. Thrale.'

A few months later her old friend writes to her in a more satisfied tone:

'*November* 13, 1783.—Since you have written to me with the attention and tenderness of ancient time, your letters give me a great part of the pleasure which a life of solitude admits. You will never bestow any share of your goodwill on one who deserves better. Those that have loved longest love best. A sudden blaze of kindness may by a single blast of coldness be extinguished, but that fondness which length of time has connected with many circumstances and occasions, though it may for awhile be suppressed by disgust or resentment, with or without a cause, is hourly revived by accidental recollection. To those that have lived long together, everything heard and everything seen recalls some pleasure communicated, some benefit conferred, some petty quarrel, or some slight endearment. Esteem of great powers, or amiable qualities newly discovered, may embroider a day or a week, but a friendship of twenty years is interwoven with the texture of life. A friend may be often found and lost, but an *old friend* never can be found, and nature has provided that he cannot easily be lost.'*

This is a fine piece of writing. We are not disposed to be irreverent; but a flippant reader might observe that, when translated into the language of common life, it means: Johnson is the friend, not Piozzi. The next, to Susan Thrale, is in a different key:

'*November* 18, 1783.—Dear Miss: Here is a whole week, and nothing heard from your house. Baretti said what a wicked house it would be, and a wicked house it is. Of

* 'Piozzi Letters,' ii. 325.

you, however, I have no complaint to make, for I owe you a letter. Still, I live here by my own self, and have had of late very bad nights; but then I have had a pig to dinner, which Mr. Perkins gave me. Thus life is chequered.'*

At this time Mrs. Thrale was very unwell, and her third daughter, Sophia, had a dangerous sickness. Johnson seems to have concerned himself much more for the latter than for the former, whose complaints he doubtless despised as sentimental and foppish lamentations. Yet she was really ill. On November 19 Miss Burney wrote: 'Dr. Pepys had a long private conference with me concerning Mrs. Thrale, with whose real state of health he is better acquainted than anybody; and sad indeed was all he said . . .' 'The 22nd,' she adds, 'I passed in sorrow for my dear unhappy friend, who sent me one letter, that came early by the Bath diligence, and another by the post. I can only tell you that I love Mrs. Thrale with a never-to-cease affection, and pity her more than ever I pitied any human being; and if I did not blame her, I could, I believe, almost die for her.'

After protesting that she has revealed the secret to no one, the prudent Fanny declares her wish to go to her friend, whose failings, if multiplied a thousandfold, would be more than counterbalanced by 'her virtues and good qualities, the generosity and feeling of her heart, and the liberality and sweetness of her disposition.'†

In the 'Memoirs,' Mme. d'Arblay has described an interview which she had about this time with Johnson, in which they joined in lamenting the widow's infatuation. On this Lord Brougham has commented in his usual trenchant style: 'Johnson, perhaps unknown to himself, was in love with Mrs. Thrale, but for Miss Burney's thoughtless folly there can be no excuse. And her father,

---

* 'Piozzi Letters,' ii. 327   † Mme. d'Arblay's 'Diary,' i. 543.

a person of the very same rank and profession with Piozzi, appears to have adopted the same senseless cant, as if it were less lawful to marry an Italian musician than an English. To be sure, Miss Burney says, that Mrs. Thrale was lineally descended from Adam de Sallzburg, who came over with the Conqueror. But assuredly that worthy, unable to write his name, would have held Dr. Johnson himself in as much contempt as his fortunate rival, and would have regarded his alliance as equally disreputable with the Italian's, could his consent have been asked.'

No doubt Mrs. Thrale was aware of the language Johnson used about her. On February 18, 1784, she writes to her Tyo: 'Johnson is in a sad way doubtless; yet he may still with care last another twelvemonth, and every week's existence is gain to him who, like good Hezekiah, wearies Heaven with entreaties for life.'*

Again, on March 23:

'You are a dear creature to write so soon and so sweetly; but we shall never meet. I see that clearly, and have seen it long. My going to London would be a dreadful expense, and bring on a thousand enquiries and inconveniences—visits to Johnson and from Cator; and where must I live for the time, too? Oh, I have desired nothing else since you wrote; but all is impossibility. Why would you ever flatter me that you might, maybe, come to Bath? I saw the unlikelihood even then; and my retired life will not induce your friends to permit your coming hither now. I fancy even my own young ladies will leave me, and I sincerely think they will be perfectly right so to do, as the world they wish to live in is quite excluded by my style of living.'†

On March 27 she wrote to Johnson:

* Mme. d'Arblay's 'Diary,' i. 558. † *Ibid.*, i. 560.

"You tell one of my daughters that you know not with distinctness the cause of my complaints. I believe she who lives with me knows them no better; one very dreadful one is, however, removed by dear Sophia's recovery. It is kind in you to quarrel no more about expressions which were not meant to offend; but unjust to suppose I have not lately thought myself dying. Let us, however, take the Prince of Abyssinia's advice, *and not add to the other evils of life the bitterness of controversy*. . . .

"All this is not written by a person in high health and happiness, but by a fellow-sufferer, who has more to endure than she can tell, or you can guess. And now let us talk of the Severn salmons, which will be coming in soon. I shall send you one of the finest, and shall be glad to hear that your appetite is good; mine has been so long *vitiated* that it endures no aliment with pleasure, but coffee and those doses of Peruvian bark or cascarilla which Dobson gives me by turns, and which are become —oddly enough—delightful to my palate."*

Johnson to her: "*April* 19, 1784.—I received in the morning your magnificent fish, and in the afternoon your apology for not sending it. I have invited the Hooles and Miss Burney to dine upon it to-morrow. . . . I am sensible of the ease that your repayment of Mr. [Crutchley] has given; you felt yourself *génée* by that debt. Is there an English word for it?

"As you do not now use your books, be pleased to let Mr. Cator know that I may borrow what I want. I think at present to take only Calmet and the Greek Anthology. When I lay sleepless, I used to drive the night along by turning Greek epigrams into Latin.

"It is time to return you thanks for your present. Since I was sick, I know not if I have not had more delicacies sent me than I had ever seen till I saw your table."†

* 'Piozzi Letters,' ii. 359.   † *Ibid.*, ii. 363.

A few days later he said: 'While I am writing, the post has brought me your kind letter. Do not think with dejection of your own condition: a little patience will probably give you health; it will cerainly give you riches, and all the accommodations that riches can procure.'*

It is not difficult to follow the working of Mrs. Thrale's mind during the period of her retirement at Bath. For some time after her arrival she was submissive, having been persuaded that it was her duty to give up Piozzi. But as she felt the isolation of her position, she began to rebel against the influence which had placed her in it. She does not seem to have resented the remonstrances of Miss Burney, whom do doubt she regarded as a mere agent; she did resent very strongly the part played by Johnson, who, though he had declined to concur in the strong measures proposed by Crutchley, had used all his authority to prevent her from going abroad. Fanny was full of sympathy and tenderness, though full also of the worldly prudence in which she had been disciplined by her father. Johnson took no pains to soothe the irritation which he had excited. Habitually rough, jealous, dictatorial, he was too much engrossed with his own ailments, and with the various opiates, cathartics, and vellications which he judged proper for their relief, to have much attention to spare for the distemper of a friend, whose case did not admit of the like drastic treatment. It is right to say that for what he considered the real evils of life—such as the sickness and loss of children, the embarrassment of debt, the prospect of death—he never wanted fellow-feeling. But though his mistress said that he knew more of physic than any doctor, he certainly was not fitted to advise as a specialist in nervous disorders.

* 'Piozzi Letters,' ii. 369.

What he had not experienced in his own person, he could not understand, nor, indeed, believe in another. Constantly complaining himself of being solitary in Bolt Court, where he had numberless visitors, he would not allow his correspondent to feel depressed at a watering-place, where she was not merely separated from her lover, but removed from nearly all her acquaintance. Thus he will close one letter with the formal exhortation: 'Take care of your own health, compose your mind, and you have yet strength of body to be well,' and end the next with such complaints as these: 'Visitors are no proper companions in the chamber of sickness. They come when I could rest or sleep; they stay till I am weary,' and so forth. 'The amusements and consolations of languor and depression are conferred by familiar and domestic companions.... Such society I had with Levet and Williams; such I had where—I am never likely to have it more.'* Can we wonder that an invalid who demanded so much sentimental sympathy, and was able to give so little in return, now and then provoked his correspondent into the use of hasty expressions? She certainly said nothing of Johnson nearly so harsh as his judgment on her, when, on May 16, 1784, he talked to Boswell of her with much concern, saying: 'Sir, she has done everything wrong, since Thrale's bridle was off her neck.'

Mrs. Thrale was not able to take Johnson's well-meant but somewhat perfunctory advice to compose her mind. Her health continued to decline. Her physician and friend, Sir Lucas Pepys, pronounced that her reason, if not her life, was in danger. At length her condition was pressed on the attention of her eldest daughter. It seems that her medical attendant in Bath insisted on the necessity of recalling Piozzi. The advice was taken. A letter was

* 'Piozzi Letters,' ii. 341. Miss Williams had died in the autumn of 1783.

despatched to Milan about the end of April, or the beginning of May, and from that time the distressed lady began to recover. About the middle of May she went to London for a week to make preparations for her marriage. This visit is mentioned in Miss Burney's diary: 'May 17.—The rest of the week I devoted almost entirely to sweet Mrs. Thrale, whose society was truly the most delightful of cordials to me, however at times mixed with bitters the least palatable. One day I dined with Mrs. Garrick to meet Dr. Johnson, Mrs. Carter, Miss Hamilton, and Dr. and Mrs. Cadogan; and one evening I went to Mrs. Vesey, to meet almost everybody. . . . But all the rest of my time I gave wholly to dear Mrs. Thrale, who lodged in Mortimer Street, and who saw nobody else. Were I not sensible of her goodness, and full of incurable affection for her, should I not be a monster? I parted most reluctantly from my dear Mrs. Thrale, whom when or how I shall see again heaven only knows; but in sorrow we parted—on my side in real affliction.'*

Mrs. Thrale returned to Bath to await her lover, and what ensued is told in the following letters:

Mrs. Thrale to Dr. Johnson.

'Bath, June 30.

'MY DEAR SIR,

'The enclosed is a circular letter which I have sent to all the guardians, but our friendship demands somewhat more; it requires that I should beg your pardon for concealing from you a connection which you must have heard of by many, but I suppose never believed. Indeed, my dear Sir, it was concealed only to save us both needless pain; I could not have borne to reject that counsel it would have killed me to take, and I only tell

* Mme. d'Arblay's 'Diary,' i. 566.

you now because all is irrevocably settled, and out of your power to prevent. I will say, however, that the dread of your disapprobation has given me some anxious moments, and though perhaps I am become by many privations the most independent woman in the world, I feel as if acting without a parent's consent till you write kindly to
'Your faithful servant.'

Circular.

'Sir,
'As one of the executors of Mr. Thrale's will, and guardian to his daughters, I think it my duty to acquaint you that the three eldest left Bath last Friday (25th) for their own house at Brighthelmstone in company with an amiable friend, Miss Nicholson, who has sometimes resided with us here, and in whose society they may, I think, find some advantages, and certainly no disgrace. I waited on them to Salisbury, Wilton, etc., and offered to attend them to the seaside myself, but they preferred this lady's company to mine, having heard that Mr. Piozzi is coming back from Italy, and judging, perhaps, by our past friendship and continued correspondence that his return would be succeeded by our marriage.
'I have the honour to be, sir,
'Your obedient servant.

'*Bath*, June 30, 1784.'

Dr. Johnson to Mrs. Thrale.

'Madam,
'If I interpret your letter right, you are ignominiously married; if it is yet undone, let us once more talk together. If you have abandoned your children and your religion, God forgive your wickedness; if you have

forfeited your fame and your country, may your folly do no further mischief! If the last act is yet to do, I who have loved you, esteemed you, reverenced you, and served you, I who long thought you the first of womankind, entreat that, before your fate is irrevocable, I may once more see you. I was, I once was, madam, most truly yours,

'SAM. JOHNSON.

'*July* 2, 1784.

'I will come down, if you permit it.'

To Dr. Johnson.

'July 4, 1784.

'SIR,

'I have this morning received from you so rough a letter in reply to one which was both tenderly and respectfully written, that I am forced to desire the conclusion of a correspondence which I can bear to continue no longer. The birth of my second husband is not meaner than that of my first; his sentiments are not meaner; his profession is not meaner; and his superiority in what he professes acknowledged by all mankind. It is want of fortune, then, that is ignominious; the character of the man I have chosen has no other claim to such an epithet. The religion to which he has been always a zealous adherent will, I hope, teach him to forgive insults he has not deserved; mine will, I hope, enable to bear them at once with dignity and patience. To hear that I have forfeited my fame is indeed the greatest insult I ever yet received. My fame is as unsullied as snow, or I should think it unworthy of him who must henceforth protect it.

'I write by coach, the more speedily and effectually to prevent your coming hither. Perhaps by my fame (and I hope it is so) you mean only that celebrity which is a consideration of a much lower kind. I care for that only as it may give pleasure to my husband and his friends.

'Farewell, dear Sir, and accept my best wishes. You have always commanded my esteem, and long enjoyed the fruits of a friendship never infringed by one harsh expression on my part during twenty years of familiar talk. Never did I oppose your will, or control your wish; nor can your unmerited severity itself lessen my regard; but till you have changed your opinion of Mr. Piozzi, let us converse no more. God bless you.'

To Mrs. Piozzi.

'London, July 8, 1784.

'Dear Madam,

'What you have done, however I may lament it, I have no pretence to resent, as it has not been injurious to me. I therefore breathe out one sigh more of tenderness, perhaps useless, but at least sincere.

'I wish that God may grant you every blessing, that you may be happy in this world for its short continuance, and eternally happy in a better state; and whatever I can contribute to your happiness I am very ready to repay, for that kindness which soothed twenty years of a life radically wretched.

'Do not think slightly of the advice which I now presume to offer. Prevail upon Mr. Piozzi to settle in England: you may live here with more dignity than in Italy, and with more security; your rank will be higher, and your fortune more under your own eye. I desire not to detail all my reasons, but every argument of prudence and interest is for England, and only some phantoms of imagination seduce you to Italy.

'I am afraid, however, that my counsel is vain, yet I have eased my heart by giving it.

'When Queen Mary took the resolution of sheltering herself in England, the Archbishop of St. Andrew's, attempting to dissuade her, attended on her journey;* and when they came to the irremeable† stream that separated the two kingdoms, walked by her side into the water, in the middle of which he seized her bridle, and with earnestness proportioned to her danger and his own affection, pressed her to return. The Queen went forward.—If the parallel reaches thus far, may it go no farther!—The tears stand in my eyes.

'I am going into Derbyshire, and hope to be followed by your good wishes, for I am, with great affection,
'Yours, etc.

'Any letters that come for me hither will be sent me.'

In a memorandum on this letter, she says: 'I wrote him a very kind and affectionate farewell.'

The following are entries in 'Thraliana':

'*Bath, July* 2, 1784.—The happiest day of my whole life, I think—Yes, quite the happiest; my Piozzi came home yesterday and dined with me; but my spirits were too much agitated, my heart was too much dilated. I was too painfully happy then; my sensations are more quiet to-day, and my felicity less tumultuous.'

Written in the margin of the last entry: 'We shall go

---

* Queen Mary left the Scottish for the English coast, on the Firth of Solway, in a fishing-boat. The incident to which Johnson alludes is introduced in Scott's ' Abbot,' where the scene is laid on the seashore.

† Johnson has the word irremeable in his ' Dictionary,' and explains it ' admitting no return.'

'Evaditque celer ripam irremeabilis undæ.'—VIRGIL, *Æn.*, vi. 425.

'The keeper dreamed, the chief without delay
   Pass'd on, and took the irremeable way.'—DRYDEN.

to London about the affairs, and there be married in the Romish Church.'

'*July* 25, 1784.—I am returned from church the happy wife of my lovely faithful Piozzi ... subject of my prayers, object of my wishes, my sighs, my reverence, my esteem. His nerves have been horribly shaken, yet he lives, he loves me, and will be mine for ever. He has sworn in the face of God and the whole Christian Church; Catholics, Protestants, all are witnesses.'

In one of her memorandum books she set down:

'We were married according to the Romish Church in one of our excursions to London, by Mr. Smith—Padre Smit, as they called him, chaplain to the Spanish Ambassador. . . . Mr. Morgan tacked us together at St. James's, Bath, 25th July, 1784, and on the first day, I think, of September, certainly the first week, we took leave of England.'*

Some years after the marriage a malignant attack on Mrs. Piozzi was published by Baretti in the *European Magazine*. In this he refers to the circumstances attending her second marriage, and alleges that when she left Bath with her three daughters for Brighton, she quitted them on some pretext at Salisbury, and posted off to town, deceiving Johnson, who continued to direct to her at Bath as usual. Baretti says that he knew this from the fact that she concealed herself in a lodging not far from his own habitation in Suffolk Street, Middlesex Hospital. His assertion would be of no importance, save for the circumstance of its having received credence from some writers unfavourable to Mrs. Piozzi, who suspect that she was guilty of a white lie in relating that she returned to Bath. But by whomsoever made or adopted, this charge seems to amount to very little. What could be more

* Hayward's 'Piozzi,' i. 226.

natural than that an impatient woman should seek to meet her returning lover at the earliest possible moment, or that she should withhold her doing so from those who had no right to control her movements? We do not defend the use of white lies under any circumstances, but if they are ever justifiable, it is when they are employed to defeat unwarranted interference. Yet, on consideration, Baretti's story is not probable. The inference drawn from it has been, that the marriage at the Spanish Embassy took place almost immediately after Piozzi's landing, and some weeks before the avowed marriage at Bath. This, however, is known not to have been the case. From a copy of the certificate found among Mrs. Piozzi's papers, it appears that the ceremony performed by Padre Smit was celebrated on July 23.

"When her first engagement with Piozzi became known," says Mr. Hayward, "the newspapers rang the changes on the amorous disposition of the widow, and the adroit cupidity of the fortune-hunter. On the announcement of the marriage, they recommenced the attack, and people of our day can hardly form a notion of the storm of obloquy that broke upon her. The repugnance of the daughters to the match was reasonable and intelligible, but to appreciate the tone taken by her friends, we must bear in mind the social position of Italian singers and musical performers at the period. 'Amusing vagabonds' are the epithets by which Lord Byron designates Catalani and Naldi in 1809, and such is the light in which they were undoubtedly regarded in 1784." Whatever passing fancies may have crossed Johnson's brain, it would be most unjust to suppose that his strong disapproval of the match was caused by personal disappointment. Many were the jokes about the philosopher's presumed wish to unite himself with the rich widow.

One wit produced an ode to Mrs. Thrale by Samuel Johnson on their approaching nuptials:

> "To rich felicity thus raised,
>   My bosom glows with amorous fire;
> Porter no longer shall be praised,
>   'Tis I myself am *Thrale's Entire.*"

Boswell, referring to these stories, says: 'I believe they were without foundation.' Mrs. Piozzi wrote on the margin of the page, 'I believe so too.'

CHAPTER IX.

Departure for the Continent—Calais—Aspect of the Country—Chantilly—The Prince of Condé—Paris—The Palais Royal—The Parisians—Beaumarchais—The English Austin Nuns—An Air Balloon—Animal Magnetism—Mont Cenis—Italian Costume—Milan—Christmas Festivities—Free Manners—The Theatre of La Scala—The Lower Classes—Cremona—The Bells—Dr. Burney—Verona—Venice—Venetian Society—The Po—Ferrara—Talassi's Visit to Streatham—Bologna—The Painters of the Bolognese School—Journey to Florence.

MRS. PIOZZI, as we have seen, left England with her husband in the early part of September, 1784. They travelled through France to Italy, where they spent nearly two years, returning through Germany and Belgium, and reaching home in the early part of 1787. Two years later Mrs. Piozzi published an account of this tour, in two volumes, 8vo., under the title of 'Observations and Reflections made in a Journey through France, Italy and Germany.' Thus her account of Continental society under the old *régime*, written without any presage of coming change, appeared in the very year which witnessed the outbreak of the French Revolution. The preface contains one brief allusion to the circumstances of her second marriage. 'I have not,' she says, 'thrown my thoughts into the form of private letters; because a work of which truth is the best recommendation should not, above all others, begin with a lie. My old acquaintance rather chose to amuse themselves with conjectures, than to flatter me with tender inquiries during my absence: our correspondence then would not have been any amusement to the public, whose treatment of me deserves every possible acknowledgment.' The last words refer to the reception of her 'Anecdotes of Dr. Johnson,' which had been published in the year 1786.

The voyage from Dover to Calais, which is now reckoned by minutes, occupied six-and-twenty hours, during which the travellers had nothing to amuse them but 'the flights of shaggs, and shoals of maycril,' and the sight of the sun rising and setting 'upon an unobstructed horizon.' After dinner at Calais, she writes, 'we set out to see Miss Grey, at her convent of Dominican Nuns, who, I hoped, would have remembered me, as many of the ladies there had seized much of my attention when last abroad: they had, however, all forgotten me, nor could call to mind how much they had once admired the beauty of my eldest daughter, then a child, which I thought impossible to forget: one is always more important in one's own eyes than in those of others; but no one is of importance to a nun, who is and ought to be employed in other speculations.'

The journey was made, of course, after the manner of those days, when, if well-to-do people proposed to go to Italy, they took a carriage and drove there. Mrs. Piozzi notes the French postillions 'with greasy nightcaps and vast jack-boots, driving the carriage harnessed with ropes, and adorned with sheepskins.' Now and then she mentions some small accident or breakage, but on the whole she gives few details of a mode of travelling then too familiar to need description. Our readers will remember how Mr. Ruskin, in his 'Præterita,' dwells on all the incidents of it with fond recollection and passionate regret.

As the travellers passed through France less than five

years before the Revolution, one or two remarks on the appearance of the country have a special interest. 'The country, as far as Montreuil, is a coarse one; "thin herbage in the plains, and fruitless fields." The cattle, too, are miserably poor and lean; but where there is no grass, we can scarcely expect them to be fat: they must not feed on wheat, I suppose, and cannot digest tobacco. Herds of swine, not flocks of sheep, meet one's eye upon the hills; and the very few gentlemen's seats that we have passed by seem out of repair, and deserted.' The banks of the Yonne, on the other hand, are described as extremely rich and fertile, but 'every town that should adorn these lovely plains exhibits, upon a nearer approach, misery; the more mortifying, as it is less expected by a spectator, who requires at least some days' experience to convince him that the squalid scenes of wretchedness and dirt in which he is obliged to pass the night, will prove more than equivalent to the pleasures he has enjoyed in the day-time. . . . The French do seem, indeed, an idle race; and poverty, perhaps for that reason, forces her way among them, through a climate that might tempt other mortals to improve its blessings; but, as the motto to the arms they are so proud of expresses it, "they toil not, neither do they spin."'

At Montreuil she is much amused by the 'pert vivacity of *la fille*, which filled up my notions of French flippancy agreeably enough; as no English wench would so have answered one, to be sure. She had complained of our avant-coureur's behaviour. "Il parle sur le haut ton, mademoiselle," said I, "mais il a le cœur bon." "Ouidà," replied she smartly, "mais c'est le ton qui fait le chanson."'

At Amiens, she observes that 'the rage for Lombardy poplars is in equal force here as about London.' At

Chantilly she visits the palace and gardens, and remembers how the tame fish had fed from her hand eleven or twelve years ago. 'The theatre belonging to the house is a lovely one; and the truly princely possessor, when he heard once that an English gentleman, travelling for amusement, had called at Chantilly too late to enjoy the diversion, instantly, though past twelve o'clock at night, ordered a new representation, that his curiosity might be gratified. This is the same Prince of Condé who, going from Paris to his country seat here for a month or two, when his eldest son was nine years old, left him fifty louis d'or as an allowance during his absence. At his return to town, the boy produced his purse, crying, "Papa, here's all the money safe; I have never touched it once." The Prince, in reply, took him gravely to the window, and, opening it, very quietly poured all the louis d'or into the street, saying, "Now, if you have neither virtue enough to give away your money, nor spirit enough to spend it, always *do this* for the future, do you hear; that the poor may at least have a *chance for it*."'

Arrived in Paris, she is chiefly struck with the cheerfulness and contentment of the people. On the boulevards, 'as wine, beer, and spirits are not permitted to be sold there, one sees what England does not even pretend to exhibit, which is gaiety without noise, and a crowd without a riot. . . . In the evening we looked at the new square called the Palais Royal, whence the Duc de Chartres has removed a vast number of noble trees, which it was a sin and shame to profane with an axe, after they had adorned that spot for so many centuries. The people were accordingly as angry, I believe, as Frenchmen can be, when the folly was first committed; the Court, however, had wit enough to convert the place into a sort of Vauxhall, with tents, fountains, shops, full of frippery, brilliant at once and worthless, to attract them; with coffee-houses surrounding it on every side; and now they are all again *merry* and *happy*, synonymous terms at Paris, though often disunited in London; and " Vive le Duc de Chartres!"

'The French are really a contented race of mortals; precluded almost from possibility of adventure, the low Parisian leads a gentle, humble life, nor envies that greatness he never can obtain. . . . They see at the beginning of their lives how that life must necessarily end, and trot with a quiet, contented, and unaltered pace down their long, straight, and shaded avenue.' Strange words to have been written less than ten years before the Reign of Terror!

The Parisians were just then 'all wild for love of a new comedy, written by Mons. de Beaumarchais, and called " Le Mariage de Figaro," full of such wit as we were fond of in the reign of Charles the Second, indecent merriment, and gross immorality; mixed, however, with much acrimonious satire, as if Sir George Etherege and Johnny Gay had clubbed their powers of ingenuity at once to divert and to corrupt their auditors; who now carry the verses of this favourite piece upon their fans, pocket-handkerchiefs, etc., as our women once did those of the " Beggar's Opera."'

At Paris Mrs. Piozzi was introduced to Goldoni, then in his eighty-fifth year, and to other cultivated Italians, among whom she desired to live as much as possible before entering their country, 'where the language will be so very indispensable.' 'Meantime I have stolen a day to visit my old acquaintance the English Austin Nuns at the Fossée, and found the whole community alive and cheerful; they are many of them agreeable women, and having seen Dr. Johnson with me when I was last abroad, inquired much for him: Mrs. Fermor, the Prioress, niece to Belinda in the "Rape of the Lock," taking occasion to tell me, comically enough, "That she believed there was but little comfort to be found in a house that harboured *poets;* for that she remembered Mr. Pope's praise made her aunt very troublesome and conceited, while his numberless caprices would have employed ten servants to wait on him; and he gave one," said she, "no amends by his talk neither, for he only sat dozing all day, when the sweet wine was out, and made his verses chiefly in the night; during which season he kept himself awake by drinking coffee, which it was one of the maids' business to make for him, and they took it by turns."

'These ladies really live here as comfortably, for aught I see, as peace, quietness, and the certainty of a good dinner every day can make them. Just so much happier than as many old maids who inhabit Milman Street and Chapel Row, as they are sure not to be robbed by a treacherous, or insulted by a favoured, servant in the decline of life, when protection is grown hopeless and resistance vain; and as they enjoy at least a moral certainty of never living worse than they do to-day: while the little knot of unmarried females turned fifty round Red Lion Square *may* always be ruined by a runaway agent, a bankrupted banker, or a roguish steward; and even the petty pleasures of sixpenny quadrille may become by that misfortune too costly for their income. *Au reste*, as the French say, the difference is small: both coteries sit separate in the morning, go to prayers at noon, and read the chapters for the day: change their neat dress, eat their little dinner, and play at small games for small sums in the evening, when recollection tires, and chat runs low.'

'All Paris, I think, myself among the rest, assembled to see the valiant brothers, Robert and Charles, mount yesterday into the air, in company with a certain Pilâtre de Rosier, who conducted them in the new-invented flying chariot fastened to an air-balloon.'

On inquiring the next day what had become of the aërial travellers, a very grave man replied, 'Je crois, madame, qu'ils sont déjà arrivés, ces messieurs là, au lieu où les vents se forment.'

From Paris they went to Lyons, where Mrs. Piozzi heard something of a subject of which our knowledge has scarcely been increased during the last hundred years. 'Some conversation here struck me as curious; the more so as I had heard the subject slightly touched upon at Paris; but faintly there, as the last sounds of an echo, while here they are all loud, all in earnest, and all their heads seem turned, I think, about something, or nothing, which they call *animal magnetism*. I cannot imagine how it has seized them so: a man who undertakes to cure disorders by the touch is no new thing; our philosophical transactions make mention of " Gretrex the stroaker," in Charles the Second's reign. The present mountebank, it is true, seems more hardy in his experiments, and boasts of being able to cause disorders in the human frame, as well as to remove them. A gentleman at yesterday's dinner-party mentioned that he took pupils, and, before I had expressed the astonishment I felt, professed himself a disciple, and was happy to assure us, he said, that though he had not yet attained the desirable power of putting a person into a catalepsy at pleasure, he could throw a woman into a deep swoon, from which no arts but his own could recover her. How difficult is it to restrain one's contempt and indignation from a buffoonery so mean, or a practice so diabolical! This folly may possibly find its way into England—I should be very sorry.'

From Lyons they went on into Italy by way of Mont Cenis. Mrs. Piozzi would have liked to pass through Switzerland, 'the Derbyshire of Europe,' as she oddly styles it, but the season was too far advanced. She gives an animated description of her feelings in crossing the Alps, 'a sensation of fulness never experienced before, a satisfaction that there is something great to be seen on earth—some object capable of contenting even fancy.' She had the satisfaction of seeing a chamois at a distance, and spoke with a fellow who had killed five hungry bears that made depredation on his pastures. 'We looked on him with reverence as a monster-tamer of antiquity, Hercules or Cadmus; he had the skin of a beast wrapt round his middle, which confirmed the fancy—but our servants, who borrowed from no fictitious records the few ideas that adorned their talk, told us he reminded *them* of *John the Baptist*. I had scarce recovered the shock of this too sublime comparison, when we approached his cottage, and found the felons nailed against the wall, like foxes' heads or spread kites in England.'

As she was carried in a chair down the Italian side of the Alps, she heard the chairmen speaking to each other of the beauties of the scene, and the change of light since they had passed by last time, 'while a fellow who spoke English as well as a native told us that, having lived in a gentleman's service twenty years between London and Dublin, he at length begged his discharge, choosing to retire and finish his days a peasant upon these mountains, where he first opened his eyes upon scenes that made all other views of nature insipid to his taste.'

At a little town in Piedmont, where they stopped for dinner, she found their room decorated with a large map of London, which, she says, 'I looked on with sensations different from those ever before excited by the same object. Amsterdam and Constantinople covered the other sides of the wall; and over the door of the chamber itself was written, as our people write the Lamb or the Lion, "Les trois Villes Hérétiques."'

They reached Turin in the middle of October, spent a few days there and at Genoa, and arrived in Milan on the 4th of November. 'The headdress of the women in this drive through some of the northern states of Italy varied at every spot; from the velvet cap, commonly a crimson one, worn by the girls in Savoia, to the Piedmontese plait round the bodkin at Turin, and the odd kind of white wrapper used in the exterior provinces of the Genoese dominions. Uniformity of almost any sort gives a certain pleasure to the eye, and it seems an invariable rule in these countries that all the women of every district should dress just alike. It is the best way of making the men's task easy in judging which is handsomest; for taste so varies the human figure in France and England, that it is impossible to have an idea how many pretty faces and agreeable forms would lose and how many gain admirers in those nations, were a sudden edict to be published that all should dress exactly alike for a year.'

At Milan they made a stay of five months, and Mrs. Piozzi had leisure to study the ways of the society to which she was introduced. 'Italians, by what I can observe, suffer their minds to be much under the dominion of the sky, and attribute every change in their health, or even humour, as seriously to its influence, as if there were no nearer causes of alteration than the state of the air, and as if no doubt remained of its immediate power, though they are willing enough here to poison it with the scent of wood-ashes within doors, while fires in the grate seem to run rather low, and a brazier full of that pernicious stuff is substituted in its place, and driven under the table during dinner. It is surprising how very elegant, not to say magnificent, those dinners are in gentlemen's or noblemen's houses; such numbers of dishes at once— not large joints, but infinite variety—and I think their cooking excellent. Fashion keeps most of the fine people out of town yet; we have, therefore, had leisure to establish our own household for the winter, and have done so as commodiously as if our habitation was fixed here for life. . . . Candour, and a good-humoured willingness to receive and reciprocate pleasure, seems indeed one of the standing virtues of Italy; I have as yet seen no fastidious contempt, or affected rejection of anything for being what we call *low;* and I have a notion there is much less of those distinctions at Milan than at London, where birth does so little for a man, that if he depends on *that,* and forbears other methods of distinguishing himself from his footman, he will stand a chance of being treated no better than him by the world. *Here* a person's rank is ascertained, and his society settled, at his immediate entrance into life; a gentleman and lady will always be regarded as such, let what will be their behaviour. . . .

'The phrase of *mistress* is here not confined to servants at all; gentlemen, when they address one, cry, *mia padrona*,* mighty sweetly, and in a peculiarly pleasing tone. Nothing, to speak truth, can exceed the agreeableness of a well-bred Italian's address when speaking to a

---

* My mistress.

lady, whom they alone know how to flatter, so as to retain her dignity, and not lose their own; respectful, yet tender; attentive, not officious; the politeness of a man of fashion *here* is *true* politeness, free from all affectation, and honestly expressive of what he really feels, a true value for the person spoken to, without the smallest desire of shining himself; equally removed from foppery on one side, or indifference on the other. The manners of the men here are certainly pleasing to a very eminent degree, and in their conversation there is a mixture, not unfrequent too, of classical allusions, which strike one with a sort of literary pleasure I cannot easily describe. Yet is there no pedantry in their use of expressions, which with us would be laughable or liable to censure: but Roman notions here are not quite extinct; and even the housemaid, or *donna di gros*, as they call her, swears by *Diana* so comically, there is no telling. They christen their boys *Fabius*, their daughters *Claudia*, very commonly.'

'The Christmas functions here were showy, and I thought well-contrived; the public ones are what I speak of: but I was present lately at a private merrymaking, where all distinctions seemed pleasingly thrown down by a spirit of innocent gaiety. The Marquis's daughter mingled in country-dances with the apothecary's prentice, while her truly noble parents looked on with generous pleasure, and encouraged the mirth of the moment. Priests, ladies, gentlemen of the very first quality, romped with the girls of the house in high good-humour, and tripped it away without the encumbrance of petty pride, or the mean vanity of giving what they expressively call *soggezione* to those who were proud of their company and protection. A new-married wench, whose little fortune of a hundred crowns had been given her by the subscription of many in the room, seemed as free with them all as the most equal distribution of birth or riches could have made her: she laughed aloud, and rattled in the ears of the gentlemen; replied with sarcastic coarseness when they joked her, and apparently delighted to promote such conversation as they would not otherwise have tried at. The ladies shouted for joy, encouraged the girl with less delicacy than desire of merriment, and promoted a general banishment of decorum; though I do believe with full as much or more purity of intention, than may be often met with in a polished circle at Paris itself.

'Such society, however, can please a stranger only as it is odd and as it is new; when ceremony ceases, hilarity is left in a state too natural not to offend people accustomed to scenes of high civilization; and I suppose few of us could return, after twenty-five years old, to the coarse comforts of *a roll and treacle.*'

The theatre excited her warmest admiration. 'Surely a receptacle so capacious to contain four thousand people, a place of entrance so commodious to receive them, a show so princely, so very magnificent to entertain them, must be sought in vain out of Italy. The centre front box, richly adorned with gilding, arms, and trophies, is appropriated to the Court, whose canopy is carried up to what we call the first gallery in England; the crescent of boxes, ending with the stage, consist of nineteen on a side, *small boudoirs,* for such they seem; and are as such fitted up with silk hangings, girandoles, etc., and placed so judiciously as to catch every sound of the singers, if they do but whisper. I will not say it is equally advantageous to the figure as to the voice; no performers looking adequate to the place they recite upon, so very stately is the building itself, being all of stone, with an immense portico, and stairs which for width you might without hyperbole drive your chariot up. An immense sideboard at the first lobby, lighted and furnished with luxurious and elegant plenty, as many people send for suppers to their box, and entertain a knot of friends there with infinite convenience and splendour. A silk curtain, the colour of your hangings, defends the closet from intrusive eyes, if you think proper to drop it; and when drawn up, gives gaiety and show to the general appearance of the whole; while across the corridor leading to these boxes another small chamber, numbered like that it belongs to, is appropriated to the use of your servants, and furnished with every conveniency to make chocolate, serve lemonade, etc.

'Can one wonder at the contempt shown by foreigners when they see English women of fashion squeezed into holes lined with dirty torn red paper, and the walls of it covered with a wretched crimson stuff? Well, but this theatre is built in place of a church founded by the famous Beatrice della Scala, in consequence of a vow she made to erect one if God would be pleased to send her a son. The church was pulled down and the playhouse erected. The Archduke lost a son that year; and the pious folks cried, "A judgment!" but nobody minded them, I believe; many, however, that are scrupulous will not go. Meantime, it is a beautiful theatre, to be sure; the finest fabric raised in modern days, I do believe, for the purposes of entertainment; but we must not be partial. While London has twelve capital rooms for the professed amusement of the public, Milan has but one; there is in it, however, a ridotto chamber for cards, of a noble size, where some little gaming goes on in carnival time; but though the inhabitants complain of the enormities committed there, I suppose more money is lost and won at one club in St. James's Street during a week than here at Milan in the whole winter.

'Every nation complains of the wickedness of its own inhabitants, and considers them as the worst people in the world, till they have seen others no better; and then, like individuals with their private sorrows, they find change produces no alleviation. . . .

'A gentleman who had long practised as a solicitor, and was retired from business, stored with a perfect knowledge of mankind so far as his experience could inform him, told me once, that whoever died before sixty years old, if he had made his own fortune, was likely to leave it according as friendship, gratitude, and public spirit dictated; either to those who had served, or those who had pleased him; or, not unfrequently, to benefit some charity, set up some school, or the like. "But let a man once turn sixty," said he, "and his natural heirs *are sure of him;*" for having seen many people, he has likewise been disgusted by many; and though he does not love his relations better than he did, the discovery that others are but little superior to them in those excellencies he has sought about the world in vain for, he begins to inquire for his nephew's little boy, whom, as he never saw, never could have offended him; and if he does not break the chain of a favourite watch, or any other such boyish trick, the estate is his for ever, upon no principle but this in the testator.

'So it is by those who travel a good deal; by what I have seen, every country has so much in it to be justly complained of that most men finish by preferring their own.'

'Here is certainly much despotic power in Italy, but, I fancy, very little oppression; perhaps authority, once acknowledged, does not delight itself always by the fatigue of exertion. "Sat est prostrasse leoni" is an old adage, with which perhaps I may be the better acquainted, as it is the motto to my own coat of arms; and unless sovereignty is hungry, for aught I see, he does not certainly *devour*.

'The certainty of their irrevocable doom, softened by kind usage from their superiors, makes, in the meantime, an odd sort of humorous drollery spring up among the common people, who are much happier here at Milan than I expected to find them; every great house giving meat, broth, etc., to poor dependents with liberal good-nature enough, so that mighty little wandering misery is seen in the streets, unlike those of Genoa, who seem mocked with the word *liberty*, while sorrow, sickness, and the most pinching want pine at the doors of marble palaces, whose owners are unfeeling as their walls.

'Our ordinary people here in Lombardy are well clothed, fat, stout, and merry, and desirous to divert themselves and their protectors, whom they love at their hearts. There is, however, a degree of effrontery among the women that amazes me, and of which I had no idea till a friend showed me one evening from my own box at the opera fifty or a hundred low shopkeepers' wives, dispersed about the pit at the theatre, dressed in men's clothes, *per disimpegno* as they called it, that they might be more *at liberty*, forsooth, to clap and hiss, and quarrel and jostle, etc. I felt shocked. "One who comes from a free government need not wonder so," said he. "On the contrary, sir," replied I, "where everybody has hopes, at least possibly of bettering his station, and advancing nearer to the limits of upper life, none except the most abandoned of their species will wholly lose sight of such decorous conduct as alone can grace them when they have reached their wish; whereas your people know their destiny, future as well as present, and think no more of deserving a higher post than they think of obtaining it."'

Mrs. Piozzi and her husband left Milan on April 6. 'Exactly five months have now since last November been passed among those who have, I hope, approved our conduct and esteemed our manners. That they should trouble themselves to examine our income, report our phrases, and listen, perhaps with some little mixture of envy, after every instance of unshakable attachment shown to each other, would be less pleasing; but that I verily believe they have at last dismissed us with general good wishes, proceeding from innate goodness of heart, and the hope of seeing again, in a year's time or so, two people who have supplied so many tables here with materials for conversation when the fountain of talk was stopped by deficiencies, and the little stream of prattle ceased to murmur for want of a few pebbles to break its course.'

From Milan the travellers went to Venice by way of Cremona, Mantua and Verona. At Cremona they climbed up the tower to see the view of the Lombard plains. 'An old man who has the care of the bells delighted much in telling us how he rung tunes upon them before the Duke of Parma, who presented him with money, and bid him ring again; and not a little was the good man amazed when one of our company sat down and played on them himself, a thing he had never before been witness to, he said, except once, when a surprising musician arrived from England, and performed the like feat. By his description of the person, and the time of his passing through Cremona, we conjectured he meant Dr. Burney.'

Verona struck her as the gayest-looking town she had ever lived in. 'I see nothing seemingly go forward here but *improvvisatori*, reciting stories or verses to entertain the populace; boys flying kites, cut square like a diamond on the cards, and called Stelle; men amusing themselves at a game called Pallamajo, something like our cricket, only that they throw the ball with a hollow stick, not with the hand, but it requires no small corporal strength, and I know not why our English people have such a notion of Italian effeminacy; games of very strong exertion are in use among them, and I have not yet felt one hot day since I left France.'

Here, however, she found an explanation of a business phrase which had puzzled her in dingy Southwark. 'That everything useful and everything ornamental, first revived in Italy, is well known; but I was never aware till now, though we talk of Italian book-keeping, that the little cant words employed in compting-houses took their original from the Lombard language, unless perhaps that of ditto, which every moment recurs, meaning "detto," or "sudetto," as that which was already said before; but this place has afforded me an opportunity of discovering what the people meant who called a large portion of ground in Southwark some years ago a "plant," above all things. The ground was destined to the purposes of extensive commerce, but the appellation of a "plant" gave me much disturbance from my inability to fathom the meaning of it. I have here found out that the Lombards call many things a "plant"; and say of their cities, palaces, etc., in familiar discourse, "che la pianta è buona, la pianta è cattiva," etc.'*

At Padua she was reminded of one of Garrick's pieces. 'A transplanted Hollander, carried thither originally from China, seems to thrive particularly well in this part of the world. The little pug dog, or Dutch mastiff, which our English ladies were once so fond of, that poor

* 'The "plant" is a good or a bad one,' etc.

Garrick thought it worth his while to ridicule them for it in the famous dramatic satire called " Lethe," has quitted London for Padua, I perceive; where he is restored happily to his former honours, and every carriage I meet here has a pug in it. That breed of dogs is now so near extirpated among us that I recollect only Lord Penryn who possesses such an animal.'

Here the coach was disposed of, and they went down the Brenta in a barge that brought them in eight hours to Venice, 'La Bella Dominante, as they call it prettily,' where they remained till May 21, with such unceasing enjoyment that Mrs. Piozzi finds on leaving that she has written more in five weeks than at Milan in five months. ' Well,' she exclaims, ' this is the first place I have seen which has been capable in any degree of obliterating the idea of Genoa la Superba, which has till now pursued me, nor could the gloomy dignity of the cathedral at Milan, or the striking view of the arena at Verona, nor the Sala di Giustizia at lettered Padua, banish her beautiful image from my mind: nor can I now acknowledge without shame, that I have ceased to regret the mountains, the chestnut groves, and slanting orange trees, which climbed my chamber-window *there*, and at *this* time, too! when

> ' " Young-ey'd Spring profusely throws
> From her green lap the pink and rose."

' . . . For it is sure there are in this town many astonishing privations of all that are used to make other places delightful; and as poor Omai the savage said, when about to return to Otaheite : " No horse there! no ass! no cow, no golden pippins, no dish of tea! Ah, missey! I go without everything—I always so content there though."

' It is really just so one lives at this lovely Venice; one has heard of a horse being exhibited for a show there, and yesterday I watched the poor people paying a penny a piece for the sight of a *stuffed one*, and am more than persuaded of the truth of what I am told here, that numberless inhabitants live and die in this great capital, nor ever find out or think of inquiring how the milk brought from terra firma is originally produced.

Of the Venetian ladies she says, 'Few remain unmarried till fifteen, and at thirty have a wan and faded look. "On ne goute pas ses plaisirs ici, on les avale," said Madame la Présidente yesterday, very judiciously,' and, indeed, Mrs. Piozzi made no attempt to deny the truth of the current account of Venetian society in the eighteenth century. She only says, in extenuation, that 'to try Venetian dames by English rules would be worse than all the tyranny complained of when some East Indian was condemned upon the Coventry Act for slitting his wife's nose; a common practice in *his* country, and perfectly agreeable to custom and the "usage du pays." Here is no struggle for female education as with us, no resources in study, no duties of family management; no bill of fare to be looked over in the morning, no account-book to be settled at noon; no necessity of reading, to supply without disgrace the evening's chat: no laughing at the card-table, or tittering in the corner if a *lapsus linguæ* has produced a mistake, which malice never fails to record. A lady in Italy is *sure* of applause, so she takes little pains to obtain it. A Venetian lady has in particular so sweet a manner naturally, that she really charms without any settled intent to do so, merely from that irresistible good-humour and mellifluous tone of voice which seize the soul, and detain it in despite of Juno-like majesty or Minerva-like wit.'

'A woman of quality, near whom I sat at the fine ball Bragadin made two nights ago in honour of this gay season, inquired how I had passed the morning. I named several churches I had looked into, particularly that which they esteem beyond the rest as a favourite work of Palladio, and called the Redentore. "You do very right," says she, "to look at our churches, as you have none in England, I know—but then you have so many other fine things—such charming *steel buttons*, for example;" pressing my hand to show that she meant no offence: "For," added she, "Chi pensa d' una maniera, chi pensa d' un altra." '*

'Late hours must be complied with at Venice, or you can have no diversion at all, as the earliest casino belonging to your soberest friends has not a candle lighted in it till past midnight. . . . The ladies, who never hardly dine at all, rise about seven in the evening, when the gentlemen are just got ready to attend them; and sit sipping their chocolate on a chair at the coffee-house door with great tranquillity, chatting over the common topics of the times; nor do they appear half so shy of each other as the Milanese ladies, who seldom seem to have any pleasure in the soft converse of a female friend. But, though certainly no women can be more charming than these Venetian dames, they have forgotten the old mythological fable that the youngest of the Graces was married to Sleep. . . .

'All literary topics are pleasingly discussed at Quirini's Casino, where everything may be learned by the conversation of the company, as Dr. Johnson said of his literary club; but more agreeably, because women are always half the number of persons admitted here.'

'Gray and Young are the favourite writers among us, as far as I have yet heard them talked over upon the Continent; the first has secured them by his residence at

* 'One person is of one mind, you know, another of another.'

Florence, and his Latin verses, I believe; the second by his piety and brilliant thoughts. Even Romanists are disposed to think dear Dr. Young very *near* to Christianity.'

The travellers left Venice with great regret, and Mrs. Piozzi exclaims: 'It is really pity ever to quit the sweet seducements of a place so pleasing, which attracts the inclination and flatters the vanity of one who, like myself, has received the most polite attentions, and been diverted with every amusement that could be devised. Kind, friendly, lovely Venetians, who appear to feel real fondness for the inhabitants of Great Britain!'

They started on May 21, returning up the Brenta to Padua, and going by way of Ferrara and Bologna to Florence, where they intended to pass the hottest months of summer. Mrs. Piozzi confessed herself disappointed with the Po, having let her imagination 'wander over all that the poets had said about it . . . but I might have recollected a comical contest enough between a literary lady once and Dr. Johnson, to which I was myself a witness; when she, maintaining the happiness and purity of a country life and rural manners, with her best eloquence, and she had a great deal, added as corroborative and almost incontestable authority, that the *poets* said so. "And didst thou not know, then," replied he, " my darling dear, that the poets lie?"'

The stateliness of Ferrara impressed them, and 'my pen was just upon the point of praising its cleanliness too, till I reflected there was nobody to dirty it. I looked half-an-hour before I could find one beggar, a bad account of poor Ferrara; but it brought to my mind how unreasonably my daughter and myself had laughed, seven years ago, at reading in an extract from some of the foreign gazettes, how the famous Improvisatore Talassi, who was in England about the year 1770, and entertained with his justly-admired talents the literati at London, had published an account of his visit to Mr. Thrale, at a villa eight miles from Westminster Bridge, during that time, when he had the good fortune, he said, to meet many celebrated characters at his country seat; and the mortification which nearly overbalanced it, to miss seeing the immortal Garrick, then confined by illness. In all this, however, there was nothing ridiculous; but we fancied his description of Streatham village truly so, when we read that he called it " Luogo assai popolato ed ameno,"* an expression apparently pompous, and inadequate to the subject; but the jest disappeared when I got into *his* town; a place which, perhaps, may be said to possess every other excellence but that of being "popolato ed ameno"; and I sincerely believe that no Ferrara man could have missed making the same or a like observation; as in this finely-constructed city, the grass literally grows in the street; nor do I hear that the state of the air and water is such as is likely to tempt new inhabitants. How much, then, and how reasonably must he have wondered, and how easily must he have been led to express his wonder, at seeing a village no bigger than that of Streatham, contain a number of people equal, as I doubt not but it does, to all the dwellers in Ferrara!'

Bologna la Grassa, though handsomely built and set in a country particularly beautiful, covered with vines and mulberry-trees, did not please the lively lady. 'This fat Bologna has a tristful look, from the numberless priests, friars, and women, all dressed in black, who fill the streets, and stop on a sudden to pray, when I see nothing done to call forth immediate addresses to heaven. Extremes do certainly meet, however, and my Lord Peter

* 'A populous and delightful place.'

in this place is so like his fanatical brother Jack, that I know not what is come to him.'

Here, however, begin her artistic criticisms, for, after the fashion of the time, the Bolognese School was the one which excited her warmest admiration, and she heaps epithets of affection and adoration upon painters whom we are far from placing in the front rank. 'Here the great Caraccis kept their school; here then was every idea of dignity and majestic beauty to be met with. . . . The boasted Raphael here does not in my eyes triumph over the wonders of this Caracci school.' Of the 'Madonna della Seggiola,' at Florence, she says that 'it wants that heavenly expression of dignity divine and grace unutterable which breathes through the school of the Caraccis.' A picture by Correggio 'lacks the taste, character and expression which are found only in the Caraccis and their school.' She speaks of 'the majestic pencil of the demi-divine Caracci;' but Guercino is her special divinity, not half, but wholly divine. 'Other painters remind one of nature, but nature when most lovely makes me think of Guercino and his works.' 'A St. John by dear Guercino is transcendent.' 'I once more half worshipped the works of divine Guercino. Nothing shall prevent my going to his birthplace at Cento, whether in our way or out of it.' When there she exclaims before a picture of his: 'How often have I said *this* is the finest picture we have seen yet! when looking on the Caraccis and their school. I will say no more; the painter's art can go no further than *this*.' With Guido she sometimes ventures to find fault, but his 'Magdalen' 'effaces every beauty, of softness mingled with distress.' Domenichino she seems to admire more as a matter of duty. His 'Diana among her Nymphs' strikes her as very laboured and very learned; and she asks irreverently: 'Why did it put me in mind of Hogarth's strolling actresses dressing in a barn?' The two volumes of her 'Journey' contain a considerable mass of art criticism, which, except as an illustration of changing fashions in art, would not much interest readers of the present day.

In spite of her æsthetic raptures, however, Mrs. Piozzi left Bologna with little regret. 'I am glad that we shall now be soon released from this, upon the whole, disagreeable town, where there is the best possible food, too, for body and mind; but where the inhabitants seem to think only of the next world, and do little to amuse those who have not yet quite done with this. . . . Those travellers who pass through will find some amends in the rich cream and incomparable dinners every day for the insects that devour them every night; and will, if they are wise, seek compensation from the company of the half-animated pictures that crowd the palaces and churches for the half-dead inhabitants who kneel in the streets of Bologna.'

They went on to Florence, 'passing apparently through a new region of the earth, or even air; clambering up mountains covered with snow, and viewing with amazement the little valleys between, where, after quitting the summer season, all glowing with heat and spread into verdure, we found cherry-trees in blossom, oaks and walnuts scarcely beginning to bud. . . . We arrived late at our inn, an English one they say it is; and many of the last miles were passed very pleasantly by my maid and myself in anticipating the comforts we should receive by finding ourselves among our own country folks, and by once more eating, sleeping, etc., *all in the English way*, as her phrase is.'

CHAPTER X.

Florence—An English Inn—Sir Horace Mann—Fruits—An Eulogium on Captain Cook—A Cardinal—The *Lingua Toscana*—Hasty Burials—Lucca—Completion and Despatch of the 'Anecdotes'—The Bagni di Pisa—Illness of Mr. Piozzi—Insects—First View of Rome—The Coliseum—The King of Sweden — Queen Christina — Dislike of Perfumes — Insanitary Streets — Escape of Mr. Piozzi from Assassination—Arrival at Naples—Vesuvius—St. Januarius—The King of Naples—The Grotto del Cane—Reminiscence of the Southwark Brewery—The Hermit of Vesuvius—Return to Rome—The Carnival—Kissing the Slipper—Anecdote of the Emperor—Angelica Kauffman — Loretto — Correggio — Return to Milan — The Emperor Joseph's Reforms— Lugano — Farewell to Italy — Innsbruck — Munich — Salzburg — Vienna—The Emperor—Metastasio—Prague—Dresden—Berlin—Antwerp—Return to England.

AT the English inn in Florence their anticipations were fully realized. ' Here are small low beds again, soft and clean, and down pillows; here are currant tarts, which the Italians scorn to touch, but which we are happy and delighted to pay not ten, but twenty times their value for, because a currant tart is so much *in the English way;* and here are beans and bacon in a climate where it is impossible that bacon should be either wholesome or agreeable; and one eats infinitely worse than one did at Milan, Venice or Bologna, and infinitely dearer too; but that makes it still more completely *in the English way.*'

'Sir Horace Mann is sick and old; but there are conversations at his house of a Saturday evening, and sometimes a dinner, to which we have been almost always asked.

'The fruits in this place begin to astonish me; such

cherries did I never yet see, or even hear tell of, as when I caught the *laquais de place* weighing two of them in a scale to see if they came to an ounce. These are, in the London street phrase, " cherries like plums," in size at least, but in flavour they far exceed them, being exactly of the kind that we call bleeding-hearts, hard to the bite, and parting easily from the stone, which is proportionately small. Figs, too, are here in such perfection that it is not easy for an English gardener to guess at their excellence; for it is not by superior size, but taste and colour that *they* are distinguished; small and green on the outside, a bright full crimson within, and we eat them with raw ham, and truly delicious is the dainty. By raw ham I mean ham cured, not boiled or roasted. It is no wonder, though, that fruits should mature in such a sun as this is; which, to give a just notion of its penetrating fire, I will take leave to tell my countrywomen is so violent that I use no other method of heating the pinching-irons to curl my hair than that of poking them out at a south window, with the handles shut in, and the glasses darkened to keep us from being actually fired in his beams.'

As visitors from England, they received an invitation to a gathering at one of the libraries 'to hear an eulogium finely pronounced upon our circumnavigator Captain Cook, whose character has attracted the attention and extorted the esteem of every European nation. Far less was the wonder that it forced my tears; they flowed from a thousand causes — my distance from England, my pleasure in hearing an Englishman thus lamented in a language with which he had no acquaintance!'

At the house of a lady in Florence 'I had the honour of being introduced to Cardinal Corsini, who put me a little out of countenance by saying suddenly: 'Well, madam, you never saw one of us red-legged partridges before, I believe; but you are going to Rome, I hear, where you will find such fellows as me no rarities." The truth is, I had seen the amiable Prince d' Orini at Milan, who was a cardinal, and who had taken delight in showing me prodigious civilities. Nothing ever struck me more than his abrupt entrance one night at our house, when we had a little music, and everybody stood up the moment he appeared. The Prince, however, walked forward to the harpsichord, and blessed my husband in a manner the most graceful and affecting; then sat the amusement out, and returned the next morning to breakfast with us, when he indulged us with two hours' conversation at least; adding the kindest and most pressing invitations to his country-seat among the mountains of Brianza, when we should return from our tour of Italy in the spring of 1786. Florence, therefore, was not the first place that showed me a cardinal.'

At Florence one of the first things to be noticed 'is the superior elegance of the language; for till we arrive here all is dialect. The *laquais de place*, who attended us at Bologna, was one of the few persons I had met then who spoke a language perfectly intelligible to me. "Are you a Florentine, pray, friend?" said I. "No, madam, but the combinations of this world having led me to talk much with strangers, I contrive to *tuscanize* it all I can, for *their* advantage, and doubt not but it will tend to my own at last."'

They spent the whole summer at Florence, and her last reflection is that 'this is no good town to take one's last leave of life in, as the body one has been so long taking care of would in twenty-four hours be hoisted up upon a common cart, with those of all the people who died the same day, and being fairly carried out of Porto

San Gallo toward the dusk of evening, would be shot into a hole dug away from the city, properly enough, to protect Florence, and keep it clear of putrid disorders and disagreeable smells. All this with little ceremony, to be sure, and less distinction; for the Grand-Duke suffers the pride of birth to last no longer than life, and demolishes every hope of the woman of quality lying in a separate grave from the distressed object who begged at her carriage door when she was last on an airing.

'Let me add that his liberality of sentiment extends to virtue on the one hand, if hardness of heart may be complained of on the other. He suffers no difference of opinions to operate on his philosophy, and I believe we heretics here should sleep among the best of his Tuscan nobles. But there is no comfort in the possibility of being buried alive by the excessive haste with which people are catched up and hurried away before it can be known almost whether all sparks of life are extinct or no.'

The travellers left Florence and the paternal despotism of the Grand-Duke on September 12, and drove through the Vale of Arno to Lucca, 'where the panther sits at the gate, and liberty is written up on every wall and door.' The capital of the little commonwealth she describes as 'larger than Salisbury, and prettier than Nottingham, the beauties of both which places it unites with all the charms peculiar to itself.' The territory she takes 'to be about the size of Rutlandshire, and their revenues about equal to the Duke of Bedford's, eighty or eighty-five thousand pounds a year.'

From Lucca they went to Pisa, and thence, with a special object, to Leghorn. During her stay in Italy Mrs. Piozzi had been busy with her first literary production. 'I have here finished that work which chiefly brought me hither, the "Anecdotes of Dr. Johnson's Life." It is from this port they take their flight for England, while we retire for refreshment to the Bagni di Pisa.'

It was perhaps the consciousness of having herself entered on a literary career that gave to her description of the baths a touch of the Johnsonian manner. 'Not only the waters here are admirable, every look from every window gives images unentertained before; sublimity happily wedded with elegance, and majestic greatness enlivened, yet softened, by taste.' Soon, however, she returns to a more familiar style. 'Mr. Piozzi has been ill, and of a putrid complaint in his throat, which above all things I should dread in this hot climate. This accident, assisted by other concurring circumstances, has convinced me that we are not shut up in measureless content, as Shakespeare calls it, even under St. Julian's Hill; for here was no help to be got in the first place, except the useless conversation of a medical gentleman, whose accent and language might have pleased a disengaged mind, but had little chance to tranquillize an affrighted one. What is worse, here was no rest to be had, for the multitudes of vermin upstairs and below. When we first hired the house, I remember my maid jumping up on one of the kitchen chairs while a ragged lad cleared *that* apartment for her of scorpions to the number of seventeen. But now the biters and stingers drive me *quite wild*, because one must keep the windows open for air, and a sick man can enjoy none of that, being closed up in the Zanzariere, and obliged to respire the same breath over and over again, which, with a sore throat and fever, is most melancholy; but I keep it wet with vinegar, and defy the hornets how I can.

'What is more surprising than all, however, is to hear that no lemons can be procured for less than twopence English apiece, and now I am almost ready to join myself in the general cry against Italian imposition . . . as I am confident they cannot even be worth twopence a hundred here, where they hang like apples in our cyder countries; but the rogues know that my husband is sick, and upon poor me they have no mercy.

'I have sent our folks out to gather fruit at a venture; and now this misery will soon be ended with his illness, driven away by deluges of lemonade, I think, made in defiance of wasps, flies, and a kind of volant beetle, wonderfully beautiful and very pertinacious in his attacks; and who makes dreadful depredations on my sugar and currant-jelly, so necessary on this occasion of illness, and so attractive to all these detestable inhabitants of a place so lovely.

'My patient, however, complaining that although I kept these harpies at a distance, no sleep could yet be obtained, I resolved when he was risen, and had changed his room, to examine into the true cause; and with my maid's assistance, unripped the mattress, which was, without exaggeration or hyperbole, *all alive* with creatures wholly unknown to me. Nondescripts in nastiness I believe they are, like maggots with horns and tails; such a race as I never saw or heard of, and as would have disgusted Mr. Leeuenhoeck himself.'

A tremendous thunderstorm completed their discomfort, and quickened their willingness 'to quit the place and its hundred-footed inhabitants. . . . I waited its abatement in a darkened room, packed up our coach without waiting to copy over the verses my admiration of the place had prompted, and drove forward to Sienna, through Pisa again, where our friends told us of the damages done by the tempest, and showed us a pretty little church just out of town, where the officiating priest at the altar was saved almost by miracle, as the lightning melted one of the chalices completely, and twisted the brazen-gilt crucifix quite round in a very astonishing manner.'

From Sienna they went towards Rome. 'The first view of Rome is wonderfully striking—

> "Ye awful wrecks of ancient times!
> Proud monuments of ages past
> Now mould'ring in decay."
> MERRY.

But mingled with every crowding, every classical idea, comes to one's recollection an old picture painted by R. Wilson about thirty years ago, which I am now sure must have been a very excellent representation.

'Well, then! here we are, admirably lodged at Strofani's in the Piazza di Spagna, and have only to choose what we will see and talk on first among this galaxy of rarities which dazzles, diverts, confounds, and nearly fatigues one.'

Her description of these occupies some sixty pages, from which it would be superfluous to quote much. A few passages have a personal interest. A visit to the Coliseum suggests to her the possibility of the unification of Italy. 'The modern Italians have not lost their taste of a prodigious theatre; were they once more a single nation they would rebuild this, I fancy. . . . I must not, however, quit the Coliseum without repeating what passed between the King of Sweden and his Roman *laquais de place* when he was here; and the fellow, in the true cant of his ciceroneship, exclaimed, as they looked up, "Ah, Maestà! what cursed Goths those were that tore away so many fine things here, and pulled down such magnificent pillars, etc." "Hold, hold, friend," replies the King of Sweden; "I am one of those cursed Goths myself, you know; but what were your Roman nobles a-doing, I would ask, when they laboured to destroy an edifice like this, and build their palaces with its materials?"'

At the Circus of Caracalla she says, 'I must not forbear mentioning his bust, which so perfectly resembles Hogarth's idle 'prentice; but why should they not be alike?

' " For blackguards are blackguards in every degree,"

I suppose, and the people here who show one things, always take delight to souse an Englishman's hat upon his head, as if they thought so too.'

'The Strada del Popolo,' she says, 'is so called with infinite propriety, for except in that strada there is little populousness enough, God knows. Twelve men to a woman even there, and as many ecclesiastics to a layman; all this, however, is fair, when celibacy is once enjoined as a duty in one profession, encouraged as a virtue in all. Where females are superfluous, and half prohibited, it were foolish to complain of the decay of population.'

'When I was told the story of Queen Christina admiring the two prodigious fountains before St. Peter's Church, and begging that they might leave off playing, because she thought them occasional, and in honour of her arrival, not constant and perpetual; who could help recollecting a similar tale told about the Prince of Monaco, who was said to have expressed his concern, when he saw the roads lighted up round London, that our King should put himself to so great an expense on his account—in good time!—thinking it a temporary illumination made to receive him with distinguished splendour.'

'The conversations of Cardinal de Bernis and Madame de Boccapaduli are what my countrywomen talk most of; but the Roman ladies cannot endure perfumes, and faint away even at an artificial rose. I went but once among them, when Memmo, the Venetian Ambassador, did me the honour to introduce me somewhere, but the conversation was soon over, not so my shame; when I perceived all the company shrink from me very oddly, and stop their noses with rue, which a servant brought to their assistance on open salvers. I was by this time more like to faint away than they—from confusion and distress; my kind protector informed me of the cause: said I had some grains of marechale powder in my hair, perhaps, and led me out of the assembly; to which no entreaties could prevail on me ever to return, or make further attempts to associate with a delicacy so very susceptible of offence.'

At the Barberini Palace this incident recurs to her. 'Nothing can equal the nastiness at one's entrance to this magazine of perfection; but the Roman nobles are not disgusted with *all sorts* of scents, it is plain; these are not what we should call perfumes indeed, but certainly *odori*, of the same nature as those one is obliged to wade through before Trajan's Pillar can be climbed.'

At Rome Mr. Piozzi had a narrow escape of being murdered. 'A man asked importunately in our antechamber this morning for the *padrone*, naming no names, and our servants turned him out. He went, however, only five doors further, found a sick old gentleman sitting in his lodging attended by a feeble servant, whom he bound, stuck a knife in the master, rifled the apartments, and walked coolly out again at noon-day; nor should we have ever heard of *such a trifle*, but that it happened just by so; for here are no newspapers to tell who is murdered, and nobody's pity is excited, unless for the malefactor when they hear he is caught.'

'On the tenth day of this month,' says Mrs. Piozzi, 'we arrived early at Naples,' but she quite forgets to say what month. It would seem, however, to have been December, 1785, and it was certainly early, for it was about two o'clock in the morning. 'Sure, the providence of God preserved us, for never was such weather seen by me since I came into the world—thunder, lightning, storm at sea, rain and wind, contending for mastery, and combining to extinguish the torches bought to light us the last stage; Vesuvius, vomiting fire, and pouring torrents of red-hot lava down its sides, was the only object visible; and *that* we saw plainly in the afternoon thirty miles off, where I asked a Franciscan friar if it was the famous volcano, "Yes," replied he; "that's our mountain, which throws up money for us, by calling foreigners to see the extraordinary effects of so surprising a phenomenon." . . .

'My poor maid had by this time nearly lost her wits with terror, and the French valet, crushed with fatigue, and covered with rain and sea-spray, had just life enough left to exclaim: "Ah, madame! il me semble que nous sommes venus ici exprès pour voir la fin du monde."'*

They secured rooms with a full view of the mountain, which called her the first night twenty times away from sleep and supper, 'though never so in want of both as at that moment, surely. . . . Upon reflection it appears to me that the men most famous at London and Paris for performing tricks with fire have been always Italians in my time, and commonly Neapolitans. No wonder, I should think, Naples would produce prodigious connoisseurs in this way. We have almost perpetual lightning of various colours, according to the soil from whence the vapours are exhaled; sometimes of a pale straw or lemon colour; often white, like artificial flame produced by camphor; but oftenest blue, bright as the rays emitted through the coloured liquors set in the window of a

* 'Lord, madam! why, we came here on purpose, sure, to see the end of the world.'

chemist's shop in London; and with such thunder! "For God's sake, Sir," said I to some of them, "is there no danger of the ships in the harbour here catching fire? Why, we should all fly up in the air directly if once these flashes should communicate to the room where any of the vessels keep their powder!" "Gunpowder, madam!" replies the man, amazed. "Why, if St. Peter and St. Paul came here with gunpowder on board, we should soon drive them out again. Don't you know," added he, "that every ship discharges her contents at such a place (naming it), and never comes into our port with a grain on board?"'

The veneration of St. Januarius struck her as the most heathenish thing she had seen in Italy. 'The Neapolitans, who are famous for blasphemous oaths, and a facility of taking the most sacred words into their mouths on every, and, I may say, on *no* occasion, are never heard to repeat *his* name without pulling off their hat, or making some reverential sign of worship at the moment. And I have seen Italians from other states greatly shocked at the grossness of these their unenlightened neighbours, particularly the half-Indian custom of burning figures upon their skins with gunpowder; these figures large, and oddly displayed, too, according to the coarse notions of the wearer.

'As the weather is exceedingly warm, and there is little need of clothing for comfort, our Lazzaroni have small care about appearances, and go with a vast deal of their persons uncovered, except by these strange ornaments. The man who rows you about this lovely bay has perhaps the angel Raphael or the Blessed Virgin Mary delineated on one brawny sunburnt leg, the saint of the town upon the other; his arms represent the Glory, or the seven spirits of God, or some strange things, while a brass medal hangs from his neck expressive of his favourite martyr.'

'The King of Spain, or *Ré Cattolico*, as these people always call him, has still much influence, and they seem to think nearly as respectfully of him as of their own immediate sovereign, who is, however, greatly beloved among them; and so he ought to be, for he is the representative of them all. He rides and rows, and hunts the wild boar, and catches fish in the bay, and sells it in the market as dear as he can, too, but gives away the money they pay him for it, and that directly; so that no suspicion of meanness, or of anything worse than a little rough merriment, can be ever attached to his truly honest, open, undesigning character.

'Stories of monarchs seldom give me pleasure, who seldom am persuaded to give credit to tales told of persons few people have any access to, and whose behaviour towards those few is circumscribed within the laws of insipid and dull routine; but this prince lives among his subjects with the old Roman idea of a window before his bosom, I believe. They know the worst of him is that he shoots at the birds, dances with the girls, eats macaroni, and helps himself to it with his fingers, and rows against the watermen in the bay, till one of them burst out o' bleeding at the nose last week with his uncourtly efforts to outdo the King, who won the trifling wager by this accident; conquered, laughed, and leaped on shore amidst the acclamations of the populace, who huzzaed him home to the palace, from whence he sent double the sum he had won to the waterman's wife and children, with other tokens of kindness. Meantime, while he resolves to be happy himself, he is equally determined to make no man miserable.'

The Grotto del Cane reminded her of a terrifying

accident which she 'once saw arise in a great brewhouse' (her first husband's, no doubt) 'from the headstrong stupidity of a workman who would go down into a vat, the contents of which had lately been drawn off, without sending his proper precursor, the candle, to inquire if all was safe. The consequence was half expected by his companions, who, hearing him drop off the steps and fall flat to the bottom, began instantly hooking him up again; but there were no signs of life. Some ran for their master, others for a surgeon, but we were nearest at hand, and, recollecting what one had read of the recovery of dogs at Naples by tossing them suddenly into the lake Agnano, we made the men carry their patient to the cooler, and, plunging him over head and ears, restored his life exactly in the manner of the Grotto del Cane experiment, which succeeded so completely in this fellow's case, I remember, that, waking after the temporary suspension, we had much ado to impress so insensible a mortal with a due sense of the danger his rashness had incurred.'

The repeated experiments with the unfortunate dog disgusted her. 'Sporting with animal life is always highly offensive. . . . Truth is, human life is lower rated in all parts of Italy than with us. They think nothing of an individual, but see him perish (excepting by the hand of justice) as a cat or dog. A young man fell from our carriage at Milan one evening. He was not a servant of ours, but a friend whom, after we were gone home, the coachman had picked up to go with him to the fireworks which were exhibited that night near the Corso. There was a crowd and an *embarras*, and the fellow tumbled off and died upon the spot, and nobody even spoke, or I believe *thought* about the matter, except one woman, who supposed that he had neglected to cross himself when he got up behind.'

The King's menagerie they found neither rich in animals nor particularly well kept. 'The bears, however, were as tame as lapdogs. There was a wolf, too, larger than ever I saw a wolf, and an elephant that played a hundred tricks at the command of his keeper, little less a beast than he.'

Of course, they climbed Vesuvius, and at the Hermitage had some talk with 'the poor, good old man, who sets up a little cross wherever the fire has stopped near his cell. . . . This hermit is a Frenchman. "J'ai dansé dans mon lit tant de fois," said he. The expression was not sublime when speaking of an earthquake, to be sure. I looked among his books, however, and found Bruyère. "Would not the Duc de Rochefoucault have done better?" said I. "Did I never see you before, madam?" said he. "Yes, sure I have, and dressed you, too, when I was a hairdresser in London, and lived with Monsieur Martinant, and I dressed pretty Miss Wynne, too, in the same street. 'Vit-elle encore? Vit-elle encore?' Ah, I am old now," continued he. "I remember when black pins first came up." This was charming, and in such an unexpected way, I could hardly prevail upon myself ever to leave the spot; but Mrs. Greathead having been quite to the crater's edge with her only son, a baby of four years old, shame rather than inclination urged me forward. I asked the little boy what he had seen. "I saw the chimney," replied he, "and it was on fire; but I liked the elephant better."'

'A *festa di ballo*, or masquerade, given here, was exceedingly gay, and the dresses surprisingly rich. *Our* party, a very large one, all Italians, retired at one in the morning to quite the finest supper of its size I ever saw. Fish of various sorts, incomparable in their kinds, composed eight dishes of the first course. We had thirty-eight set on the table in that course, forty-nine in the second, with wines and dessert truly magnificent, for all which Mr. Piozzi protested to me that we paid only three shillings and sixpence a-head English money; but for the truth of that he must answer.'

The travellers left Naples after a stay of three months, and returned to Rome, to which fifty pages more of the 'Observations' are devoted. They arrived in time for the three last days of the carnival. 'One high joke seems to consist in the men putting on girls' clothes. A woman is somewhat a rarity at Rome, and strangely superfluous, as it should appear by the extraordinary substitutes found for them on the stage. It is more than wonderful to see great strong fellows dancing the women's parts in these fashionable dramas—pastoral and heroic ballets, as they call them; but these clumsy *figurantes*, all stout, coarse-looking men, kicking about in hooped petticoats, were to me irresistibly ridiculous. The gentlemen with me, however, both Italians and English, were too much disgusted to laugh.'

They attended the 'various functions that really make Rome a scene of perpetual gala during the Holy Week, which an English friend here protested to me he had never spent with so little devotion in his life before. . . . Even the *Miserere* has much of its effect destroyed from the admission of too many people. Crowd and bustle, and struggle for places, leave no room for any ideas to range themselves, and, least of all, serious ones; nor would the opening of our sacred music in Westminster Abbey, when nine hundred performers join to celebrate *Messiah's* praises, make that impression which it does upon the mind, were not the King, and Court, and all the audience, as still as death when the first note is taken.'

'The Pope powders his hair like any other of the

Cardinals, and is, it seems, the first who has ever done so. When he takes the air it is in a fashionable carriage, with a few, a very few, guards on horseback, and is by no means desirous of making himself a show. Now and then an old woman begs his blessing as he passes; but I almost remember the time when our Bishops of Bangor and St. Asaph were followed by the country people in North Wales full as much or more, and with just the same feelings. One man in particular we used to talk of who came from a distant part of our mountainous province, with much expense in proportion to his abilities, poor fellow, and terrible fatigue. He was a tenant of my father's, who asked him how he ventured to undertake so troublesome a journey. "It was to get my good Lord's blessing," replied the farmer. "*I hope it will cure my rheumatism.*" Kissing the slipper at Rome will probably, in a hundred years more, be a thing to be thus faintly recollected by a few very old people, and it is strange to me it should have lasted so long. No man better knows than the present learned and pious successor of St. Peter that St. Peter himself would permit no act of adoration to his own person.'

They went to see Raphael's 'Transfiguration,' and Mrs. Piozzi heard an anecdote of the Emperor Joseph. 'It was the first thing the Emperor did visit when he came to Rome, and so a Franciscan friar, who shows it, told us. He saw a gentleman walking into church, it seems, and, leaving his friends at dinner, went out to converse with him. "Pull aside the curtain, sir," said the stranger, "for I am in haste to see this masterpiece of your immortal Raphael." "I was as willing to be in a hurry as *he*," says the friar, "and observed how fortunate it was for us that it could not be moved, otherwise we had lost it long ago. 'For, Sir,' said I, 'they would have carried it away from poor Monte Citoria to some finer *temple* long ago; though, let me tell you, this is an elegant Doric building, too, and one of Bramante's best works, much admired by the English in particular. I hope, if it please God now that I should live but a very little longer, I may have the honour of showing it the Emperor.'" "Is he expected?" inquired the gentleman. "Every day, Sir," replies the friar. "And well now," cries the foreigner, "what sort of man do you expect to see?" "Why, sir, you seem a traveller; did *you* ever see him?" quoth the Franciscan. "Yes, sure, my good friend, very often indeed. He is as plain a man as myself, has good intentions, and an honest heart; and I think you would like him if you knew him, because he puts nobody out of their way."

'This dialogue, natural and simple, had taken such hold of our good *religieux's* fancy, that not a word would he say about the picture, while his imagination was so full of the Prince and of his own amazement at the salutation of his companions when returning to the refectory. "Why, Gaetano," cried they, "thou hast been conversing with Cæsar!" I, too, liked the tale, because it was artless, and because it was true.'

Of the Vatican Library, 'to her perpetual regret,' she saw scarcely anything. 'Neither book nor MS. could I prevail on the librarian to show me, except some love-letters from Henry the Eighth of England to Anne Boleyn, which he said were most likely to interest *me*. They were very gross and indecent ones, to be sure; so I felt offended, and went away in a very ill humour.'

'I must not quit Rome, however, without a word of Angelica Kauffman, who, though neither English nor Italian, has contrived to charm both nations, and show her superior talents both here and there. Beside her paintings, of which the world has been the judge, her conversation attracts all people of taste to her house, which none can bear to leave without difficulty and regret.'

They left Rome on April 19, 1786. 'The first night of our journey was spent at Otricoli, where I heard the cuckoo sing in a shriller, sharper note than he does in England. I had never listened to him before since I left my own country, and his song alone would have convinced me I was no longer in it. . . . The next day's drive carried us forward to Terni, where a severe concussion of the earth, suffered only three nights since, kept all the little town in terrible alarm; the houses were deserted, the churches crowded, supplications and processions in every street, and people singing all night to the Virgin under our window.'

Next morning, going to see the Falls, they found that 'the earthquake had twisted the torrent out of its proper channel, and thrown it down another neighbouring rock, leaving the original bed black and deserted, as a dismal proof of the concussion's force.'

'At Foligno the people told us that it was the quality of those waters to turn the clothing of many animals white, and accordingly all the fowls looked like those of Dorking. I had, however, no taste of their beauty, recollecting that when I kept poultry some accident poisoned me a very beautiful black hen, the breed of Lord Mansfield at Caen Wood. She recovered her illness, but at the next moulting season her feathers came as white as the swan's. "Let us look," says Mr. Sh——, "if all the women here have got gray hair."'

'At Loretto it is very entertaining to see inscriptions in twelve different tongues, giving an account of the miraculous removal and arrival here of the Santa Casa.

I was delighted with the Welsh one; and our conductor said there came not unfrequently pilgrims from the Vale of Clwyd, who in their turns told the wonders of their holy well.'

'Ravenna l'Antica tired more than it pleased us,' is her sole mention of that wonderful place. No doubt her appetite for sightseeing was nearly satisfied. 'A charming lady of our country, for whom I have the highest esteem, protests she shall be happy to get back to London, if it is only for the relief of sitting still, and resolving to see no more sights; exchanging *fasto, fiera,* and *frittura* for a muffin, a mop, and a morning newspaper—three things equally unknown in Italy as the other three among us.'

Coming to Bologna, Mrs. Piozzi complains of it again as 'hot, and loud, and pious, though less empty of occupation than last time; for here is a new Gonfaloniere chosen in to-day, and the drums beat, and the trumpets sound, and some donations are distributed about, much in the proportions Tom Davies describes Garrick's to have been; small pieces of money, and large pieces of cake, with quantities of meat, bread, and birds, borne about the town in procession, to make display of *his* bounty, who gives all this away at the time he is elected into office.'

They found it difficult to get to Padua, the roads being very bad. 'Had we come three days sooner we might have seen the transit of Mercury from Abate Toaldo's observatory; but our own transit took up all our thoughts, and it is a very great mercy that we are come safe at last. I think it was as much as four bulls and six horses could do to drag us into Rovigo. . . . Now we are hastening to Venice, and shall leave our cares and our coach behind, in a city which admits of neither.' Floating down the

Brenta, Mrs. Piozzi read Merry's ' Paulina,' ' that glorious poem.' The poet's glories have so entirely faded that few people remember even his name. At Venice the travellers rested till June 12, and, returning to Padua, observed how surprisingly quick had been the progress of summer. 'In these countries vegetation is so rapid that everything makes haste to come and more to go. Scarce have you tasted green peas or strawberries before they are out of fashion; and if you do *not* swallow your pleasures, as Madame la Présidente said, you have a chance to miss of getting any pleasures at all. Here is no mediocrity in anything—no moderate weather, no middle rank of life, no twilight; whatever is not night is day, and whatever is not love is hatred; and that the English should eat peaches in May, and green peas in October, sounds to Italian ears as a miracle. They comfort themselves, however, by saying that they *must* be very insipid, while *we* know that fruits forced by strong fire are at least many of them higher in flavour than those produced by sun; the pineapple particularly, which West Indians confess eats better with us than with them. Figs and cherries, however, defy a hot-house, and grapes raised by art are worth little except for show. Peaches, nectarines, and ananas are the glory of a British gardener, and no country but England can show such.'

At Parma Mrs. Piozzi does not refuse to admire Correggio's pictures, though with the customary reference to the higher merits of the Caracci. 'Correggio,' she says, ' was perhaps one of the most powerful geniuses that has appeared on earth. Destitute of knowledge, or of the means of acquiring it, he has left glorious proofs of what uninstructed man may do, and is, perhaps, a greater honour to the human species than those who, from fermenting erudition of various kinds, produce performances of more complicated worth. The "Fatal Curiosity" and "Pilgrim's Progress" will live as long as the "Prince of Abyssinia" or "Les Aventures de Télémaque," perhaps; and who shall dare say that Lillo, Bunyan, and Antonio Correggio were not *naturally* equal to Johnson, Michael Angelo, and the Archbishop of Cambray? Have I said enough, or can enough be ever said, in praise of a painter whose works the great Annibale Caracci delighted to study, to copy, and to praise?'

Returning to Milan, 'where we have cool apartments and warm friends,' they observed how much the general look of the place was improved in the last fifteen months. The reforming Emperor Joseph had been at work, and the town was become neater, the ordinary people smarter, the roads round their city mended, and the beggars cleared away from the streets. 'We did not find, however, that the people we talked to were at all charmed with these new advantages: their convents demolished, their processions put an end to, the number of their priests, of course, contracted, and their church plate carried by cartloads to the mint; holidays forbidden, and every saint's name erased from the calendar, excepting only St. Peter and St. Paul; whilst those shopkeepers who worked for monasteries, and those musicians who sung or played in oratorios, are left to find employment how they can—cloud the countenances of all, and justly; as such sudden and rough reforms shock the feelings of the multitude; offend the delicacy of the nobles; make a general stagnation of business, and of pleasure, in a country where *both* depend upon religious functions, and terrify the clergy into no ill-grounded apprehensions of being found in a few years more wholly useless, and as such dismissed.'

They went to see the Lake of Lugano, and were

speedily made aware that they had crossed the frontier into Switzerland. 'Our cicerone there, in reply to the question asked in Italy three times a day, I believe— "Che principe fà qui la sua residenza?"*—replied that they were plagued with no *principi* at all, while the thirteen cantons protected all their subjects; and though, as the man expressed it, only half of them were *Christians*, and the other half *Protestants*, no church or convent had ever wanted respect; while their town regularly received a monthly governor from every canton, and was perfectly contented with this ambulatory dominion.'

After a visit to Bergamo they returned to Milan, and began their preparations for quitting Italy. 'We are now cutting hay here for the last time this season, and all the environs smell like spring on this 15th September, 1786. The autumnal tint, however, falls fast upon the trees, which are already rich with a deep yellow hue. A wintery feel upon the atmosphere early in a morning, heavy fogs about noon, and a hollow wind towards the approach of night, make it look like the very last week of October in England, and warn us that summer is going. The same circumstances prompt me, who am about to forsake this her favourite region, to provide furs, flannels, etc., for the passing of those Alps which look so formidable when covered with snow even at their present distance. Our swallows are calling their clamorous council round me while I write; but the butterflies still flutter about in the middle of the day. and grapes are growing more wholesome, as with us, when the mornings begin to be frosty.'

A week later they quitted Milan with some tears, took a still more tender farewell of Verona, and, passing the Tyrolese Alps, came to Trent. There she remarks upon

* 'What Prince makes his residence here?'

the pleasing sight ' of two nations, not naturally congenial, living happily together, as the Germans and Italians here do.' At Innsbruck they find themselves 'cruelly distressed for want of language'; but it is 'no small comfort to find one's self once more waited on by clean-looking females, who make your bed, sweep your room, etc., while the pewters in the little neat kitchens, as one passes through, amaze me with their brightness, that I feel as if in a new world, it is *so* long since I have seen any metal but gold unencrusted by nastiness, and gold *will* not be dirty.

'The clumsy churches here are more violently crowded with ornaments than I have found them yet, and for one crucifix or Madonna to be met with on Italian roads, here are at least forty. An ill-carved, and worse painted figure of a bleeding Saviour, large as life, meets one at every turn; and I feel glad when the odd devotion of the inhabitants hangs a clean shirt, or laced waistcoat over it, or both.'

'The women that run about the town, meantime, take the nearest way to be warm, wrapping themselves up in cloth clothes, like so many fishermen at the mouth of the Humber, and wear a sort of rug cap grossly unbecoming. But too great an attention to convenience disgusts as surely as too little; and while a Venetian wench apparently seeks only to captivate the contrary sex, these German girls as plainly proclaim their resolution not to sacrifice a grain of personal comfort for the pleasure of pleasing all the men alive.'

At Munich Mrs. Piozzi is in no humour to be pleased with German art, and goes to see the galleries with little hope of entertainment. 'The patient German is seen in all they shew us, from the painting of Brueghel to the music of Haydn. A friend here who speaks good Italian showed us a collection of rarities, among which was a picture formed of butterflies' wings, and a set of boxes one within another, till my eyes were tired with trying to discern, and the patience of my companions was wearied with counting them, when the number passed seventy-three. This amusement has at least the grace of novelty to recommend it.'

'An old nobleman came to dine with us yesterday in a dressed coat of fine, clean, white broad-cloth, laced all down with gold, and lined with crimson satin, of which likewise the waistcoat was made, and laced about with a narrower lace, but pretty broad, too; so that I thought I saw the very coat my father went in to the old King's birthday five-and-thirty years ago.'

At Salzburg she goes to the Benedictine convent 'seated on the top of a hill above the town, of exceeding antiquity, founded before the conquest of England by William the Norman; under which lie its founder and protectors, the old Dukes of Bavaria, which they are happy to shew travellers, with the registered account of their young Prince Adam, who came over to our island with William and gained a settlement. They were pleased when I proved to them that his blood was not yet wholly extinct among us. . . . The taste of gardening seems just what ours was in England before Stowe was planned, and they divert you now with puppets moved by concealed machinery, as I recollect their doing at places round London, called the Spaniard at Hampstead and Don Saltero's at Chelsea.'

Arriving at Vienna, she is surprised to find 'many devotional figures and chapels left in the streets, which, from the tales told in Austrian Lombardy, one had little reason to expect; but the Emperor is tender even to the foibles of his Viennese subjects, while he shows little feeling to Italian misery.'

'On the 1st of November we tried at an excursion into Hungary, where we meant to have surveyed the Danube in all its dignity at Presburgh, and have heard Haydn at Esterhazie. But my being unluckily taken ill prevented us from prosecuting our journey further than a wretched village, where I was laid up with a fever, and disappointed my company of much hoped-for entertainment. It was curious, however, to find one's self within a few posts of the places one had read so much of; and the words " Route de Belgrade " upon a finger-post gave me sensations of distance never felt before. . . . It was a melancholy country that we passed through, very bleak and dismal, and, I trust, would not have mended upon us had we gone further. The few people one sees are all ignorant, and can all speak Latin—such as it is—very fluently.'

Of the Emperor Joseph and his ways Mrs. Piozzi gives some account. 'He rises at five o'clock every morning, even at this sharp season; writes in private till nine; takes some refreshment then, and immediately after calls his Ministers, and employs the time till one professedly in state affairs; rides out till three; returns and studies alone, letting the people bring his dinner at the appointed hour; chooses out of all the things they bring him one dish, and sets it on the stove to keep hot, eating it when nature calls for food, but never detaining a servant in the room to wait; at five he goes to the corridor just near his own apartment, where poor and rich, small and great, have access to his person at pleasure, and often get him to arbitrate their lawsuits, and decide their domestic differences, as nothing is more agreeable to him than finding himself considered by his people as their father, and dispenser of justice over all his extensive dominions. His attention to the duties he has imposed upon himself is so great that, in order to maintain a pure impartiality in his mind towards every claimant, he suffers no man or woman to have any influence over him, and forbears even the slight gratification of fondling a dog, lest it should take up too much of his time. The Emperor is a stranger upon principle to the joys of confidence and friendship, but cultivates the acquaintance of many ladies and gentlemen, at whose houses (when they see company) he drops in, and spends the evening cheerfully in cards or conversation, putting no man under the least restraint; and if he sees a new comer-in look disconcerted, goes up to him and says kindly: "Divert yourself your own way, good sir, and do not let me disturb you." His coach is like the commonest gentleman's of Vienna; his servants distinguished only by the plainness of their liveries; and, lest their insolence might make his company troublesome to the houses where he visits, he leaves the carriage in the street, and will not even be driven into the courtyard, where other equipages and footmen wait. A large dish of hot chocolate thickened with bread and cream is a common afternoon's regale here, and the Emperor often takes one, observing to the mistress of the house how acceptable such a meal is to him after so wretched a dinner.

'A few mornings ago showed his character in a strong light. Some poor women were coming down the Danube on a float, the planks separated, and they were in danger of drowning. As it was very early in the day, and no one awake upon the shore, except a sawyer that was cutting wood, who, not being able to obtain from his phlegmatic neighbours that assistance their case immediately required, ran directly to call the Emperor, who he knew would be stirring, and who came flying to give that help which, from some happy accident, was no longer wanted. But Joseph lost no good humour on the occasion; on the contrary, he congratulated the women on their deliverance, praising at the same time and rewarding the fellow for having disturbed him.

'My informer told me, likewise, that if two men dispute about any matter till mischief is expected, the wife of one of them will often cry out: "Come, have done—have done directly, or I'll call our master, and he'll make you have done."'

German art did not please Mrs. Piozzi, and German exclusiveness offended her. 'Our architecture here can hardly be expected to please an eye made fastidious from the contemplation of Michael Angelo's works at Rome, or Palladio's at Venice; nor will German music much delight those who have been long accustomed to more simple melody, though intrinsic merit, and complicated excellence will always deserve the highest note of praise. Whoever takes upon him to underrate that which no one can obtain without infinite labour and study, will ever be censured, and justly, for refusing the reward due to deep research; but if a man's taste leads him to like Cyprus wine, let him drink *that*, and content himself with commending the old hock.

'Apropos, we hear that Sacchini, the Metastasio of musical composers, is dead; but nobody at Vienna cares about his compositions. Our Italian friends are more candid; they are always talking in favour of Bach and Brueghel, Handel and Rubens.'

At Vienna Mrs. Piozzi made the acquaintance of the Mesdemoiselles de Martinas, ladies of fashion, very eminent for their musical abilities, in whose family the Italian poet Metastasio had lived for sixty-five years. 'They set his poetry and sing it very finely, appearing to recollect his conversation and friendship with infinite tenderness and delight. He was to have been presented to the Pope the very day he died, I understand, and in the delirium which immediately preceded dissolution he raved much of the supposed interview. Unwilling to hear of death, no one was ever permitted even to mention it before him; and nothing put him so certainly out of humour as finding that rule transgressed even by his nearest friends. Even the small-pox was not to be named in his presence, and whoever *did* name that disorder, though unconscious of the offence he had given, Metastasio would see him no more. The other peculiarities I could gather from Miss Martinas were these: That he had contentedly lived half a century at Vienna, without ever even wishing to learn its language; that he had never given more than five guineas English money in all that time to the poor; that he always sat in the same seat at church, but never paid for it, and that nobody dared ask him for the trifling sum; that he was grateful and beneficent to the friends who began by being his protectors. but ended much his debtors, for solid benefits, as well as for elegant presents, which it was his delight to be perpetually making them, leaving to them at last all he had ever gained without the charge even of a single legacy; observing in his will that it was to them he owed it, and other conduct would in him have been injustice. Such were the sentiments, and such the conduct of this great poet, of whom it is of little consequence to tell that he never changed the fashion of his wig, the cut or colour of his coat, so that his portrait taken not very long ago looks like those of Boileau or Molière at the head of their works. His life was arranged with such methodical exactness, that he rose, studied, chatted, slept, and dined at the same hours for fifty years together, enjoying uninterrupted health, which probably gave him that happy sweetness of temper, or habitual gentleness of manners, which never suffered itself to be ruffled, but when his sole injunction was forgotten, and the death of any person whatever was unwittingly mentioned before him. No solicitation had ever prevailed on him to dine from home, nor had his nearest intimates ever seen him *eat* more than a biscuit with his lemonade, every meal being performed with even mysterious privacy to the last. When his end approached by steps so very rapid, he did not in the least suspect that it was coming; and Mademoiselle Martinas has scarcely yet done rejoicing in the thought that he escaped the preparations he so dreaded. His early passion for a celebrated singer is well known upon the Continent; since that affair finished, all his pleasures have been confined to music and conversation. He had the satisfaction of seeing the seventieth edition of his works, I think they said, but am ashamed to copy out the number from my own notes, it seems so *very* strange; and the delight he took in hearing the lady he lived with sing his songs was visible to everyone. An Italian Abate here said, comically enough, "Oh! he looked like a man in the state of beatification always when Mademoiselle de Martinas accompanied his verses with her fine voice and brilliant finger." The father of Metastasio was a goldsmith at Rome, but his son had so devoted himself to the family he lived with, that he refused to hear, and took pains not to know, whether he had in his latter days any one relation left in the world.'

The travellers left Vienna on November 23, and went to Prague, but Mrs. Piozzi has little to say of it. 'Dr. Johnson was very angry with a gentleman at our house once, I well remember, for not being better company, and urged that he had travelled into Bohemia and seen

Prague. "Surely," added he, "the man who has seen Prague might tell us something new, and something strange, and not sit silent for want of matter to put his lips in motion!" *Horresco referens!* I have now been at Prague, as well as Doctor Fitzpatrick, but have brought away nothing very interesting, I fear.'

On December 4 they arrived at Dresden, having found the roads so bad that at Aussig they put their 'shattered coach on board a bark, and floated her down to Dresden, whither we drove forward in the little carts of the country, called chaises, but very rough and with no springs, as our very old-fashioned curricles were about the year 1750.'

Dresden pleased Mrs. Piozzi better than other German cities. 'The general air and manner, both of place and people, puts one in mind of the pretty clean parts of our London, about Queen Square, Ormond Street, Lincoln's-Inn-Fields, and Southampton Row.'

The gallery, with its famous collection of Italian pictures, is of course noticed at length. 'The gaiety and good-humour of the Court are much desired by the Saxons, who have a most lofty notion of Princes, and repeat all they say, and all that is said of them, with a most venerating affection. I see no national partiality to England, however, as in many other parts of Europe, though our religions are so nearly allied: and here is a spirit of subordination beyond what I have yet been witness to—an aunt kissing the hand of her own niece (a baby not six years old), and calling her "*ma chère comtesse!*" —carried it as high, I think, as it can be carried.'

With Berlin Mrs. Piozzi was not much enchanted. It was, she said, the first place of any consequence she had felt in a hurry to run away from. At Potsdam they saw the tomb of Frederick the Great, who had died but a few months before. On January 13, 1787, they set off for

Hanover, and thence hastened to Brussels, 'very weary of living on the high roads of *Teuchland* all winter long.' Antwerp she found 'a dismal, heavy-looking town—*so* melancholy! the Scheld shut up! the grass growing in the streets! those streets so empty of inhabitants!' Here her many 'reflections upon painting' find a conclusion in some warm expressions of admiration for the masterpieces of Rubens. They went by way of Lille to Calais, and found themselves once more in the Ship Inn at Dover.

CHAPTER XI.

Macaulay's Account of the Flight to Italy—Obloquy—Insults from Baretti—Continuing Regard for Johnson—His Death—Projected Work on Him—The Florence Miscellany—The 'Anecdotes'—Rupture with Boswell—Inaccuracies in the 'Anecdotes'—Show Resentment against Johnson—Walpole's Censures—Sale of the Book—Peter Pindar—Bozzy and Piozzi—Extracts—Miss Thrale—The Piozzis Return to England—Their Reception—Miss Seward's Impressions of Mrs. Piozzi and her Husband.

YET Mrs. Piozzi's life on the Continent was not a period of unmixed enjoyment. Lord Macaulay says that 'she fled from the laughter and hisses of her countrymen and countrywomen to a land where she was unknown, hastened across Mont Cenis, and learned while passing a merry Christmas of concerts and lemonade-parties at Milan that the great man with whose name hers is inseparably associated had ceased to exist.' There is a good deal of extravagance about both parts of this sentence. Dr. Birkbeck Hill calls the former part of it 'a monstrous exaggeration.' Yet it is true that a vast amount of gossip, most of it idle, but some malignant, had been expended on her marriage. The newspapers and magazines assailed her with offensive personalities, and inserted epigrams, neither witty nor decent, at the expense of the fortune-hunter and the amorous widow. What Johnson termed 'an adumbration' of his first letter denouncing her union with Piozzi appeared in the *Gentleman's Magazine*. These attacks pursued her abroad. On November 3, 1784, she writes in her diary:

'Yesterday I received a letter from Mr. Baretti, full of the most flagrant and bitter insults concerning my late marriage with Mr. Piozzi, against whom, however, he can bring no heavier charge than that he disputed on the road with an innkeeper concerning the bill in his last journey to Italy; while he accuses me of murder and fornication in the grossest terms, such as I believe have scarcely ever been used even to his old companions in Newgate, whence he was released to scourge the families which cherished, and bite the hands that have since relieved him. Could I recollect any provocation I ever gave the man, I should be less amazed; but he heard, perhaps, that Johnson had written me a rough letter, and thought he would write me a brutal one.'*

Yet she continued to write not unkindly of Johnson.

'*Milan, 27th November,* 1784.—I have got Dr. Johnson's picture here, and expect Miss Thrale's with impatience. I do love them dearly, as ill as they have used me, and always shall. Poor Johnson did not *mean* to use me ill. He only grew upon indulgence till patience could endure no further.'†

In a letter to Mr. Lysons, from Milan, dated December 7, 1784, she says: ' Do not neglect Dr. Johnson: you will never see any other mortal so wise or so good. I keep his picture in my chamber, and his works on my chimney.'‡

Meanwhile Johnson was writing to Hawkins that the woman he had once called ' his mistress ' had now ' become a subject for her enemies to exult over, and for her friends, if she has any left, to forget or pity '; and he was telling Miss Burney, at her last interview with him, that he drove that despicable person, whose eldest daughter had visited him the day before, entirely from his mind, burning every

* Hayward's ' Piozzi,' i. 267.   † *Ibid.,* i. 248.   ‡ *Ibid.*

letter of hers on which he could lay his hand. He had passed the first part of the summer at Oxford, with the master of his old college; thence he had gone to Lichfield and Ashbourne; and, after another visit to Dr. Adams, had returned in the middle of November to London, where he died of dropsy on December 13, 1784. He could not have complained of being neglected in his last illness by the woman he was driving from his mind, even had she been in England. As to the 'merry Christmas of concerts and lemonade-parties,' Mr. Hayward remarks: 'An Italian concert is not a merry meeting; and a lemonade-party, I presume, is a party where, instead of *eau sucrée*, as at Paris, the refreshment handed about is lemonade—not an enlivening drink at Christmas.'* Probably Lord Macaulay referred to the Christmas entertainment which Mrs. Piozzi attended as a traveller, and which, as we have seen, she did not regard with complete satisfaction or approval.

In January, 1785, she complains of a fresh outburst of insolence to her in the English newspapers, for which the death of Johnson had furnished an excuse. By the end of the month she had begun to contemplate publishing an account of her acquaintance with the Doctor. 'Six persons,' she writes, 'have already undertaken to write his life, I hear, of whom Sir John Hawkins, Mr. Boswell, Tom Davies, and Dr. Kippis are four. Piozzi says he would have me add to the number, and so I would, but that I think my anecdotes too few, and am afraid of saucy answers if I send to England for others. The saucy answers *I* should disregard, but my heart is made vulnerable by my late marriage, and I am certain that, to spite me, they would insult my husband.'†

Boswell was first in the field with his 'Journal of a Tour to

* Hayward's 'Piozzi,' i. 265. † *Ibid.*, i. 269.

the Hebrides with Samuel Johnson, LL.D.,' which appeared at the end of September, 1785. This book had great success, three editions being published within the twelvemonth. It led to a public rupture between the author and Mrs. Piozzi. In his 'Journal' Boswell makes Johnson say of Mrs. Montagu's 'Essay on Shakspeare': 'Reynolds is fond of her book, and I wonder at it; for neither I, nor Beauclerk, nor Mrs. Thrale could get through it.' On reading this, Mrs. Piozzi published a letter to Mrs. Montagu, disclaiming the unflattering opinion thus imputed to her. The matter is referred to in a letter, dated March 6, 1786, from Horace Walpole to his correspondent Sir Horace Mann, the British Minister at Florence:

'I have lately been lent a volume of poems composed and printed at Florence, in which another of our exheroines, Mrs. Piozzi, has a considerable share; her associates three of the English bards who assisted in the little garland which Ramsay the painter sent me. The present is a plump octavo; and if you have not sent me a copy by our nephew, I should be glad if you could get one for me: not for the merit of the verses, which are moderate enough, and faint imitations of our good poets but for a short and sensible and genteel preface by La Piozzi, from whom I have just seen a very clever letter to Mrs. Montagu, to disavow a jackanapes who has lately made a noise here, one Boswell, by anecdotes of Dr. Johnson. In a day or two we expect another collection by the same Signora.'*

The volume of poems mentioned in the foregoing extract was 'The Florence Miscellany,' the production of what was called the Della Crusca School, the principal members of which were Merry, Greathead, and Parsons, the associates of Mrs. Piozzi above referred to. The

* 'Letters,' ix. 44.

Piozzis had entertained Parsons, and received complimentary verses from him, at Milan. 'We met again,' writes the lady, 'the following summer at Florence, where we were living in a sort of literary coterie with Mr. and Mrs. Greathead, Mr. Merry, whom his friends called Della Crusca, and a most agreeable *et cetera* of English and Italians.' It was against this school that William Gifford some years later directed his satires of the Baviad and Mæviad. In the former of these the author names the female poet of the 'Miscellany':

> 'See Thrale's gray widow with a satchel roam,
> And bring in pomp laborious nothings home.'

The other collection expected from her by Walpole was her 'Anecdotes of the late Samuel Johnson, during the last twenty years of his life.' This little book was finished at Florence, transcribed for the press at Leghorn, and forwarded thence to London, where it was revised by Sir Lucas Pepys and Mr. Lysons, under the advice of Dr. Hinchcliffe, Bishop of Peterborough, and Dr. Lort,* and was finally published by Cadell at the end of March, 1786. Most of the anecdotes were written from memory, which will explain and excuse a good many inaccuracies. She accounts for the inferiority of her work to Boswell's when she says: 'A trick, which I have seen played on common occasions, of sitting steadily down at the other end of the room, to write at the moment what should be said in company, either by Dr. Johnson or to him, I never practised myself, nor approved of in another. There is something so ill-bred, and so inclining to treachery in this conduct, that were it commonly adopted, all confidence would soon be exiled from society, and a conversation assembly-room would become tremendous as a court of justice.'† This reflection was of course aimed at

---
* Michael Lort, D.D., an eminent collector of books.
† 'Anecdotes,' p. 44.

Boswell. It stung him deeply, as appears from the terms in which he refers to it: doubtless it contributed much to embitter the quarrel which had already arisen between them, and accounts for his eagerness to fasten a mistake on the lady at every possible opportunity. Miss Seward, who was herself subsequently involved in controversy with Boswell, has remarked with much force that the censures on Mrs. Piozzi's carelessness of truth, which the biographer constantly attributes to his hero, are absolutely in conflict with the high esteem which Johnson expresses for her in his printed letters.

Mrs. Piozzi's disavowal of having concurred in Johnson's expression of contempt for Mrs. Montagu's essay was repeated by her in a postscript to her 'Anecdotes,' and was met by Boswell by a letter published in the *Gazetteer* on April 17, 1786.

After all, the errors in the 'Anecdotes,' which several years of patient research enabled Boswell to expose in his 'Life of Johnson,' are by no means so numerous or so gross as has sometimes been represented. We shall find space for a few examples. Take as a first instance the following:

Mrs. Piozzi wrote: 'When I one day lamented the loss of a first cousin, killed in America, "Prithee, my dear," said he, "have done with canting: how would the world be worse for it, I may ask, if all your relations were at once spitted like larks, and roasted for Presto's supper?" Presto was the dog that lay under the table.' Against this Boswell quotes the version given by Baretti: 'Mrs. Thrale, while supping very heartily upon larks, laid down her knife and fork, and abruptly exclaimed, "Oh, my dear Johnson! do you know what has happened? The last letters from abroad have brought us an account that our poor cousin's head was taken off by a cannon-ball."

Johnson, who was shocked both at the fact and her light, unfeeling manner of mentioning it, replied: "Madam, it would give you very little concern if all your relations were spitted like those larks, and dressed for Presto's supper."'

In a marginal note on this passage, Mrs. Piozzi wrote: 'I never addressed Johnson so familiarly in my life. I never did eat any supper, and there were no larks to eat.' In a further note she adds: 'Never was a hot dish seen on the table after dinner at Streatham Park.' In this statement she is confirmed by Miss Burney, who, in a passage already quoted, says that no supper was the rule at Thrales's. Even had Baretti, therefore, been a credible and unprejudiced witness, his testimony must in this case have been rejected. When the Thrales were giving evening parties Johnson told the mistress of the house that though few people might be hungry after a late dinner, she should keep a supply of cakes and sweetmeats on a side table.

Again, Mrs. Piozzi writes: 'He once bade a very celebrated lady (Hannah More) who praised him with too much zeal, perhaps, or perhaps too strong an emphasis (which always offended him), consider what her flattery was worth before she choked him with it.' Boswell characterizes this story as a perversion, on the authority of Malone, who supplied the biographer with a number of qualifying circumstances, which the latter considers to have taken off the edge of the reproof. Yet these circumstances do not seem to make much difference; and here again we may appeal to Miss Burney, who in one passage of her Diary repeats a story which she had from Mrs. Thrale about Hannah More, substantially identical with that given in the 'Anecdotes,' and, in another passage occurring shortly afterwards, records that Mrs. Thrale, in her presence, said to Johnson: 'We have told her what you said to Miss More, and I believe that makes her afraid;' and that he replied: Well, and if she was to serve me as Miss More did, I should say the same thing to her.'

We can make room for only one instance more. 'Mrs. Piozzi,' says Boswell, 'has given a similar misrepresentation of Johnson's treatment of Garrick in this particular (as to the club), as if he had used these contemptuous expressions: "If Garrick does apply, I'll blackball him. Surely one ought to sit in a society like ours

'"Unelbowed by a gamester, pimp, or player."'

The lady retorts, 'He did say so, and Mr. Thrale stood astonished.' Johnson was constantly depreciating the profession of the stage. The biographer himself gives us the following :—BOSWELL: 'There, sir, you are always heretical; you never will allow merit to a player.' JOHNSON: 'Merit, sir, what merit? Do you respect a rope-dancer or a ballad-singer?'

When we turn from the matter of the 'Anecdotes' to the tone in which they speak of their subject, we cannot but perceive a constant struggle going on in the mind of the writer, between her old feelings of regard for Johnson, and the resentment which his recent behaviour to her had occasioned. Hers was an extremely sweet temper, but the sweetest of tempers must have been soured for a time by the affronts which he had heaped on her in relation to her second marriage; hence we cannot be surprised at such a paragraph as the following, which occurs at the close of a passage of which we have already extracted the earlier portions :

"Veneration for his virtue, reverence for his talents, delight in his conversation, and habitual endurance of a yoke my husband first put upon me, and of which he contentedly bore his share for sixteen or seventeen years, made me go on so long with Mr. Johnson; but the perpetual confinement I will own to have been terrifying in the first years of our friendship, and irksome in the last; nor could I pretend to support it without help, when my coadjutor was no more. To the assistance we gave him, the shelter our house afforded to his uneasy fancies, and to the pains we took to soothe or repress them, the world, perhaps, is indebted for the three political pamphlets, the new edition and correction of his Dictionary, and for the Poets' Lives, which he would scarce have lived, I think, and kept his faculties entire, to have written, had not incessant care been exerted at the time of his first coming to be our constant guest in the country; and several times after that, when he found himself particularly oppressed with diseases incident to the most vivid and fervent imaginations. I shall for ever consider it as the greatest honour which could be conferred on anyone, to have been the confidential friend of Dr. Johnson's health; and to have in some measure, with Mr. Thrale's assistance, saved from distress at least, if not from worse, a mind great beyond the comprehension of common mortals, and good beyond all hope of imitation from perishable beings.'*

With respect to the literary merits of this production, it is not possible to differ very much from the severe estimate expressed by Walpole, whatever we may think of the latter's judgment in other respects. On March 28, 1786, he wrote to Mann: 'Two days ago appeared Madame Piozzi's "Anecdotes of Dr. Johnson." I am lamentably disappointed—in her, I mean; not in him. I had conceived a favourable opinion of her

* 'Anecdotes,' 293.

capacity. But this new book is wretched; a high-varnished preface to a heap of rubbish, in a very vulgar style, and too void of method even for such a farrago. Her panegyric is loud in praise of her hero; and almost every fact she relates disgraces him. She allows and proves he was arrogant, yet affirms he was not proud: as if arrogance were not the flower of pride. A man may be proud, and may conceal it; if he is arrogant, he declares he is proud. She, and all Johnson's disciples, seem to have taken his brutal contradictions for *bons-mots*. Some of his own works show that he had, at times, strong, excellent sense; and that he had the virtue of charity to a high degree is indubitable; but his friends (of whom he made a woeful choice) have taken care to let the world know, that in behaviour he was an ill-natured bear, and in opinions as senseless a bigot as an old washerwoman—a brave composition for a philosopher!'*

Good or bad, the book met with immediate and great success. The first edition was exhausted on the day of publication, so that when the King sent for a copy in the evening there was none to be had. In April Hannah More wrote to her sister that Mrs. Piozzi's book was much in fashion, and was indeed entertaining, though she complained of the author for having needlessly printed some of Johnson's rough speeches. She had before begged Boswell to mitigate some of their departed friend's asperities, and had received from James the answer that he would not cut off his claws, nor make a tiger a cat to please anybody. The public interest in all relating to Johnson, and the dispute between the rival collectors of anecdotes, kept attention fixed on the matter. 'The Bozzi, etc., subjects,' wrote Hannah More later in April, 'are not exhausted, though everybody seems heartily sick of them.

* 'Letters,' ix. 46.

Everybody, however, conspires not to let them drop. That, the Cagliostro, and the Cardinal's necklace spoilt all conversation, and destroyed a very good evening at Mr. Pepys' last night.' At the end of the same month Walpole wrote to Mann :

'All conversation turns on a trio of culprits—Hastings, Fitzgerald, and the Cardinal de Rohan. . . . So much for tragedy. Our comic performers are Boswell and Dame Piozzi. The cock biographer has fixed a direct lie on the hen, by an advertisement in which he affirms that he communicated his manuscript to Madam Thrale, and that she made no objection to what he says of her low opinion of Mrs. Montagu's book. It is very possible that it might not be her real opinion, but was uttered in compliment to Johnson, or for fear he should spit in her face if she disagreed with him ; but how will she get over her not objecting to the passage remaining ? She must have known, by knowing Boswell, and by having a similar intention herself, that his Anecdotes would certainly be published; in short, the ridiculous woman will be strangely disappointed. As she must have heard that the whole first impression of her book was sold the first day, no doubt she expects, on her landing, to be received like the Governor of Gibraltar, and to find the road strewed with branches of palm. She and Boswell, and their hero, are the joke of the public. A Dr. Wolcot,* *soi-disant* Peter Pindar, has published a burlesque eclogue, in which Boswell and the Signora are the interlocutors, and all the absurdest passages in the works of both are ridiculed. The print-shops teem with satiric prints on them ; one, in which Boswell, as a monkey, is riding on Johnson, the

---

* Dr. John Wolcot, previously preacher to a congregation of negroes in Jamaica, had settled in London as a physician, and made his first appearance as Peter Pindar in 1782.

bear, has this witty inscription, "My friend *delineavit*." But enough of these mountebanks.'*

We give some extracts from the burlesque referred to by Horace, which is written in the vein of humour that came into vogue in the period succeeding Charles Churchill. The oddity and boldness of the author's style, the easy flow of his irregular verse, and the pungency of his lampoons, procured him celebrity in an age which cared more for vigour than refinement.

'Bozzy and Piozzi; or, The British Biographers,' is an excellent specimen of Peter Pindar's peculiar manner, and is nearly free from the grossness which disfigures much of his work. It is entitled 'A Town Eclogue,' and describes a contest between the speakers for the honour of writing Johnson's life:

> At length rushed forth two candidates for fame—
> A Scotchman one, and one a London Dame:
> *That* by th' emphatic Johnson christened Bozzy;
> *This*, by the Bishop's license, Dame Piozzi,
> Whose widowed name, by topers loved, was Thrale,
> Bright in the annals of Election Ale—
> A name by marriage that gave up the ghost,
> In poor Pidocchio,† no, Piozzi, lost.
> Each seized with ardour wild the gray-goose quill,
> Each set to work the intellectual Mill,
> That pecks of Bran so coarse began to pour
> To one poor solitary grain of flour.
>
> Forth rushed to light their books; but who should say
> Which bore the palm of Anecdote away?
> This to decide, the rival wits agreed
> Before Sir John their tales and jokes to read,
> And let the Knight's opinion in the strife
> Declare the properest pen to write Sam's life:
> Sir John, renowned for musical palavers,
> The Prince, the King, the Emperor of quavers.‡
> *   *   *   *   *

---

* 'Letters,' ix. 49.
† 'Pidocchio' signifies in Italian what we now call 'a nameless insect.'
‡ *Vide* his 'History of Music.'

Madame Piozzi.

The Doctor said, 'In literary matters
A Frenchman goes not deep—he only smatters;'
Then asked what could be hoped for from the dogs,
Fellows that lived eternally on frogs.

Bozzy.

In grave procession to St. Leonard's College,
Well stuffed with every sort of useful knowledge,
We *stately* walked as soon as supper ended:
The Landlord and the Waiter both attended.
The landlord, skilled a piece of grease to handle,
Before us marched, and held a tallow candle;
A lantern (some famed Scotchman its creator)
With equal grace was carried by the waiter.
Next morning from our beds we took a leap,
And found ourselves much better for our sleep.

Madame Piozzi.

I asked him if he knocked Tom Osborn down,
As such a tale was current through the Town.
Says I, 'Do tell me, Doctor, what befell.'
'Why, dearest lady, there is nought to tell:
I pondered on the properest mode to treat him;
The dog was impudent, and so I beat him.
Tom, like a fool, proclaimed his fancied wrongs;
Others that I belaboured held their tongues.'

Bozzy.

Lo! when we landed on the Isle of Mull,
The megrims got into the Doctor's skull:
With such bad humours he began to fill,
I thought he would not go to Icolmkill;
But lo! those megrims (wonderful to utter!)
Were banished all by tea and bread-and-butter!

Madame Piozzi.

Travelling in Wales, at dinner-time we got on
Where, at Lleweny, lives Sir Robert Cotton;
At table, our great Moralist to please,
Says I, 'Dear Doctor, aren't those charming peas?'
Quoth he, to contradict, and *run his rig*,
'Madam, they possibly might please a pig.'

Bozzy.

Of thatching well the Doctor knew the art,
And with his threshing-wisdom made us start;
Described the greatest secrets of the Mint,
And made folks fancy that he had been in't.
Of hops and malt 'tis wondrous what he knew;
As well as any brewer he could brew.

MADAME PIOZZI.

In ghosts the Doctor strongly did believe,
And pinned his faith on many a liar's sleeve.
He said to Dr. Lawrence, 'Sure I am
I heard my poor dear mother call out "Sam"'!
'I'm sure,' said he, 'that I can trust my ears;
And yet my mother had been dead for years.'

BOZZY.

When young ('twas rather silly, I allow),
Much was I pleased to imitate a cow.
One time, at Drury Lane, with Doctor Blair,
My imitations made the playhouse stare.
So very charming was I in my roar,
That both the galleries clapped and cried 'Encore!'
Blessed by the general plaudit and the laugh,
I tried to be a jackass and a calf.
But who, alas! in *all* things can be great?—
In short, I met a terrible defeat.
So vile I brayed and bellowed, I was hissed;
Yet all who *knew* me *wondered* that I missed.
Blair whispered me, 'You've lost your credit now;
Stick, Boswell, for the future to the cow.'

At length the contest between the rivals turns to an angry dispute :

MADAME PIOZZI.

Who told of Mistress Montagu the lie—
So palpable a falsehood? Bozzy—fie!

BOZZY.

Who would have said a word about Sam's wig,
Or told the story of the peas and pig?
Who would have told a tale so very flat,
Of Frank the Black, and Hodge the mangy cat?

MADAME PIOZZI.

I'm sure you've mentioned many a pretty story
Not much redounding to the Doctor's glory.
Now for a *saint* upon us you would palm him—
First murder the poor man, and then *embalm* him!

BOZZY.

Well, Ma'am, since all that Johnson said or wrote
You hold so sacred, how have you forgot
To grant the wonder-hunting world a reading
Of Sam's Epistle, just before your wedding,
Beginning thus, in strains not formed to flatter :
'Madam, *If that most ignominious matter
Be not concluded*'——* Farther shall I say?
No ; we shall have it from yourself some day,

---

* Referring to the 'adumbration' of Johnson's letter above mentioned.

> To justify your passion for the *Youth*,
> With all the charms of eloquence and truth.
>
> MADAME PIOZZI.
>
> What was my marriage, Sir, to you or him?
> *He* tell me what to do!—a pretty whim!
>
> * * * * *
>
> The folks who paid respects to Mistress Thrale
> Fed on her pork, poor souls! and swilled her ale,
> May sicken at Piozzi, nine in ten—
> Turn up the nose of scorn; but, pray, what then?
>
> * * * * *
>
> When they, poor owls! shall beat their cage, a jail,
> I, unconfined, shall spread my peacock tail;
> Free as the birds of air, enjoy my ease,
> Choose my own food, and see what climes I please.
> I suffer only—if I'm in the wrong;
> So now, you prating puppy, hold your tongue!*

Mrs. Piozzi wrote from Venice in May, 1786: 'Cadell says he never published a work the sale of which was so rapid, and the rapidity of so long continuance. I suppose the fifth edition will meet me at my return.' And from Milan, in July: 'If Cadell would send me some copies I should be very much obliged to him. 'Tis like living without a looking-glass never to see one's own book so.'

In December, 1786, her friend Dr. Lort wrote to Bishop Percy: 'I had a letter lately from Mrs. Piozzi, dated Vienna, in which she says that, after visiting Prague and Dresden, she shall return home by Brussels, whither I have written to her; and I imagine she will be in London early in the New Year. Miss Thrale is at her own house at Brighthelmstone, accompanied by a very respectable companion, an officer's widow, recommended to her as such.'

The lady, Miss Nicholson, whom Mrs. Piozzi had selected as the companion of her three eldest daughters during her absence, soon left them; or, says Mr. Hayward, 'according to another version, was summarily dismissed by Miss Thrale (afterwards Viscountess Keith), who, for-

---

* Works of Peter Pindar, i. 341, *et seq.*

tunately, was endowed with high principle, firmness, and energy. This young lady called to her aid an old nurse-maid named Tib, who had been much trusted by her father, and with this homely but respectable duenna she shut herself up at the house at Brighton, limited her expenses to her allowance of £200 a year, and resolutely set about the course of study which seemed best adapted to absorb attention and prevent her thoughts from wandering.' Hebrew, mathematics, and perspective are said to have been included in the list of her studies. On coming of age, and being put into possession of her fortune, she hired a house in London, and took her two eldest sisters to live with her.*

The Piozzis arrived, as expected, early in March, 1787, and took a house in Hanover Square. 'On reaching London,' she wrote afterwards, 'we drove to the Royal Hotel, in Pall Mall, and, arriving early, I proposed going to the play. There was a small front box, in those days, which held only two; it made the division, or connection, with the side boxes, and, being unoccupied, we sat in it, and saw Mrs. Siddons act Imogen, I well remember, and Mrs. Jordan, Priscilla Tomboy. Mr. Piozzi was amused, and the next day was spent in looking at houses, counting the cards left by old acquaintances, etc. The lady-daughters came, behaved with cool civility, and asked what I thought of *their* decision concerning Cecilia, then at school. No reply was made, or a gentle one; but she was the first cause of contention among us. The lawyers gave her into my care, and we took her home to our new habitation in Hanover Square, which we opened with music, cards, etc., on, I think, the 22nd of March. Miss Thrales refused their company, so we managed as well as we could. Our affairs were in good

* Hayward's 'Piozzi,' i. 234.

order, and money ready for spending. The World, as it is called, appeared good-humoured, and we were soon followed, respected, and admired.'

Mr. Cator, in whose hands her pecuniary matters had been placed at her going abroad, had ably discharged his trust, and his management had been loyally seconded by her husband's economy, with the result that, on their return, they found the mortgage paid off, and £1,500 in the bank. On May 1 she wrote: 'We were not wrong to come home, after all, but very right. The Italians would have said we were afraid to face England, and the English would have said we were confined abroad in prisons or convents, or some stuff.' A few days later: 'We had a fine assembly last night indeed: in my best days I never had a finer; there were near a hundred people in the rooms, which were besides much admired. . . . The summer months sent us about visiting and pleasuring.'

Miss Seward writes from Lichfield in October, 1787: 'I am become acquainted with Mr. and Mrs. Piozzi. Her conversation is that bright wine of the intellect which has no lees. Dr. Johnson told me truth when he said she had more colloquial wit than most of our literary women; it is indeed a fountain of perpetual flow. But he did not tell me truth when he asserted that Piozzi was an ugly dog, without particular skill in his profession. Mr. Piozzi is a handsome man, in middle life, with gentle, pleasing, unaffected manners, and with very eminent skill in his profession. Though he has not a powerful or fine-toned voice, he sings with transcending grace and expression. I am charmed with his perfect expression on his instrument. Surely the finest sensibilities must vibrate through his frame, since they breathe so sweetly through his song.'

CHAPTER XII.

Life in England—Publication of the Letters—Opinions on them—Baretti's Libels—Mrs. Piozzi's Character of him after his Death—'The Sentimental Mother'—The Blues Ashamed—The Book of Travels—Walpole's Sentence—Miss Seward's Opinion—Samuel Rogers—Conduct of the Daughters—Mrs. Piozzi and Miss Burney—Return to Streatham Park—Gaieties there—Mr. Piozzi lays out Money—Society in London—Dr. Parr—Boswell's Life Published—Boswell's Attack on her—Walpole sides with her—'British Synonymy'—Gifford's Opinion on It—Walpole's Criticism—Removal to Wales—Brynbella—Piozzi's Amiable Character—His Prudent Economy—Adoption of an Heir—Sir John Salusbury—'Retrospection'—Piozzi's Gout—Her Care of him—Her Irrepressible Spirits—Miss Thrale marries Lord Keith—A Visit from Dr. Burney—Death of Piozzi—His Will.

'PREVAIL on Mr. Piozzi to settle in England' had been Johnson's parting advice to his mistress. It corresponded exactly with Mr. Piozzi's intentions, for 'he always,' says his wife, ' preferred this island to any other place!'

On New Year's Day, 1788, she wrote: "How little I thought this day four years that I should celebrate this 1st of January, 1788, here at Bath, surrounded with friends and admirers! The public partial to me, and almost every individual whose kindness is worth wishing for, sincerely attached to my husband.

"Mrs. Byron* is converted by Piozzi's assiduity—she really likes him now, and sweet Mrs. Lambert told everybody at Bath she was in love with him.

"I have passed a delightful winter in spite of them, caressed by my friends, adored by my husband, amused

* Mrs. Byron was the wife of the admiral ("Foul-weather Jack") and the poet's grandmother.

with every entertainment that is going forward; what need I think about three sullen misses? . . . And yet!"

In the spring of this year she published the 'Letters to and from Dr. Johnson.' In the preface she says: 'The good taste by which our countrymen are distinguished, will lead them to prefer the native thoughts and unstudied phrases scattered over these pages, to the more laboured elegance of his other works, as bees have been observed to reject roses, and fix upon the wild fragrance of a neighbouring heath. The main value of these letters consists in the additional illustrations they afford of his conduct in private life, and of his opinions on the management of domestic affairs.'

The 'Letters' were published on March 8. 'Cadell,' writes the editor a few days afterwards, 'printed 2,000 copies, and says 1,000 are already sold. The book is well spoken of on the whole, yet Cadell murmurs. I cannot make out why.' Boswell mentions as a proof of the high estimation set on anything which came from Johnson's pen, that Mrs. Piozzi sold the copyright of this collection for £500. We need say little about these 'Letters,' from which we have made frequent extracts. Boswell states that Horace Walpole thought Johnson a more amiable character after reading his letters to Mrs. Thrale, though he was never one of the Doctor's admirers. Miss Burney, on the other hand, thought that they were injurious to his memory. Johnson himself wished them to be preserved, and he must have known that, if preserved, they would surely be given to the world. Probably the publication was premature. At all events, it drew down several attacks on Mrs. Piozzi. Foremost among her assailants was the malignant Baretti, who was provoked by a passage in one of the published letters in which Johnson wrote: 'Poor B——i! do not quarrel with him; to neglect him a little will be sufficient. He means only to be frank and manly and independent, and perhaps, as you say, a little wise. To be frank, he thinks, is to be cynical, and to be independent is to be rude. Forgive him, dearest lady, the rather because of his misbehaviour I am afraid he learned part of me.'* This was more than enough to make Italian blood boil. Baretti retaliated by three papers in the *European Magazine*, assailing Mrs. Piozzi with the coarsest brutality. There he calls her 'the frontless female, who goes now by the mean appellation of Piozzi, La Piozzi, as my fellow-countrymen term her, who has dwindled down into the contemptible wife of her daughter's singing master.' The attack contained much more insolent abuse, but the writer refrained from repeating in the magazine the worst charges which he had hurled against her in the private letter before referred to. 'I could not have suspected him,' wrote Miss Burney, 'of a bitterness of invective so cruel, so ferocious.'

Baretti died in May, 1789, and the placable nature of the woman he had calumniated is shown by the comment on that event which she inserted in 'Thraliana':

'Baretti is dead. Poor Baretti! I am sincerely sorry for him, and as Zanga says, "If I lament thee, sure thy worth was great." He was a manly character, at worst, and died, as he lived, less like a Christian than a philosopher, refusing all spiritual or corporeal assistance, both which he considered useless to him; and perhaps they were so. He paid his debts, called in some single acquaintance, told him he was dying, and drove away that panada conversation which friends think proper to administer at sick bedsides, with becoming steadiness, bid him write his brothers word that he was dead, and gently desired a woman who waited to leave him quite

* 'Piozzi Letters,' i. 277.

alone. No interested attendant watching for ill-deserved legacies, no harpy relatives, clung round the couch of Baretti. He died!

> '"And art thou dead? so is my enmity:
> I war not with the dead!"'

'Baretti's papers—manuscripts, I mean—have been all burnt by his executors without examination, they told me. So great was his character as a mischief-maker, that Vincent and Fendall saw no nearer way to safety than that hasty and compendious one. Many people think 'tis a good thing for me, but, as I never trusted the man, I see little harm he could have done me.'*

Respecting some others of her old acquaintance, she wrote at the beginning of 1789:

'Mrs. Siddons dined in a coterie of my unprovoked enemies yesterday at Porteous's. She mentioned our concerts, and the Erskines lamented their absence from one we gave two days ago, at which Mrs. Garrick was present, and gave a good report to the *Blues*. Charming *Blues!* blue with venom, I think; I suppose they begin to be ashamed of their paltry behaviour. Mrs. Garrick, more prudent than any of them, left a loophole for

---

* Hayward, i. 316. 'Among Mrs. Piozzi's papers,' says Mr. Hayward, 'was found a sketch of Baretti's character, written for *The World* newspaper, in which she quotes as applicable to him four lines from Pope's version of the description of Menelaus in the Iliad:

> '" So burns the vengeful Hornet, soul all o'er,
> Repulsed in vain, and thirsty still for gore;
> Bold son of air and heat on angry wings,
> Untamed, untired, he turns, attacks, and stings."'

The comparison of Baretti to the hornet,' continues Mr. Hayward, 'was truer than she anticipated: *animamque* in vulnere ponit. Internal evidence leads almost irresistibly to the conclusion that he was the author or prompter of "The Sentimental Mother, a Comedy in Five Acts. The Legacy of an Old Friend, and his Last Moral Lesson to Mrs. Hester Lynch Piozzi. London, 1789." The principal *dramatis personæ* are Mr. Timothy Tunskull, a respectable and complacent nonentity; Lady Fantasma Tunskull, vain, affected, silly, and amorous to excess; two Misses Tunskull; and Signor Squalici, the lady's gallant, and in league with her to cheat the daughters of their patrimony.

returning friendship to fasten through, and it *shall* fasten; that woman has lived a *very wise life*, regular and steady in her conduct, attentive to every word she speaks and every step she treads; decorous in her manners and graceful in her person. My fancy forms the Queen just like Mrs. Garrick; they are countrywomen, and have, as the phrase is, had a hard card to play; yet never lurched by tricksters nor subdued by superior powers, they will rise from the table unhurt either by others or themselves . . . having played a *saving game*. I have run risks to be sure, that I have; yet—

> ' " When, after some distinguished leap,
> She drops her pole and seems to slip,
> Straight gath'ring all her active strength,
> She rises higher half her length;"

and better than *now* I have never stood with the world in general, I believe.' Soon afterwards she says: ' Mrs. Montagu wants to make up with me again. I dare say she does; but I will not be taken and left even at the pleasure of those who are much nearer and dearer to me than Mrs. Montagu.'

In June, 1789, she published her book of travels. The extracts which we have given from this book will enable our readers to form their own opinion of its merits. It seems, as the author says, to have been, upon the whole, exceedingly well liked and much read; but the colloquial negligence of the style provoked the animadversion of the critics. Walpole, according to his wont, was unsparingly severe. ' It was said that Addison might have written his travels without going out of England. By the excessive vulgarisms so plentiful in these volumes, one might suppose the writer had never stirred out of the parish of St. Giles. Her Latin, French, and Italian, too, are so miserably spelt, that she had better have studied her own language before she floundered into other tongues. Her friends plead that she piques herself on writing as she talks. Methinks, then, she should talk as she would write. There are many indiscretions, too, in her work of which she will, perhaps, be told, though Baretti is dead.'*

Anna Seward, in a more friendly spirit, mingled warm praise with her blame. On December 21, 1789, she writes:

'Suffer me now to speak to you of your highly ingenious, instructive, and entertaining publication; yet shall it be with the sincerity of friendship, rather than with the flourish of compliment. No work of the sort I ever read possesses, in an equal degree, the power of placing the reader in the scenes and amongst the people it describes. Wit, knowledge, and imagination illuminate its pages—but the infinite inequality of the style! Permit me to acknowledge to you what I have acknowledged to others, that it excites my exhaustless wonder, that Mrs. Piozzi, the child of genius, the pupil of Johnson, should pollute, with the vulgarisms of unpolished conversation, her animated pages!—that, while she frequently displays her power of commanding the most chaste and beautiful style imaginable, she should generally use those inelegant, those strange *dids* and *does* and *thoughs* and *toos*, which produce jerking angles, and stop-short abruptness, fatal at once to the grace and ease of the sentence; which are in language what the rusty black silk handkerchief and the brass ring are upon the beautiful form of the Italian countess she mentions, arrayed in embroidery and blazing in jewels.'†

* In a letter to Mrs. Carter, dated June 13, 1789, 'Letters,' ix. 179. On June 30 he returns to the charge in a letter to Miss Berry: 'If you could wade through two octavos of Dame Piozzi's *though's* and *so's* and *I trow's*, and cannot listen to seven volumes of Scheherezade's recitations, I will sue for a divorce *in foro Parnassi*.'—' Letters,' ix. 184.

† In order to assign their due weight to the strictures of the fair lady who

The style of the 'Observations' was, in fact, an attempt by an unqualified writer to substitute something more easy and idiomatic for the sustained language and formal constructions of the Johnsonian style. The experiment was not successful, as it hardly would have been, by whomsoever tried, within five years from the dictator's death.

Shortly after the publication of the 'Journey' she set out, with her husband and youngest daughter, on an excursion to Scotland.* 'We had been all over Scotland,' she wrote of a later season, 'except the Highlands, where we were afraid of carrying Cecy because of her unsteady health.' We have two notes from her to Mr. Lysons, written from Edinburgh in July, 1789. In one she says: 'I am glad the book swims, poor thing! What does Dr. Lort say of it? Yet he would have written himself, I fear, had it much pleased him.' In the other: 'I wish Cadell had sent my money to Drummond's before he left London; but I warrant he forbore only because he felt that it was too little for such a book, so means to do something handsome just at harvest season; and "the genteel thing is the genteel thing at any time," as Goldsmith's bear-leader says in the play.'†

Samuel Rogers met with them during this trip. In his 'Table Talk' we read:

---

was once known as 'The Swan of Lichfield,' we should have some acquaintance with the style which she herself affected. In her 'Memoirs of Dr. Darwin,' she tells us that the doctor, about the year 1777, purchased 'a little wild umbrageous valley, a mile from Lichfield, irriguous from various springs, and swampy from their plenitude.' This he soon dressed up into a very neat imitation of Paradise, and then, having till now 'restrained his friend Miss Seward's steps to this her always favourite scene,' he allowed her to visit it, when, the lady informs us, 'she took her tablets and pencil, and, seated on a flower-bank in the midst of that luxurious retreat, wrote the following verses, while the sun was gilding the glen, and while birds of every plume poured their song from the bough.' Certainly Mrs. Piozzi never attained to this elegance of diction.

* Hayward's 'Piozzi,' ii. 226. † P. 45.

'My acquaintance with Mr. and Mrs. Piozzi began at Edinburgh, brought about by the landlord of the hotel where they and I were staying. He thought that I should be gratified by "hearing Mr. Piozzi's performance," and they called upon me, on learning from the landlord who I was, and that Adam Smith,* Robertson, and Mackenzie had left cards for me.

'I was afterwards very intimate with the Piozzis, and visited them often at Streatham. The world was most unjust in blaming Mrs. Thrale for marrying Piozzi; he was a very handsome, gentlemanly, and amiable person, and made her a very good husband. In the evening he used to play to us most beautifully on the piano. Her daughters never would see her after that marriage, and (poor woman!) when she was at a very great age, I have heard her say that "she would go down upon her knees to them, if they would only be reconciled to her."'

That the poet was in error in the last statement appears from what has been already mentioned, and Mr. Hayward's inquiries seem to have proved that Mrs. Piozzi's accounts scarcely did her daughters justice: 'On the return of Mr. and Mrs. Piozzi, Miss Thrale made a point of paying them every becoming attention, and Piozzi was frequently dining with her. Latterly she used to speak of him as a very worthy sort of man, who was not to blame for marrying a rich and distinguished woman who took a fancy to him. The other sisters seem to have adopted the same tone, and so far as I can learn, no one of them is open to the imputation of filial unkindness, or has suffered from maternal neglect in a manner to bear out Dr. Burney's forebodings by the result. Occasional expressions of querulousness are matters of course in family differences, and are seldom totally sup-

---

* Adam Smith died on July 17, 1790, after a protracted illness.

pressed by the utmost exertion of good feeling and good sense.'*

We have the following notes from her pen in the year 1790:

'*March* 18, 1790.—I met Miss Burney at an assembly last night, 'tis six years since I had seen her; she appeared most fondly rejoiced. In good time! and Mrs. Locke, at whose house we stumbled on each other, pretended that she had such a regard for me, etc. I answered with ease and coldness, but in exceeding good humour, and we talked of the King and Queen, his Majesty's illness and recovery . . . and all ended, as it should do, with perfect indifference.'

'I saw Master Pepys,† too, and Mrs. Ord, and only see how foolish and how mortified the people do but look.'

'Barclay and Perkins live very genteelly. I dined with them at our brewhouse one day last week. I felt so oddly in the old house where I had lived so long.'

'The Pepyses find out that they have used me very ill. . . . I hope they find out that I do not care. Seward, too, sues for reconcilement underhand . . . So they do all, and I sincerely forgive them, but like the linnet in "Metastasio"—

'"Cauto divien per prova
Nè più tradir si fa!"'

'"When lim'd, the poor bird thus with eagerness strains,
Nor regrets torn wing, while his freedom he gains;
The loss of his plumage small time will restore,
And once tried the false twig—it shall cheat him no more."'‡

In the summer of this year, Streatham Park, unoccupied by tenants, called them home.

'*July* 28, 1790.—We have kept our seventh wedding day and celebrated our return to this *house* with pro-

---

* Hayward's 'Piozzi,' i. 256.
† This is Sir W. Pepys, mentioned above.
‡ Hayward, i. 203.

digious splendour and gaiety. Seventy people to dinner. . . . Never was a pleasanter day seen, and at night the trees and front of the house were illuminated with coloured lamps that called forth our neighbours from all the adjacent villages to admire and enjoy the diversion. Many friends swear that not less than a thousand men, women, and children might have been counted in the house and grounds, where, though all were admitted, nothing was stolen, lost, or broken, or even damaged—a circumstance almost incredible, and which gave Mr. Piozzi a high opinion of English gratitude and respectful attachment.'

Mr. Piozzi, she says, with more generosity than prudence, spent £2,000 in 1790 on the repairs and refurnishing of the house, and, she adds, 'we had danced all night I recollect, when the news came of Louis Seize's escape from, and recapture by, his rebel subjects.' This, of course, was at midsummer, 1791.

Her Diary furnishes a large list of persons who visited at her house in the years succeeding her return from Italy. The names of Burke, Reynolds, Boswell, Dr. Burney and his daughter, Mrs. Boscawen, Mrs. Crewe, Lord Westcote, Miss Streatfield, and some others no longer occur; but we still find mention of Dr. Lort, Sir Lucas Pepys, Dr. Hinchcliffe, Bishop of Peterborough, Mr. Selwin, Sir Philip Clerk, Mrs. Byron, Arthur Murphy, Mrs. Siddons; and to these are now added: Lord Fife, the Kembles, the Greatheads, Mr. Parsons, Miss Seward, Miss Lee, Lord Huntingdon, Lord Dudley, Lord Cowper, Lord Pembroke, Lord Deerhurst, Mrs. Locke, Mrs. Hobart, Lady Betty Cobb and her daughter, the Marquis Araciel, Count Martinengo, Count Moltze, and many more.

In December, 1790, she wrote: 'Dr. Parr and I are in

correspondence, and his letters are very flattering. I am proud of his notice, and he seems pleased with my acknowledgments of esteem ; but in the meantime I have lost Dr. Lort.'*

Boswell's 'Life of Johnson' appeared in May, 1791, and of course fell at once under her notice. She writes a few days afterwards in ' Thraliana ' :

"I have been now laughing and crying by turns, for two days, over Boswell's book. That poor man should have a *bon bouillon* and be put to bed .... he is quite light-headed; yet madmen, drunkards, and fools tell truth, they say .... and if Johnson was to me the back friend he has represented .... let it cure me of ever making friendship more with any human being."

"25th *May*, 1791.—The death of my son, so suddenly, so horribly produced before my eyes, now suffering from the tears then shed .... so shockingly brought forward in Boswell's two-guinea book, made me very ill this week, very ill indeed; it would make the modern friends all buy the work, I fancy, did they but know how sick the *ancient* friends had it in their power to make me; but I had more wit than tell any of 'em. And what is the folly among all these fellows of wishing we may know one another in the next world. . . . Comical enough! when we have only to expect deserved reproaches for breach of confidence and cruel usage. Sure, sure, I hope, rancour and resentment will at least be put off in the last moments . . . sure, surely, we shall meet no more, except on the Great Day when each is to answer to other and before other. . . . After that, I hope to keep better company than any of them."†

The death of young Henry Thrale is, in fact, mentioned by Boswell in no unfeeling terms, but the reflections on

* He died November 5, 1790. † Hayward, i. 342.

Mrs. Thrale's veracity, which he ascribes to his hero, depend entirely on James's envious and hostile testimony. Walpole, to whom Johnson was always a bear, and his biographer a jackanapes, ranges himself on the side of the lady:

"Boswell's book is gossiping; but, having numbers of proper names, would be more readable, at least by me, were it reduced from two volumes to one; but there are woful *longueurs*, both about his hero and himself, the *fidus Achates*; about whom one has not the smallest curiosity. But I wrong the original Achates: one is satisfied with his fidelity in keeping his master's secrets and weaknesses, which modern led-captains betray for their patron's glory and to hurt their own enemies; which Boswell has done shamefully, particularly against Mrs. Piozzi, and Mrs. Montagu, and Bishop Percy. Dr. Blagden says justly, that it is a new kind of libel, by which you may abuse anybody, by saying some dead person said so-and-so of somebody alive."*

In 1794 she produced another book in two volumes, entitled 'British Synonymy,' an imitation of Girard's 'Synonimes Français.'† The truculent Gifford, who about this time published his 'Baviad' and 'Mæviad,'‡ assailed the 'Synonymy' and its author in unmeasured terms:

---

* 'Letters,' ix. 318.
† The 'Synonymy' was translated in Paris, with some omissions, in 1804.
‡ The 'Baviad' appeared in 1794, the 'Mæviad' in 1795. 'She one evening,' says Mr. Mangin, 'asked me abruptly if I did not remember the scurrilous lines in which she had been depicted by Gifford in his "Baviad" and "Mæviad." And, not waiting for my answer, for I was indeed too much embarrassed to give one quickly, she recited the verses in question, and added: "How do you think 'Thrale's grey widow' revenged herself? I contrived to get myself invited to meet him at supper at a friend's house" (I think she said in Pall Mall), "soon after the publication of his poem, sate opposite to him, saw that he was perplexed in the extreme, and, smiling, proposed a glass of wine as a libation to our future good fellowship. Gifford was sufficiently a man of the world to understand me, and nothing could be more courteous and entertaining than he was while we remained together."'—'Piozziana,' p. 4.

"To execute it with any tolerable degree of success required a rare combination of talents, among the least of which may be numbered neatness of style, acuteness of perception, and a more than common accuracy of discrimination; and Mrs. Piozzi brought to the task a jargon long since become proverbial for its vulgarity, an utter incapability of defining a single term in the language, and just as much Latin from a child's Syntax as sufficed to expose the ignorance she so anxiously labours to conceal. 'If such a one be fit to write on Synonimes, speak.' Pignotti himself laughs in his sleeve; and his countrymen, long since undeceived, prize the lady's talents at their true worth."

Walpole on this occasion showed himself a somewhat more indulgent censor, admitting that there was some merit in the illustrative matter, though he found nothing deserving notice in the definitions. 'Here and there she does not want parts, has some good translations, and stories that are new, particularly an admirable *bon-mot* of Lord Chesterfield.'* We may cite this passage as a specimen of the book. The writer is dealing with the words *symbol, type, emblem*, etc.:

'In these latter days the taste for EMBLEMS and emblematical DEVICES, which are all of Oriental original, is fallen into decay from the mere propagation of literature, as beacons are useless in a broad noonday sun. The last I recollect was when the famous witty Lord Chesterfield was sent ambassador to some foreign Court, I forget which. The nobleman *Envoyé de Louis Quinze* at the same place, being called upon for a health, drank that of his master under the EMBLEM of the sun—taken by his predecessor—(the scene of our story is laid at a public feast)—when the Russian, standing up, begged leave

* 'Letters,' ix. 434.

to toast his Empress under the EMBLEM of a rising moon. Next came Great Britain in turn; and it was then Lord Chesterfield, though unaccustomed to such DEVICES, showed his promptness of invention, by saying readily, "I'll give you, gentlemen, as my King's EMBLEM, then, *Joshua, the leader of Heaven's chosen host, at whose command the sun and moon stopped in the midst of their career.*"*

Walpole, who had heard most things, says that he had never heard this anecdote before. His characteristic comment is: 'The story, I dare to say, never happened, but was invented by the Earl himself, to introduce his reply. The sun never was the emblem of Louis Quinze, but of Louis Quatorze; in whose time his Lordship was not Ambassador, nor the Czarina Empress; nor, foolish as some ambassadors are, could two of them propose devices for toasts, as if, like children, they were playing at pictures and mottoes; and what the Signora styles a *public feast*, the Earl, I conclude, called a *great dinner* then. I have picked out a motto for her work in her own words, and written it on the title-page: "Simplicity cannot please without eloquence!"'

Other critics found enough value in the work to make them suspect that the great lexicographer, though dead, was somehow speaking through its pages. On January 2, 1795, the author wrote in 'Thraliana':

'My "Synonyms" have been reviewed at last. The critics are all civil, for aught I see, and nearly just, except when they say that Johnson left some fragments of a work upon Synonymy, of which God knows I never heard till now one syllable; never had he and I, in all the time we lived together, any conversation upon the subject.'†

The entry just quoted is dated Denbigh. About this time the writer and her husband quitted Streatham for

---

* 'Synonymy,' ii. 291.   † Hayward's 'Piozzi,' i. 337.

the lady's property in North Wales. We have reached the close of Mrs. Piozzi's London life. If she lost some friends by her second marriage, she replaced them by others. The editor of the early diary of Frances Burney, lately published, says that Mrs. Piozzi withdrew from those of her friends who were intimate enough to show disapprobation of what she had done. How far this is true may be gathered in part from what has been related above. How much of the coolness which arose between her and the Burneys was due to her, and how much to them, it is not quite easy to decide. Miss Burney says that Mrs. Piozzi broke off the intimacy, but Dr. Burney had brought up his family in excessive awe of public opinion. It seems clear from numerous passages in the d'Arblay diary that Fanny never met her ancient Tyo after she became Mrs. Piozzi, never even heard her name mentioned, without a feeling of nervous apprehension. Mrs. Piozzi has left an account of her removal from her old home:

'We went on spending our money *at* and *upon* Streatham Park, till old Mr. Jones and the wise Marquis Trotti advised Piozzi to make the tour of North Wales, and see *my* country, *my* estate, etc. I stayed with dear Mrs. Siddons, at Rose Hill, while our friends made their ramble, and came back as much delighted with Denbighshire and Flintshire as Mr. Thrale had been disgusted with them. This was charming. Piozzi had fixed upon a spot, and resolved to build an Italian villa on the banks of the Clwyd. Even Mr. Murphy applauded the project, and we drew in our expenses, preparing to engage in brick and mortar. . . . Mr. Piozzi built his pretty villa in North Wales, and, conforming to our religious opinions, kindly set our little church at Dymerchion in a state it never before enjoyed, spending sums of money on its decoration, and making a vault for my ancestors and for ourselves to repose in. I wrote verses for the opening of our tiny temple, and dear Piozzi set them most enchantingly to music. . . . The house, our dwelling-house I mean, was built from a design of its elegant master's own hand, and he set poor old Bâchygraig up too; repaired and beautified it, and to please his silly wife, gilt the Lleweny lion on its top. The scroll once held in his paw was broke and gone. . . . Mr. Piozzi built the house for me, he said; my own old château, Bâchygraig by name, though very curious, was wholly uninhabitable, and we called the Italian villa he set up as mine in the Vale of Clwyd, Brynbella, or the beautiful brow, making the name half Welsh and half Italian, as we were.'

Till he was disabled by the gout, Piozzi's principal occupation was his violin, and it was her delight to listen to him. She more than once observed to the Vicar: 'Such music is quite heavenly.' 'I am in despair,' cried out the village fiddler; 'I may now stick my fiddle in my thatched roof, for a greater performer is come to reside in the parish.' 'The existing superstition of the country,' wrote Mr. Hayward, 'is that his spirit, playing on his favourite instrument, still haunts one wing of Brynbella.' If he designed the building, his architectual taste does not merit the praises she lavished on it. The exterior is not prepossessing; but there is a look of comfort about the house; the interior is well arranged; the situation, which commands a fine and extensive view of the upper part of the Clwyd, is admirably chosen; the garden and grounds are well laid out, and the walks through the woods on either side, especially one called the Lovers' Walk, are remarkably picturesque. Altogether, Brynbella may be fairly held to merit the appellation of a 'pretty villa.' The name implies a compliment to Piozzi's country as well as to his taste; for she meant it to typify the union between Wales and Italy in his and her own proper persons.

Whilst Piozzi lived, her affairs were faithfully and carefully administered. Although they built Brynbella, spent a good deal of money on Streatham, and lived handsomely, they never wanted money. He had a moderate fortune, the produce of his professional labours, and left it neither impaired nor materially increased, to his family. With peculiar reference probably to her habits of profuse expenditure, he used to say that 'white moneys were good for ladies, yellow for gentlemen.' He took the guineas under his especial charge, leaving only the silver to her. This was a matter of notoriety in the neighbourhood, and the tenants, to please her or humour the joke, sometimes brought bags of shillings and sixpences in part payment of their rents.

There is hardly a family of note or standing, within visiting distance of their place, that has not some tradition or reminiscence to relate concerning them; and all agree in describing him as a worthy, good sort of man, obliging, inoffensive, kind to the poor, principally remarkable for his devotion to music, and utterly unable, to his dying day, to familiarize himself with the English language or manners. It is told of him that, being required to pay a turnpike toll near the house of a country neighbour whom he was on his way to visit, he took it for granted that the toll went into his neighbour's pocket, and proposed setting up a gate near Brynbella, with the view of levying toll in his turn.

About the end of the century she wrote from Brynbella: 'Dear Mr. Piozzi, who takes men out of misery so far as his power extends in this neighbourhood, feels flattered and encouraged by your very kind approbation. He has been getting rugs for the cottagers' beds to keep them warm this winter, while we are away, and they all take me into their sleeping-rooms when I visit them *now*, to show how comfortable they live. As for the old hut you so justly abhorred, and so kindly noticed—it is knocked down, and its coarse name too, Polticho; we call it Cottage-o'-the-Park. Some recurrence to the original derivation in soup season will not, however, be much amiss, I suppose.'

Tom Moore mentioned an anecdote of Piozzi, who, upon calling upon some old lady of quality, was told by the servant she was "indifferent." "Is she, indeed?" answered Piozzi, huffishly; "then pray tell her I can be as indifferent as she;" and walked away.*

In a letter, dated January, 1799, to a Welsh neighbour, Mrs. Piozzi says: " Mr. Piozzi has lost considerably in purse by the cruel inroads of the French in Italy, and of all his family driven from their quiet homes, has at length, with difficulty, saved one little boy, who is now just turned of five years old. We have got him here (Bath) since I wrote last; and his uncle will take him to school next week, for as our John has nothing but his talents and education to depend upon, he must be a scholar, and we will try hard to make him a very good one.

" My poor little boy from Lombardy said, as I walked him across our market, 'These are sheep's heads, are they not, aunt? I saw a basket of men's heads at Brescia.'

" As he was by a lucky chance baptized, in compliment to me, John Salusbury, five years ago, when happier days smiled on his family, he will be known in England by no other, and it will be forgotten he is a foreigner. A lucky circumstance for one who is intended to work his way

* Hayward.

among our islanders by talent, diligence, and education."

The boy was to be naturalized and make his career in this country; 'and then we shall see,' says the adoptive mother, 'whether he will be more grateful and natural and comfortable than the Misses Thrale have been to their parent.'

And now the restless little lady engaged in the last and most ambitious of her literary labours. She undertook to write a 'Review of the Most Striking and Important Events, Characters, Situations, and their Consequences, which the Last Eighteen Hundred Years have presented to the View of Mankind.' This was an enterprise about as hopeful as the 'History of Human Error,' to which Mr. Caxton devoted his life, or the 'Key to all Possible Mythologies,' whereby the Reverend Isaac Casaubon expected to achieve immortality. However, Mrs. Piozzi did complete her task, and in January, 1801, published 'Retrospection,' in two volumes, quarto, containing together rather more than a thousand pages. The book was of course a failure; and by the needless cruelty of fate, the bulky volumes were disfigured by innumerable press errors, which the author accounted for by her 'being obliged to print on New Year's Day, during an insurrection of the printers.' 'The *Critical Review*,' she says, 'laid hold of these errors with an acuteness sharpened by malignity.' Yet anyone who takes the trouble to turn over a few of those multitudinous leaves will be repaid by lighting on some curious trait of character or manners, some quaint legend, or some interesting piece of unfamiliar history told in a lively and entertaining manner. We have found in one place the story of the Pied Piper of Hamelin,* set forth with brief details, which are to Browning what Shakspeare's Italian sources are to

* See vol. i., p. 418.

Shakspeare. The developments of liturgical worship had evidently a strong attraction for our author, who returns to these matters with a frequency and zest which might induce the belief that she was a Ritualist born out of due time.

It was just about the date of the publication of this work that she entertained at Brynbella the young Lord Henry Petty, afterwards Lord Lansdowne, who repeated to Mr. Hayward his recollection of the visit:

"When in my youth I made a tour in Wales—times when all inns were bad, and all houses hospitable—I put up for a day at her house, I think in Denbighshire. I remember her taking me into her bedroom to show me the floor covered with folios, quartos, and octavos, for consultation, and indicating the labour she had gone through in compiling an immense volume she was then publishing, called 'Retrospection.' She was certainly what was called, and is still called, blue, and that of a deep tint, but good-humoured and lively, though affected; her husband, a quiet, civil man, with his head full of nothing but music."*

When Piozzi's gout became serious, they usually spent their winters in Bath. The period of his decline was long, and he was waited on by his wife with unwearied patience and affection. But her vivacity never left her, and the elasticity of her spirits bore up against every kind of depression. Hearing that Hannah More's health had broken down under a controversial attack, she wrote in December, 1801: 'We shall go to Bath next month, and then I will try to comfort her. A sister in affliction may have peculiar chance for success; but, I don't know how it is, I never was in affliction. My countenance, unlike that of old Hamlet's ghost, was more—much more in

* Hayward, i. 345.

anger than in sorrow; and so grew less like a ghost, I do believe, in proportion as my critics charged me with loss of youth and beauty. They had need be very young and handsome themselves to make such nonsense tolerated.'

A lady who met her on her way to Wynnstay in January, 1803, describes her as 'skipping about like a kid, quite a figure of fun, in a tiger-skin shawl, lined with scarlet, and *only* five colours upon her head-dress—on the top of a flaxen wig a bandeau of blue velvet, a bit of tiger ribbon, a white beaver hat and plume of black feathers—as gay as a lark.'

Time goes on, however, and on January 31, 1807, we have the following:

'That quack lady who magnetizes the people in London is accused of her (a patient's) death, I observe, and many patients *do* come here oppressed by the half-broiled beef and hot buttered ale with which physicians say that Miss Prescott loads those who place themselves under her care. But poor Mr. Piozzi is as ill as *they* can be, though he prefers boiled mutton and macaroni to all that a table can offer him; and he is in bed now with gout on his breast, hands, arms, etc., a cough beside shaking his harassed frame to pieces. You may be sure I never quit him, except for an hour's walk o' mornings, when I go out to hear what passes, and bring him accounts how Buonaparte was first to turn about, and *Le Troisième des Fuyards* that got safe into Warsaw.'*

Miss Thrale's marriage with Lord Keith took place in 1808, and is thus mentioned in 'Thraliana':

'The "Thraliana" is coming to an end; so are the Thrales. The eldest is married now. Admiral Lord Keith the man; a *good* man for aught I hear; a *rich* man

* Hayward, ii. 266.

for aught I am told; a *brave* man we have always heard; and a *wise* man I trow by his choice. Elphinstone is no new name, and it is an excellent one for a charade.'*

Notwithstanding the somewhat sarcastic tone of this notice, there was no breach between the writer and her daughters, for in a letter dated in August of this year, she speaks of their having spent some days at Brynbella a few days before.

During this summer Dr. Burney writes to his daughter, Madame d'Arblay, who was then living in France:

"Last autumn I had an alarming seizure in my left hand; and mine being pronounced a *Bath case*, on Christmas Eve I set out for that city, and after remaining there three months I found my hand much more alive, and my general health considerably amended.

"During my invalidity at Bath, I had an unexpected visit from your Streatham friend, of whom I had lost sight for more than ten years. When her name was sent in I was much surprised, but desired she might be admitted; and I received her as an old friend, with whom I had spent much time very happily, and never wished to quarrel. She still looks well, but is grave, and candour itself; though still she says good things, and writes admirable notes and letters, I am told, to my granddaughters C. and M., of whom she is very fond.† We shook hands very cordially, and avoided any allusion to our long separation and its cause. The Caro Sposo still lives, but is such an object from the gout that the account of his sufferings made me pity him sincerely; he wished, she told me, "to see his old and worthy friend," and *un beau matin* I could not refuse compliance with his

---

* Her third daughter, Sophia, had been married in 1807 to Mr. Merrick Hoare. The fourth daughter, Cecilia, had become Mrs. Mostyn some years previously; we have not been able to ascertain the exact date of her marriage.

† C. and M. were Charlotte and Marianne Frances, daughters of Dr. Burney's fourth daughter, Charlotte Ann, by her first marriage.

wish. She nurses him with great affection and tenderness, never goes out or has company when he is in pain.'*

In some of her notes she says: 'Piozzi's fine hand upon the organ and pianoforte deserted him. Gout, such as I never knew, fastened up his fingers, distorting them into every dreadful shape. . . . A girl, shown to him as a musical wonder of five years old, said, " Pray, sir, why are your fingers wrapped up in black silk so?" " My dear," replied he, " they are in mourning for my voice." " Ah, me!" cries the child, " *is she dead ?*" He sung an easy song, and the baby exclaimed, " Ah, sir! you are very naughty—you tell fibs!" Poor dears! and both gone now! When life was gradually, but perceptibly, closing round him at Bath, 1808, I asked him if he would wish to converse with a Romish priest—we had full opportunity there. " By no means," said he. " Call Mr. Leman, of the Crescent." We did so: poor Bessy ran and fetched him. Mr. Piozzi received the blessed Sacrament at his hands; but recovered sufficiently to go home and die in his own house.'

The last entry in the six manuscript books composing ' Thraliana ' runs:

'*March* 30, 1809.—Everything most dreaded has ensued. . . . All is over, and my second husband's death is the last thing recorded in my first husband's present. Cruel Death!'

Piozzi was buried in a vault constructed by his wife's desire in Dymerchion Church. There is a portrait of him (period and painter unknown) still preserved amongst the family portraits at Brynbella. It is that of a good-looking man of about forty, in a straight-cut brown coat with metal buttons, lace frill and ruffles, and some leaves of music in his hand.

* Printed in Madame d'Arblay's ' Diary,' iv. 185.

'He left Brynbella to his widow,' she says, 'and everything else, never naming his nephew in his will, only leaving among his father's children £6,000 in the three per cent., being the whole of his savings during the twenty-five years he had shared and enjoyed my fortune.' Her daughters being amply provided for, and the eldest having, she says, declined the Welsh estate, she fixed her care, as well as her affections, on her adopted son. Referring to the later years of her life with Piozzi, she wrote at the end of her life: 'Had we vexations enough? We had certainly many pleasures. The house in Wales was beautiful, and the boy was beautiful too. Mr. Piozzi said I had spoiled my own children and was spoiling his. My reply was, that I loved spoiling people, and hated anyone I could not spoil.'

In spite of spoiling, the youth did not turn out badly. In June, 1810, she wrote of him to Dr. Gray:* 'He is a boy of excellent principle. Education at a private school has an effect like baking loaves in a tin. The bread is more insipid, but it comes out *clean*.' Yet she carried her indulgence so far that, when he was at college, instead of suffering him to travel to and from the University by coach, she insisted on his taking a post-chaise. In after-years she wrote to her last-named correspondent: 'You remember me hoping and proposing to make dear Salusbury a gentleman, a Christian, and a scholar: and when one has succeeded in the first two wishes, there is no need to fret if the third does fail a *little*.'

* Dr. Robert Gray, who was made Bishop of Bristol in 1827, and died in 1834, was distinguished by piety, learning, and a wide knowledge of general literature. He was the author of 'The Key to the Old Testament and the Apocrypha,' and 'Connection between the Sacred Writings and the Literature of the Jewish and Heathen Authors,' works which Mrs. Piozzi much admired and often referred to in her correspondence with him.

CHAPTER XIII.

Cession of Brynbella — Subsequent Life — Lavish Expenditure—Sir James Fellowes—Attempt to Dispose of Streatham—A Bath Cat—The Streatham Portraits Sold by Auction—Improvement in London — Bath Life — Mr. Mangin's Account of her—Her Handwriting—Rouge—Anecdotes of Johnson—Acquirements—Literary Conversation at Bath—Sir William Pepys—Miss Hawkins—Fickleness of Public Taste—Bennet Langton—Fazio—Miss O'Neill—The Conway Episode — Renewed Acquaintance with Madame d'Arblay—Moore's Impression of her—Celebration of her Eightieth Birthday—Her Death and Will—Madame d'Arblay's Parallel between her and Madame de Staël—Mr. Hayward's Criticism—His Estimate of Mrs. Piozzi —Sayings and Anecdotes.

MRS. PIOZZI continued to live at Brynbella until 1814, when she gave up the house and property to her adopted son on his marriage. From that time she resided principally at Bath and Clifton, occasionally visiting Streatham, or making summer excursions to the seaside. Rightly or wrongly, she considered that Piozzi's behaviour to her demanded the sacrifice she made. Here is her account of the matter: 'Unexampled generosity! And true love ! Could I do less than repay it to the child whose situation in life I now felt responsible for ? I bred him with his friends at Oxford, yet he stood alone, *insulated* in a nation where he had no natural friend. Incapacitated to return where his religion would have rendered him miserable, and petted, and spoiled, till any profession would have been painful, what could I do ? The boy had, besides all this, formed an attachment to his friend's sister. What could I do ? I gave them my estate, and resolving that Mr. Thrale's daughters should suffer as little as possible by this arrangement, I repaired and new-fronted their house at Streatham Park.'

Her expenditure at Streatham was not indeed wholly voluntary, but it was doubtless carried much further than necessity required. On November 27, 1814, she writes to Dr. Gray:

'Streatham Park was worth anyone's seeing six months ago. Upon some threats concerning dilapidation, I set heartily to work, new-fronted the house, new-fenced the whole of the hundred acres completely round; repaired stables, out-buildings, barns which I had no use for, and hot-houses which are a scourge to my purse, a millstone round my neck. £6,500 sterling just covers my expenses, of which £4,000 are paid; but poor old dowager as I am, the remainder kept me marvellous low in pocket, and drives me into a nutshell here at Bath, where I used to live gay and grand in Pulteney Street. Direct, however, Post Office, when you are kind enough to write, and I shall get your letter. Count Lieven is my tenant, and pays me liberally, but so he should, for his dependents smoke their tobacco in my nice new beds, and play a thousand tricks that keep my steward, who I have left there, in perpetual agony. I am famous for *tenants*, you know.'*

Besides this lavish outlay, she distressed herself by her habits of profuse personal expenditure. Whether living at Streatham or Bath, she constantly entertained very large parties. She was, in fact, one of those persons who never learn the value of money, and as, after her cession of the Welsh estate, she had nothing left but a life income, she found it difficult as she grew old to obtain sufficient credit, and it is said that executions were sometimes levied on her goods. She does not seem, however, to

* Hayward, ii. 269.

have ever regretted her liberality to her adopted son. Before she died she had the satisfaction of seeing him Sheriff of his county, and on carrying up an address, he was knighted, and became Sir John Salusbury Piozzi Salusbury.

From about the beginning of the year 1815 she appears to have become intimate with two of her latest friends: Sir James Fellowes, whom she made one of her executors, and Mr. Mangin, the author of 'Piozziana.' The former seems to have been early in her confidence in matters of business. When her acquaintance with him began, she seems to have been deeply in debt. In the summer of 1815 she came to town to try to sell her interest in Streatham Park to her daughters, but received, as she tells Sir James, 'a cold, short note from Mr. Merrick Hoare, who married one of the sisters, to say that Lord Keith, who married the other, wished to decline purchasing; so here I am no whit nearer disposing of Streatham Park than when I sat still in Bath. Money spent and nothing done; but bills thronging in every hour. Mr. Ward, the solicitor, has sent his demand of £116 18s. 3d., I think, for expenses concerning Salusbury's marriage. I call that the *felicity* bill; those which produce nothing but infelicity all refer to Streatham, of course.' . . . 'Well, now,' she continues, 'the rest of this letter shall be like other people's letters, and say how hot the streets are, and how disagreeable London is in the summer months, and how sincerely happy I should have been to pass the next six or seven weeks at Sidmouth, but that—Oh, such speeches are *not* like other people's letters at all—but that I have not (with an income of £2,000 a year) £5 to spend on myself, so encumbered am I with debts and taxes. Leak says he must pay £40 property tax now, this minute. He is a good creature, and will be a bitter loss to his poor mistress, whenever we part; although the keeping him, and his wife, and his child is dreadful, is it not? Since, however, in mental as in bodily plagues, despondency brings on ruin faster than it would come of itself:

> '"What yet remains? but well, what's left to use,
> And keep good-humoured still, whate'er we lose."'*

In October, 1815, she writes to the same friend from Bath:

'I have had a nice dish of flattery dressed to my taste this morning. That grave Mr. Lucas brought his son here, that he might see the *first woman in England*—forsooth. So I am now grown one of the curiosities of Bath, it seems, and *one of the antiquities*.

'This evening a chair will carry me to Mrs. Holroyd's, to meet two other females, whom Richardson taught the town to call old tabbies, attended, says he, by young *grimalkins*. Now that's wrong; because they are young tabbies, and when grown gray are *gris malkins*, I suppose. Is not this fine nonsense for the first woman? Prima Donna, in good time!'

In the course of the next few months, she had succeeded in getting rid of her expensive house, and wrote to Dr. Gray from Gay Street, Bath:

'My affairs here being all settled, Streatham Park disposed of, and my poor steward, Leak, being dead, I have got a pretty neat house and decent establishment for a widowed lady, and shall exist a true Bath cat for the short remainder of my life, hearing from Salusbury of his increasing family, and learning from the libraries in this town all the popular topics—Turks, Jews, and ex-Emperor Buonaparte—remembering still that now my debts are all paid, and my income set free, which was so

* Hayward, ii. 288.

long sequestered to pay repairs of a house I was not rich enough to inhabit, and could not persuade my daughters to take me:

> '"Malice domestic, foreign levy—nothing
> Can touch me further,"

as Macbeth says of Duncan when he is dead. Things will at worst last *my* time, I suppose.'

Before possession of Streatham Park was given to the purchaser, the collection of portraits there was sold by action. The sale took place in the spring, and is thus referred to in a letter from Madame d'Arblay to her son, dated April 30, 1816:

'Your uncle has bought the picture of my dearest father at Streatham. I am truly rejoiced it will come into our family, since the collection for which it was painted is broken up. Your uncle has also bought the Garrick, which was one of the most agreeable and delightful of the set. To what recollections, at once painful and pleasing, does this sale give birth! In the library, in which those pictures were hung, we always breakfasted; and there I have had as many precious conversations with the great and good Dr. Johnson as there are days in the year. Dr. Johnson sold the highest of all! 'Tis an honour to our age, that £360! My dear father would have been mounted higher, but that his son Charles was there to bid for himself, and, everybody must have seen, was resolved to have it. There was besides, I doubt not, a feeling for his lineal claim and pious desire.'*

In 1817 she was in town, and on her return wrote: 'The improvements in London amused me very much,

---

* Printed in Mme. d'Arblay's 'Diary,' iv., at p. 302. According to a list of the prices, with which Mrs. Piozzi furnished Mr. Mangin, Dr. Johnson sold for £378, that being the highest price, while Dr. Burney produced £84, and Baretti went for £31 10s., which was the least sum paid for any of the pictures. —'Piozziana,' p. 51.

and such a glare is cast by the gas-lights, I knew not where I was after sunset. Old Father Thames, adorned by four beautiful bridges, will hardly remember what a poor figure he made eighty years ago, I suppose, when gay folks went to Vauxhall in barges, an attendant barge carrying a capital band of music playing Handel's " Water Music "—as it has never been played since.'*

The following letter refers to an event of which our grandfathers, and the fathers of some among us, used to speak with the strongest feeling :

'*Bath, November* 11, 1817.—My dear Dr. Gray's kind letter arrived the same day as the Queen ;† and such a day of gaiety and triumph Bath certainly never did witness. Now, Lord be praised, and let us keep our wits! was *my* exclamation; the delight of the people was boundless. Everybody was on the *alerte;* numbers of women (who had been presented) left their names, and some had a notion she would send for others who did *not.* Madame d'Arblay, *ci-devant* Miss Burney, was believed by many to have a claim on her remembrance; and some prepared to sing, and some to read, and some to talk. The illumination was more gaudy than I ever saw London exhibit; and a prodigious expense was incurred by subscriptions to pillars, arches, and I know not what besides. The Mayor and Corporation put on new dresses, the cooks prepared a magnificent repast, and Death‡ uninvited came to the dinner. The Duke of Clarence really could not articulate the fatal words that extinguished hope and merriment ; he threw the paper to Lord Camden, and left the room—it was empty in five minutes. All this in one short week!'§

Mr. Mangin describes her as he knew her in her later days. After giving the account of her personal appearance,

---

* Hayward, ii. 281. † Queen Charlotte.
‡ The death of the Princess Charlotte. § Hayward, ii. 272.

to which we have referred in a former chapter, he proceeds:

'Her writing was, even in her eightieth year, exquisitely beautiful; and one day, while conversing with her on the subject of education, she observed that "all misses nowadays wrote so like each other that it was provoking," adding: "I love to see individuality of character, and abhor sameness, especially in what is feeble and flimsy." Then, spreading her hand, said she: "I believe I owe what you are pleased to call my good writing to the shape of this hand, for my uncle, Sir Robert Cotton, thought it was too manly to be employed in writing like a boarding-school girl, and so I came by my vigorous, black manuscript."

'Her countenance is constantly in my recollection; but could I have forgotten it, I should have been reminded of its striking features by a good miniature of her in my possession. This was her gift to me in her seventy-seventh year, accompanied by some lines of her own composition, enclosed in the case containing this valuable memorial. She gave the ingenious artist, Roche, of Bath, many sittings, and enjoined him to make the painting in all respects a likeness; to take care to show her face deeply rouged, which it always was, and to introduce the trivial deformity of the lower jaw, of which mention has been made before.'*

Respecting the rouge, Mr. Mangin has written in another place: 'She carefully put it upon her cheeks every day before she went out, and sometimes before she would admit a visitor—or sometimes in his presence. One day I called early at her house, and as I entered her drawing-room, she passed me, saying: "Dear sir, I will be with you in a few minutes; but, while I think of it, I

* 'Piozziana,' p. 8.

must go to my dressing-closet and paint my face, which I forgot to do this morning." Accordingly, she soon returned, wearing the requisite quantity of bloom; which, it must be noticed, was not in the least like that of youth and beauty. I then said that I was surprised she should so far sacrifice to fashion as to take that trouble. Her answer was that, as I might conclude, her practice of painting did not proceed from any silly compliance with Bath fashion, or any fashion; still less, if possible, from the desire of appearing younger than she was, but from this circumstance, that in early life she had worn rouge, as other young persons did in her day, as part of dress, and after continuing the habit for some years discovered that it had introduced a dead yellow colour into her complexion, quite unlike that of her natural skin, and that she wished to conceal the deformity.'*

'She told a story incomparably well; omitting everything frivolous or irrelevant, she would throw into her narrative a gentle imitation—not *mimicry*—of the parties concerned, at which they might themselves have been present without feeling offended.

'In this way she once, I remember, gave us two scenes, one at Streatham, and the other, I think, in London. The first referred to one of Johnson's eccentric habits. A large company had just sat down to the dinner-table, where Johnson's chair was, however, still vacant; for, though the doctor had been descending the stairs, he was not yet withinside the door, "So," said Mrs. Piozzi, "I supposed there was something wrong, and making my

---

* 'Piozziana,' p. 212. In her earlier life the rouge must have assisted in making her look much younger than she really was. Thus, when Charlotte Burney, Fanny's younger sister, was introduced to her in 1777 or 1778, she wrote: 'I fancy she (Mrs. Thrale) is about thirty, though she hardly looks twenty-eight, for she is blooming and pretty enough to prove that nature has not been a little partial to her.'—'Early Diary of F. Burney,' ii. 280. Yet she was then over thirty-six at least.

excuses, started up, and ran in search of my loiterer; and there was he in the passage, indulging in one of his strange whims; stepping forward, drawing back his leg, and then another step! I scolded him soundly, not for affectation nor absence of mind, for, to do him justice, of all such absurdities he was incapable; but for pursuing a queer practice at a time when others were waiting. At length I got him in, and after dinner he made up ample amends by his talk, as he did invariably." In telling this she bent her neck sideways, looking solemn, and stepped to and fro, so as to transmit, I have no doubt, a very good notion of Johnson's air.'

The other anecdote told by Mr. Mangin relates to her old jealousy of Miss Streatfield. Mrs. Piozzi said:

'Johnson was, on the whole, a rigid moralist; but he could be ductile, I may say servile; and I will give you an instance. We had a large dinner-party at our house; Johnson sat on one side of me and Burke on the other; and in the company there was a young lady to whom I, in my peevishness, thought Mr. Thrale superfluously attentive, to the neglect of me and others; especially of myself, then near my confinement, and dismally low-spirited; notwithstanding which, Mr. Thrale very unceremoniously begged of me to change place with Sophy, who was threatened with a sore throat, and might be injured by sitting near the door. I had scarcely swallowed a spoonful of soup when this occurred, and was so overset by the coarseness of the proposal that I burst into tears, said something petulant—that perhaps erelong the lady might be at the head of Mr. Thrale's table, without displacing the mistress of the house, etc., and so left the apartment. I retired to the drawing-room, and for an hour or two contended with my vexation, as I best could, when Johnson and Burke came up. On seeing them, I resolved to give a *jobation* to both, but fixed on Johnson for my charge, and asked him if he had noticed what passed, what I had suffered, and whether, allowing for the state of my nerves, I was much to blame? He answered, "Why, possibly not; your feelings were outraged." I said, "Yes, greatly so; and I cannot help remarking with what blandness and composure you *witnessed* the outrage. Had this transaction been told of others, your anger would have known no bounds; but towards a man who gives good dinners, etc., you were meekness itself!" Johnson coloured, and Burke, I thought, looked foolish; but I had not a word of answer from either.'*

Mr. Mangin recollected her showing him a valuable china bowl, in the inside of which was pasted a slip of paper, and on it written, "With this bowl Hester Lynch Salusbury was baptized, 1740."†

The author of 'Piozziana' doubtless exaggerates her acquirements when he says: 'She not only read and wrote Hebrew, Greek and Latin, but had for sixty years constantly and ardently studied the Scriptures and the works of commentators in the original languages.' She was indeed an omnivorous reader, but there is nothing, so far as we are aware, to show that she knew more of Hebrew or Greek than the characters. Among her printed letters there is one to Sir James Fellowes, in

* 'Piozziana,' p. 20.
† *Ibid.*, p. 167. According to Mr. Hayward, the bowl came into the possession of the Mr. Salusbury who placed her papers in Mr. Hayward's hands, and the exact words on the slip of paper were: 'In this basin was baptized Hester Lynch Salusbury, 16th January, 1740-41, O.S., at Bodville in Carnarvonshire.' This Mr. Salusbury's father copied from the original bit of paper (probably of her own handwriting), which was worn only by time. In those days, and even much later, it was common to baptize infants privately, without much regard for there being "great cause or necessity for it," as the rubric ordains. The best china bowl in the house (which served as the punch-bowl at supper-time), was used on these occasions.—'Early Diary of F. Burney,' ii. 87.

which, referring to the captain of the host of Jabin, King of Canaan, she writes the name Sisera in Hebrew letters, and instructs her correspondent that the termination in *a* does not in Hebrew feminize a name, any more than the termination in *o* renders a name masculine in the Greek! This wears a learned air, but probably the latter piece of information has no more recondite source than the former. In one of Johnson's letters to her he says: 'I have learned since I left you, that the names of two of the Pleiades were Coccymo and Lampado;'* alluding, Mrs. Piozzi says, to a search made at that time by the Streatham coterie for female names ending in *o*. The old joke of inviting a friend to *eta beta pi*, which she was fond of repeating, and fathered on Hogarth, was Greek enough in those days for a lady or an artist; but the capacity to enjoy it would scarcely be accepted at Girton or Newnham as affording sufficient proof of scholarship. The fame of Sophy Streatfield in her peculiar field of distinction was never challenged by Mrs. Piozzi, and though, in the second half of her life, she added greatly to her reading, there is no reason to suppose that she enlarged her knowledge of the learned languages.

Her chief resource for literary conversation, in her closing years, seems to have been Mr. Mangin. The old set she had known in Bath forty years before had wellnigh disappeared. Dr. Harrington, the last survivor of them, had long passed his eightieth year. Her own memory, too, was no longer what it had been. The writer of 'Piozziana' mentions a discussion which he had with her respecting the authorship of the well-known lines :

> 'To die is landing on some silent shore,
> Where billows never break, nor tempests roar :
> Ere well we feel the friendly stroke, 'tis o'er !'

---

* 'Piozzi Letters,' i. 32.

She had spoken of these verses as Dryden's, on the authority of a passage in Warton, when Mr. Mangin pointed out to her that Warton was mistaken, and that the lines in question occur in Garth's 'Dispensary.'* She would hardly have been thus at fault when she was at Bath with Miss Burney, in 1780.

She seldom visited London in the last few years of her life. There the fame which her social talents had procured her gradually died out. As late as 1825, her old friend Sir William Pepys told Miss Wynn that he never met with any other human being who possessed the talent of conversation in an equal degree. But very few people then remembered the days of which Miss Lætitia Hawkins wrote when she said: 'I have heard it said that into whatever company she fell, Mrs. Thrale could be the most agreeable person in it.'† As early as 1809, when Piozzi died, his death was mentioned in the *Gentleman's Magazine* as that of 'the husband of Mrs. Piozzi, the once justly celebrated Mrs. Thrale.' *Autres temps autres mœurs.* The conversation which is considered brilliant in one age is generally found tedious in the next. The Earl of Norwich, who ranked as the wit of Charles I.'s Court, was voted a bore at the Court of Charles II. And Mrs. Piozzi was not the only member of the old Streatham circle who experienced the fickleness of the capital's esteem. She wrote in 1817: 'The Dean of Winchester's account of Bennet Langton coming to town some few years after the death of Dr. Johnson, and finding no house where he was even asked to dinner, was exceedingly comical. Mr. Wilberforce dismissed him with a cold "Adieu, dear sir; I hope we shall meet in heaven!" How capricious is the public taste! I remember when to have Langton in a man's house stamped him at once a literary character.'‡

* Canto iv., 225-7.   † 'Memoirs,' i., n. 56.   ‡ Hayward, ii. 370.

Yet the clever, bright-eyed, alert little old lady continued to be admired by her personal acquaintance down to the latest days of her long life. When the son of Sir Francis Milman, the physician, had written a play, she was invited to contribute an epilogue, but prudently declined. The piece referred to was Dean Milman's fine play 'Fazio,' in which an actor named Conway performed with Miss O'Neill, afterwards Lady Becher. Conway had also the honour of acting Romeo and Jaffier to the Juliet and Belvidera of the same celebrated actress. Mrs. Piozzi has left her impressions of the latter when she visited Bath in the summer of 1818:

'Miss O'Neill has fascinated all eyes; no wonder: she is *very* fair, very young, and innocent-looking; of gentlest manners in appearance certainly, and lady-like to an exactness of imitation. The voice and emphasis are not delightful to my old-fashioned ears; but all must feel that her action is quite appropriate. Where passionate love and melting tenderness are to be expressed she carries criticism quite away. The scene with Stukely disappointed me; I hated to see indignation degenerate into shrewishness, and hear so lovely a creature *scold* the man in a harsh accent—such as *you now* are hearing in the street! My aristocratic prejudices, too, led me to think she under-dressed her characters; one is used to fancy an audience entitled to respect from all public performers; and Belvidera's plain black gown, and her fine hair twisted up, as the girls do for what they call an *old cats'* card-party, pleased me not.'*

To another correspondent she wrote of Miss O'Neill's visit: 'Our ladies are all in hysterics, our gentlemen's hands quite blistered with clapping, and her stage companions worn to a thread with standing up like chairs in

* 'Piozziana,' p. 91.

a children's country dance, while she alone commands the attention of such audiences as Bath never witnessed till now. The box-keepers said last night that the numbers Kean drew after him were nothing to it.'

For Conway Mrs. Piozzi presently conceived a sentimental attachment. 'The actor,' says Mr. Hayward, ' was six feet high, and a very handsome man to boot; but his advantages were purely physical: not a spark of genius animated his fine features and commanding figure, and he was battling for a moderate share of provincial celebrity when Mrs. Piozzi fell in with him at Bath.' It was rumoured, after her death, that she had wished to marry him, and had offered Sir John Salusbury a large sum of ready money to restore Brynbella, that it might be settled on Conway. But the latter part of this story is certainly untrue; she never had much money at command, and though it has been stated that Conway once showed a letter from her, offering him marriage, it seems more reasonable, on the whole, to suppose that her attachment was merely an old woman's warm friendship for a young man whom she admired.

To complete the account of this episode, we may mention here that Conway threw himself overboard and was drowned on a voyage from New York to Charleston, in 1828, and that fourteen years after his death seven letters purporting to have been addressed to him by Mrs. Piozzi were published in London. The genuineness of these letters is doubtful, and Mr. Hayward remarks that, taken as they stand, they do not amount to very much, while the change of three or four sentences would alter their entire tenor.

In the early part of 1818, the long estrangement between Madame d'Arblay and Mrs. Piozzi came to an end, and from that time till the death of the latter occa-

sional letters passed between them, some of which are printed in Madame d'Arblay's Diary. In one of these letters, Mrs. Piozzi says: 'Fell, the bookseller in Bond Street, told me a fortnight or three weeks ago, that Miss Streatfield lives where she did in his neighbourhood, Clifford Street, S. S., still.' In a later one: 'The once charming S. S. had inquired for me of Nornaville and Fell, the Old Bond Street booksellers, so I thought she meditated writing, but was deceived.' In the summer of 1818, Mrs. Piozzi spent some time with Sir John Salusbury at Brynbella, and in the following spring we hear of her in London. Moore writes in his diary, April 28, 1819:

'Breakfasted with the Fitzgeralds. Took me to call on Mrs. Piozzi; a wonderful old lady; faces of other times seemed to crowd over her as she sat: the Johnsons, Reynoldses, etc. Though turned eighty, she has all the quickness and intelligence of a gay young woman.'

She celebrated her eightieth birthday by a concert and a ball and supper to between six and seven hundred people, at the Kingston Assembly Rooms, Bath. Her health was proposed by Admiral Sir James Saumarez, and was drunk with three times three. The supper was provided by Tully, who was then the Gunter of Bath. The hostess exhorted her guests to profit to the utmost by Tully's Offices; she led off the dancing with her adopted son, Sir John Salusbury, and, Mangin says, with 'astonishing elasticity.' The next day the friends who called expecting to hear that she had exerted herself too much, found her not only quite well, but full of jokes and lively sallies of wit. Speaking of fatigue, she said: 'This sort of thing is greatly in the mind, and I am almost tempted to say the same of growing old at all, and especially as regards those usual concomitants of age: laziness, defective sight, and ill-temper.'

In May, 1821, while travelling from Penzance to Clifton, she met with an accident and broke her leg. The fall proved fatal. She died after an illness of ten days, with very little suffering. Her daughters, Lady Keith and Mrs. Hoare, reached Clifton in time to be recognised, and to take an affectionate farewell of her. On hearing of their arrival, she remarked cheerfully: 'Now I shall die in state.' Her unmarried daughter, Susan, came only just before she expired. Mrs. Mostyn, the youngest daughter, does not appear to have been present. She had breathed her last before her adopted son could come over from Brynbella. These circumstances are mentioned in a letter by Mrs. Pennington, of the Hot Wells, Clifton, who is mentioned in Miss Seward's correspondence as the beautiful and agreeable Sophia Weston. Mrs. Pennington told Mr. Mangin that the dying woman's last words were: 'I die in the trust and the fear of God.'* When visited by her old medical attendant, Sir George Gibbs, of Bath, being unable to articulate, she traced the outline of a coffin in the air with her hand, and then lay calmly down.†

Mrs. Piozzi was buried in the little church of Dymerchion, in Flintshire. With the exception of some family pictures and trifling mementoes to her daughters, and a watch to Conway, she left all her real and personal property to Sir John Salusbury Piozzi Salusbury, appointing him and Sir James Fellowes executors of her will, which was dated the 29th March, 1816. A memorandum signed by Sir James Fellowes runs thus: 'After I had read the will, Lady Keith and her two sisters, present, said they had long been prepared for the contents and for such a disposition of the property, and they acknowledged the validity of the will.'‡

* 'Piozziana,' p. 6.   † *Ibid.*, p. 8.   ‡ Hayward, i. 364.

In the autumn of 1857, soon after Mrs. Mostyn's death, her collection of curiosities and relics of Mrs. Piozzi and Dr. Johnson was sold at Silwood Lodge, Brighton. An odd volume of 'Saurin on the Bible,' with a memorandum by Dr. Johnson on the title-page, and some manuscript notes by Mrs. Piozzi, fetched £42 at this sale. The teapot which used to stand on Mrs. Piozzi's table, and from which Dr. Johnson drank innumerable cups of the cheering fluid, was bought at the same time by Mrs. Marryatt. It held more than three quarts, and was of Oriental porcelain, painted and gilt.

On receiving the news of her old friend's death, Madame d'Arblay wrote in her Diary: 'I have lost now, just lost, my once most dear, intimate, and admired friend, Mrs. Thrale Piozzi, who preserved her fine faculties, her imagination, her intelligence, her powers of allusion and citation, her extraordinary memory, and her almost unexampled vivacity, to the last of her existence. She was, in truth, a most wonderful character for talents and eccentricity, for wit, genius, generosity, spirit, and powers of entertainment. She had a great deal both of good and not good, in common with Madame de Staël Holstein. They had the same sort of highly superior intellect, the same depth of learning, the same general acquaintance with science, the same ardent love of literature, the same thirst for universal knowledge, and the same buoyant animal spirits, such as neither sickness, sorrow, nor even terror, could subdue. Their conversation was equally luminous, from the sources of their own fertile minds, and from their splendid acquisitions from the works and acquirements of others. Both were zealous to serve, liberal to bestow, and graceful to oblige; and both were truly high-minded in prizing and praising whatever was admirable that came in their way. Neither of them was delicate nor polished, though each was flattering and caressing; but both had a fund inexhaustible of good humour, and of sportive gaiety, that made their intercourse with those they wished to please attractive, instructive, and delightful; and though not either of them had the smallest real malevolence in their compositions, neither of them could ever withstand the pleasure of uttering a repartee, let it wound whom it might, even though each would serve the very person they goaded with all the means in their power. Both were kind, charitable, and munificent, and therefore beloved; both were sarcastic, careless, and daring, and therefore feared. The morality of Madame de Staël was by far the most faulty, but so was the society to which she belonged; so were the general manners of those by whom she was encircled.'*

Doubtless Madame d'Arblay, who for a short time had been intimate with Madame de Staël, considered that she was paying her ancient Tyo a high compliment in comparing her with the greatest female writer she herself had known. But the parallel wholly fails: it afforded Mr. Hayward scope for the exercise of his peculiar talent; and it is impossible, we think, to dispute the justice of his criticism:

'The superiority in the highest qualities of mind will be awarded without hesitation to the Frenchwoman, although M. Thiers terms her writings the perfection of mediocrity. . . . But her tone of mind was so essentially and notoriously masculine, that when she asked Talleyrand whether he had read her "Delphine," he answered, "Non, madame, mais on m'a dit que nous y sommes tous les deux déguisés en femmes." This was a material drawback on her agreeability; in a moment of excited con-

* Madame d'Arblay's 'Diary,' iv. 461.

sciousness she exclaimed that she would give all her fame for the power of fascinating.'

After quoting Byron's petulant remarks about her, which he summed up in the words, 'She would have made a great man,' Mr. Hayward proceeds:

'This is just what Mrs. Piozzi never would have made. Her mind, despite her masculine acquirements, was thoroughly feminine; she had more tact than genius, more sensibility and quickness of perception than depth, comprehensiveness, or continuity of thought. But her very discursiveness prevented her from becoming wearisome; her varied knowledge supplied an inexhaustible store of topics and illustrations; her lively fancy placed them in attractive lights; and her mind has been well likened to a kaleidoscope, which, whenever its glittering and heterogeneous contents are moved or shaken, surprise by some new combination of colour or of form. She professed to write as she talked; but her conversation was doubtless better than her books, her main advantages being a well-stored memory, fertility of images, aptness of allusion, and *apropos*.'

He continues: 'Her verses are advantageously distinguished amongst those of her blue-stocking contemporaries by happy turns of thought and expression, natural playfulness, and an abundant flow of idiomatic language. But her facility was a fatal gift, as it has proved to most female aspirants to poetic fame, who rarely stoop to the labour of the file. Although the first rule laid down by Goldsmith's connoisseur is far from universally applicable to productions of the pencil or the pen, all fruitful writers would do well to act upon it, and what Mrs. Piozzi could do when she took pains is decisively proved by her "Streatham Portraits."

'She was wanting in refinement, which very few of the

eighteenth-century wits and authors possessed according to more modern notions; and she abounded in vanity, which, if not necessarily a baneful or unamiable quality, is a fruitful source of folly, and peculiarly calculated to provoke censure or ridicule. In her, fortunately, its effects were a good deal modified by the frankness of its avowal and display, by her habits of self-examination, by her impulsive generosity of character, and by her readiness to admit the claims and consult the feelings of others. To seek out and appreciate merit, as she appreciated it, is a high merit in itself.

'Her piety was genuine, and old-fashioned politicians, whose watchword is "Church and King," will be delighted with her politics. Literary men, considering how many curious inquiries depend upon her accuracy, will be more anxious about her truthfulness, and I have had ample opportunities of testing it; having not only been led to compare her narratives with those of others, but to collate her own statements of the same transactions or circumstances at distant intervals or to different persons. She was very fond of writing marginal notes, and after annotating one copy of a book, would take up another and do the same. I have never detected a substantial variation in her narratives, even in those which were more or less dictated by pique; and as she generally drew upon the "Thraliana" for her materials, this, having been carefully and calmly compiled, affords an additional guarantee for her accuracy.

'Her taste for reading never left her or abated to the last. In reference to a remark (in Boswell) on the irksomeness of books to people of advanced age, she writes: "Not to me at eighty years old: being grieved that year (1819) particularly, I was forced upon study to relieve my mind, and it had the due effect. I wrote this note in 1820."'

We give a few specimens of her sayings and anecdotes:

'I hate a general topic, as a pretty woman hates a general mourning when black does not become her complexion.'

'Life is a schoolroom, not a playground.'

In allusion to the rage for scientific experiment in 1811 : 'Never was Nature so put to the rack, and never, of course, was she made to tell so many lies.'

'Science (*i.e.*, learning) which acted as a sceptre in the hand of Johnson, and was used as a club by Dr. Parr, became a lady's fan when played with by George Henry Glasse.'

When gaslights were first introduced into London, she quoted from Milton :

> '" From the arched roof,
> Pendent by subtle magic, many a row
> Of starry lamps, and blazing cressets, fed
> With naphtha and asphaltus yielded light
> As from a sky."'

'Hope is drawn with an anchor always, and commonsense is never strong enough to draw it up.'

'The poppy which nature sows among the corn, to show us that sleep is as necessary as bread.'

When complaint was made of the scanty dresses worn by fashionable ladies, she said : 'As you have always acknowledged the British belles to exceed those of every other nation, you may now say with truth that they *outstrip* them.'

'The heat has certainly exhausted my faculties, and I have but just life enough left to laugh at the fourteen tailors who, united under a flag with *Liberty and Independence* on it, went to vote for some of these gay fellows. I forget which ; but the motto is ill-chosen, said I : they should have written up, *Measures, not Men.*'

'You will think me as stupid as Lord Carlisle's cook,

who begged permission to examine the library one day, because, says he, I have been told when a child about Nelson's "Feasts and Fasts," and 'tis time to read it in earnest and fix upon some good recipes.'

'Dr. Johnson used to beg for Samuel Boyce; but did not relate, till after his decease, how, when he had procured a guinea, and laid it out in roast beef and port wine, Boyce quarrelled with him, because he had forgotten their favourite sauce; "and how can a man eat roast beef," said he, "without mushrooms or catsup?"'

'A lady once asked me at Streatham Park to lend her a book. "What sort of a book would you like?" said I. "An abridgment," was the unexpected reply; "the last pretty book I had was an abridgment."'

'"White figs in England as good," says Sir William Temple, "as any of that sort in Italy." The art of cultivating them must have been lost, for our figs now resemble not in any wise those of Italy.'

'There is a story of Sir Roger L'Estrange going to see Lee, the poet, when confined for lunacy. The first expressing his concern to see his old friend in so dull a place, "Ay, sir," replied the other:

'"Manners may alter, circumstances change;
But I am strange Lee still, and you Le Strange!"'

THE END.

www.ingramcontent.com/pod-product-compliance
Lightning Source LLC
Chambersburg PA
CBHW020233240426
43672CB00006B/506